LIFE STYLE
INDIAN TRIBES
(Locational Practice)

LIFE STYLE
INDIAN TRIBES
(Locational Practice)

Vol. I

DR. S.T. DAS

GIAN PUBLISHING HOUSE
New Delhi-110002

Life Style: Indian Tribes

ISBN : 81-212-0058-X

Second Edition Published in 2000
First Edition Published in 1993
in India by Gyan Publishing House
5, Ansari Road
New Delhi-110002

Printed at Goyal Offset Works, Delhi

PREFACE

ANTHROPOLOGY has waited a hundred years for a full account of the different tribes of India, but Verrier Elwin, J.H. Hutton, H. Risley and S.C. Ray has paid the debt as fully as any other author, who had to work on many Indian Tribes after its tribal life and organisation had largely gone.

The people of India include a very large number of primitive tribes who subsist on hunting, fishing or by simple form of agriculture. These people are called Aboriginal Tribes. The tribal groups are presumed to form the oldest ethnological sector of the national population. The term 'Adivasis' has recently become current to designate these groups. These groups are the earliest inhabitants or indigenous people of our country.

There are apparent cultural differences and locational practices between the life-styles of the Indian Tribes but historically there is a basic unity in thought and philosophy among these people, born and brought up in environment of diversity through the length and breadth of the country. What these differences are ? And what threads of fundamental commonness are inherent in the overall tribal system, custom and locational practice ? Can the questions be answered by a study of this book ?

There are hundreds of aboriginal tribes in India who are still living with their ancient life style happily and joyfully. It is not possible to give in a single book the locational practices of each and every tribe. Only about those few tribes have been discussed here, whose peculiar characteristics of locational practice in general differs from other tribes. The book has been written to highlight the following features of the tribes :

(a) The principles of distinct element of tribes have been discussed.

(b) Those tribes have been included on which the effect of welfare schemes and the acculturalization due to plain people are much visible.

(c) The effect of ill-conceived tribal reforms and the conflict created in their way of life have been highlighted.

It is not yet too late to save the tribes from the fate which an ever-hasty and unregulated process of uplift and civilization has brought upon tribal people. Most of the tribes still live as far as possible on forest produce and the spoils of the chase. But due to ever-increasing restriction on the use of the forest, these forest tribes are slowly but surely dying out, partly from famine and partly from loss of interest in life.

These tribes are compelled to leave their attractive and charming traditional local practices and life style. Due to the effect of various factors not only we are destructing our basic tradition but we are nourishing or creating a culture in which the very existence of these colourful tribes will be lost.

During the last twenty years that have elapsed since the publication of my earlier work on the Aboriginal Tribes of the World in Hindi, I have continued my investigation and research into the locational practice and life-style of different tribes of India. The considerable portion of the result of those investigations are embodied in two volumes.

Since lost two decades I was thinking of writing a sane, clear, scientific, sympathetic, and comprehensive book on locational practice of the most important tribes of India. This is of prime importance to the students of anthropology and to the administrator who seeks or should seek to understand the forces which govern human activities and it is full of charm and interest for the general reader who desire to know something at once accurate and intelligible of the people of India.

The students of anthropology soon learns that the secret of his science is "to see life steadily and to see it whole." No belief exists in isolation. Every custom is but a part of a whole and neither the whole nor the parts can be justly appraised unless their functions, interdependence and organic relations are made clear, recorded faithfully, synthesised, intelligently surveyed and explained. The nature of man, the nature of spiritual beings, the nature of phenomena and natural processes, as viewed and understood by the tribes are of deepest interest and are faithfully presented here.

In a book like this, I must acknowledge the assistance I have received from various authorities, writers and critics, who have afforded valuable suggestions and those whose works have helped me to draw inspiration. Omission if any was not deliberate.

In presenting this book, I cannot refrain from expressing my profound gratitude to J.H. Hutton, Verrier Elwin and Rai Bahadur Sarat Chandra Ray whose works and census reports made my work easier.

Special mention may be made to Mr. Jyoti Kumar Sarma, P. Pugh, K.P. Bahadur, T.S. Gangte, Principal, Chura Chandrapur College, Manipur, Dr. H. Kamkhenthang, Sr. Research Officer, Tribal Welfare Deptt, Manipur, Ms. Jaya Hazarika, Tinsukia College, Assam, Dr. D.N. Mazumdar, reader, Anthropology, Guwahati University and N.K. Jain, Director, Directorate of Tribal Development and Backward Classes, Manipur for valuable material help and friendly suggestions. I am grateful to them. I would also like to pay my gratitude to S. Barkataki, Raghuvir Sinha, Dr. S.S. Sashi and Dr. Hari Mohan, whose works have helped me to present this book.

Among those who have encouraged me most in this monumental work, was Prof. K.K. Mazumdar, Deptt. of Geography, University of Delhi. He not only gave me his fullest cooperation but inspired me to write a book on the locational practices of Indian Tribes. I am also indebted to my sincere friend Dr. B.K. Roy, Deputy Registrar General of India. He lent me many tribal monographs from his office. I record my gratitude to them.

Last but not least, I would also like to record my sincere thanks to Shri Raj Mani Tiwari, Director, Central Hindi Directorate, Ministry of Human Resource Development, Govt. of India and Shri O.P. Aggarwal, Assistant Director, for their constructive help at official level.

I have also to mention my deep love and affection that I owe to my loving daughters Nivedita and Sunandita for their unending help and cooperation throughout the preparation of this book. The final chapters of this book were written by Nivedita. She deserves my deepest affection. My wife Mina has shared the challenge of rethinking and reworking on the manuscript at every stage. My all love, intellectual and personal; are to her.

I am also thankful to M/s Gian Publishing House for their above average standard publication. Without their sincere help, it would not have been possible for the book to see the light of the day.

S.T. DAS

133-E
Kamla Nagar,
Delhi-110007

LIST OF ILLUSTRATIONS

CONTENTS

CHAPTER I

INTRODUCTION

THE PEOPLE of India include a very large number of primitive tribes who subsist on hunting, fishing or by simple form of agriculture. Various authorities have described them by different names. Sir Herbert Risley and Lacey, Mr. Elwin and Shri A.V. Thakar called them 'Aboriginals' ; Sir Baines included them under the category of 'Hill Tribes' ; Mr. Grigson regards them as 'Hill Tribes or wilder aboriginals', while Mr. Shoobert called them 'aborigines'. They have been regarded as 'animists', by Tallents, Sedgwick, Martin and Dr. Hutton calls them as 'primitive tribes'. Mr. Baines calls them 'jungle people, forest tribes or folk'. Mr. Elwin calls the Baigas, the 'original owners of the country'. The eminent Indian anthropologist and sociologist, Dr. Ghurye calls them 'Backward Hindus'. Dr. Das and Das rename them as 'Submerged humanity'.

The tribal groups are presumed to form the oldest ethnological sector of the national population. The term 'Adivasis' (Adi=original ; Vasi=inhabitant) has recently become current to designate these groups.

The origin of Indian Scheduled Tribes has been traced to such races as the Proto-Australoids, who one time practically covered the whole of India ; secondly, the Mongolians who are still located mostly in Assam and North-Eastern India and finally, to a limited extent, also to the Negritos strain as indicated by frizzy hair, among the Andamanese and the Kadars of the South-West India.

The Scheduled Tribes of India are the earliest inhabitants or indigenous people of the country, who were unable to defend themselves and were gradually forced to receds before the invading hoards of such people, as the Dravidians, Indo-Aryans and Mongolians coming from the west, North-west and

North-east respectively, who were not only superior in numerical strength but also in mechanical equipment. The indigenous people thus took shelter in the mountain depths and thick jungles, where a considerable number of them are still found and have been estimated to be about ten million. Those who were left behind on the plains gradually disappeared either by absorption or by acculturalization.

Though these original tribes in India have been divided and sub-divided into a large number of sub-tribes, all mutually exclusive, each having the endogamous and exogamous clans with their own names and their own culture, customs, locational practice and life-style.

The most common features of all these tribes are :

(1) They live away from the civilized world in the inaccessible parts lying in the forests and hills.
(2) They belong either to one of the three stocks—Negritos, Australoids or Mongoloids.
(3) Speak their own tribal dialect.
(4) Follow primitive occupation.
(5) They are largely carnivorous.
(6) They live either naked or semi-naked.
(7) They have nomadic habits and love for drink and dance.
(8) Profess primitive religion known as 'Animism' in which the worship of ghosts and spirits is the most important elements.

We know that religion in the abstract can and must be handled dispassionately without prejudice or passion—and we are learning that despite controversy and sectarianism—Religion in the concrete is "a mode of behaviour, a system of intellectual beliefs and a system of feelings" held by and current among human beings who form a society, live in a definite part of the world and are therefore to be studied by constant reference to history, geography, social and economic conditions and to the universal facts of psychology. The tribes of India live in different parts of India which has its special characteristics and their views as to the nature of Nature, of the world in which and by which they live and move and have their beings, are based upon their experience, personal and communal, of their peculiar environment.

They speak different languages which belongs to various language family. They are in constant contact with Hindu and Hinduised groups. There are features in their intellectual beliefs, their traditional beliefs, their tacitly assumed and unquestioned beliefs, which apart from resemblances due to the common elements of the universal pattern—are unmistakably borrowed from their tribal and Hindu neighbours. We must endeavour to know why this feature and not another was selected for adoption, and whether or in what direction the features so selected have been modified and adapted.

To understand the main currents in Indian culture, one has to probe the colourful world of the tribal people in different parts of the country who are generally considered the original inhabitants of the land. The legends, literature, customs and traditions, speak volumes about the wealth of splendour and creativity of these people that have, concomitantly, influenced even those in the vicinity who have chosen to don the garb of sophistication.

There are apparent cultural differences and locational practices between the life styles of the tribal people of India, but historically, there is a basic unity in thought and philosophy among these people born and brought up in environments of diversity through the length and breadth of the country. What these differences are and what threads of fundamental commonness are inherent in the overall tribal system ? Can the questions be answered by a study of this book.

Anthropology has waited a hundred years for a full account of the different tribes of India, but Mr. Verrier Elwin has paid the debt as fully as any single author who had to work on many tribes after its tribal life and organisation had largely gone. Even the tongue the tribal people now speak is not their own, for there seems to be no doubt but the different speech which they carried with them from the plains to their fastnesses in the hills, and that mixture of their language with Indo-Aryan, Indo-Mongoloid or Dravidian, are the result of linguistic borrowings which have supplanted and effaced an earlier language.

Language, of course, is no safe indication of race and the primitive tribes of India, even if the Mongolian fringes be eliminated, show very great variation when examined by the test of the Co-efficient of Racial Likeness. The Co-efficient of Racial Likeness is by no means an entirely satisfactory criterion of racial affinity, but one would have expected a greater degree of propinquity between such tribes as Bhils, Gonds, Gaddis, Pangwals, etc., than is actually found. In any case the tribal people of India clearly belong to one of the oldest strata of race in India. There is much to suggest that these tongues entered India from the north-west, north and from the south-east and east.

Other items of culture appear among different tribes in India, sometimes very distant, suggesting isoleted survivals of some very ancient culture or cultures now submerged except in remote corners of India, many of which offer links with similar survivals in south-east Asia and Oceania. Thus the use of stilts at one of their festivals of the agricultural year, possibly originating in an attempt to make the crop grow high by the force of goodly ensample, appears again among the Lepcha of the eastern Himalayas, the Angami Nagas of Nagaland and in the Indian Archipelago. The use of tattoo with the idea that it is necessary for the sake of recognition in another world appears again in Chhota Nagpur, in North-eastern States of India and in Borneo. Probably, if it were known, this association of tattoo is frequent in India. A big and pendulous ear seems to have once been greatly admired at any rate from North-eastern India to Formosa and South-eastwards far into the Pacific.

But perhaps the most striking of these survivals of ancient culture among the tribe is the social organisation which makes it proper for grandparent to marry grandchild. The occurrence among the Chhota Nagpur tribes and in the north-eastern tribes and in other societies in India, of a 'joking relationship' between grandparents and grand children, which makes possible a freedom and even licence in conversation that would be quite improper between parents and child, has led to the inference being drawn that at some earlier date a marriage system was in force in which, like the four-class system of Australia, made marriage between grandparent and grandchild not only permissible but socially approved. But in India, in Baiga we find a man still marrying not only his classifactory granddaughter—generally, it seems, his wife's sister's son's daughter—but actually his own daughter's daughter, while the union of a woman with her son's son is also mentioned as a regular practice.

In other respect the Baiga marriage system appears to be in a state of disruption or at least of transition. There is a division into localized and to some extent endogamous groups which are spoken of by the word ordinarily used by Hindus for caste. These endogamous groups are divided into exogamous territorial divisions, but also into clans which are theoretically exogamous but practically not so. Mr. Elwin considers that the exogamous clan is a recent borrowing from the Gond and that the territorial division is the older exogamous grouping, but he also finds traces of an older exogamous clan which, like those of the Gonds, is totemic, while even among the Gond totems, there seems to be traces of two system, for the Markam clan is named after the mango but has the tortoise for its totem. Perhaps it is of some significance that the Gond totems seems to be all animal while the Baiga totems that survive are vegetables.

The remarkable thing about the Baiga endogamy is that it exhibits some of the features of the caste system in what is perhaps a more ancient form than that familiar to us from Hinduism.

Generally speaking the rules of commensality and intermarriage between Baiga tribal groups suggest rather the sort of society from which the caste system may have taken rise, than the society which is characterized by and is dependent on caste to-day.

No doubt Adivasi culture is intrinsically linked to the economic, social and environmental aspects of Adivasi life. There is a clear evidence of changing trends in Adivasi art forms. Some have retained the purity of the original, mainly because of their isolated existence, but the influence of urban culture was evident in the dress, dance and social comments of many others.

The mute message of Adivasis, relayed through their art form, is clear. They do not want computers. They want the forest, the wild animals and birds that have inspired them and sustained them through centuries. Despite their surface urbanisation, every song, dance and other art form of the Adivasis eloquently speak of the circle of life and harmony therein.

The life of the tribal people is simple and placid and often hard. But they have a rich cultural legacy—a myriad, myths and legends which are interesting though rather strange. In the same manner as other communities cherishes the stories of their epic or religious books, the tribal people like to relate or listen to the stories of their history. They have usually emotional reactions to their environment, but to older generation, their mythological tales appear to cover almost every aspect of their life.

The ghotul—the village dormitory—is a central institution in the life and culture of the Muria, a tribe in Madhya Pradesh. But unlike dormitories found among primitive people elsewhere, it is a highly disciplined and democratic organisation. It is one of most highly developed and carefully organised in the world. It is a school which provides co-education in every sphere of tribal life, and it is here that boys and girls start at an early age to train for marriage. For what is a village guard-room for the Nagas, a boy's club among the Oraon, a refuge for temporary sexual association in Indonesia, is for the Muria the centre of social and religious life.

But according to differences in climate and vegetation which lead men to one kind of activity, type of society and even of religious belief in one region and to different activities, social institutions and beliefs in other regions. Social change is not a mechanical addition or subtraction but the integration of the new among the old. Every advance therefore, depends on the pre-existing pattern and must fit into it, and in doing so an intrusive element will probably undergo changes itself, so that any practice however similar in its general character will play a different part in the general life of each separate people.

It is clear that both the spread of knowledge and customs from one people to another, that is *diffusion*, and the part any element plays in the life of the people, that is its *functional relations*, are extremely important in influencing the final pattern of human life in any one region or among any group. These active cultural factors operate on the relatively static materials of race and physical environment. In order to appreciate these matters it is necessary, however, to obtain a fairly full and balanced picture of actual people. By considering as a whole the life of a number of tribes, grouped according to their region, some of their life style and locational practices in relation between the trilogy, habitat, economy and society will be explored.

CHAPTER II

TRIBES : A DISTINCT ELEMENT

J.H. HUTTON, the renowned anthropologist believed that at least the tribals if not the exterior castes who were as backward—formed a distinct element in the Indian population which was not amenable to normal constitutional processes but which required a strategy of intervention by the government to protect their rights and promote their welfare. So he enumerated in 1931 Census all primitive tribes "whatever, their numbers and irrespective of the percentage provision for individual tabulation of caste. This made him possible to give the accurate number of an identifiable tribal unit, though it was not easy to indicate the extent to which such unit remained primitive in its habit. But Hutton was prone to describe tribal religion as the "Surplus material not yet built into the temple of Hinduism" and to highlight the process of the tribes being swallowed up by this religion. But according to latest report about one-third of tribes adhere to tribal religion. The majority of the remainder is Hindus, there are also some Christians, Buddhist and Muslims.

But there are other factors, too, of which the census authorities were only dimly aware, namely the transformation of the tribe into the peasant, as a result of transfer of technology by and the acceptance of the fact of Jati more of the latter. The economic dimension which did not fall within the ambit of the British census authorities to explore was as important, if not more, than the social. According to 1981 census, Hinduism claiming 87 per cent and Christianity 7 per cent of adherents among tribes. Even so, Hutton, J.P. Mills and those who have written about this subject seem to have under-estimated the autonomy of tribal society and of it's religion. Tribal religions have not disappeared. Many elements of tribal religion are as alive, even vigorous, as ever. As studies have recently shown trIbal religion has not lost its distinct identity in spite of its long years of interaction with Hinduism and Christianity. It has maintained its system of religious beliefs and practices including propitiation of spirit, magic and witchcraft and the priesthood. Recent trends even suggest revival of many of pristine elements of tribal religion by those who have gone out of its fold. Therefore, the prevalent assumption that the survival of tribal religion is at stake needs to be reconsidered.

Much the same observation may also apply to the status of tribal languages, in spite of the dominance of the languages of various states and increasing incidence of bilingualism among tribes. The role of economic factor appears to have been over-emphasised by Hutton and that of acculturation somewhat ignored by him. To day non-tribals are also turning bilingual picking up a tribal language or two. Non-tribal languages have emerged as the language of trade, exchange, and the under world of magic and witchcraft.

In areas of tribal preponderance tribal languages have survived. The Munda languages still hold sway : the number of speakers of Gondi fell slightly. The Oraons of Madhya Pradesh have regained the linguistic status in 1961, they had lost earlier but Bhumji of Orissa have lost theirs. Many tribal movements in recent years have demonstrated renewed interest in their language and script.

Non-tribal Laws

It has been found that their position in surroundings of a more developed culture presents certain problem for academicians. As long as a primitive tribe remains in isolation conducting its own affairs according to its own laws and customs it presents no problem except that required to prevent raiding or other forms of aggression on more civilised or less warlike neighbours.

Where communications are meagre or non-existent contact with the outer world will be so slow that the effect of its impact will not be rapid enough for observation and no change will take place in the primitive community except the gradual adaptation and alteration resulting from the intercourse on the fringes of the area inhabited. Changes of this kind involving a very slow change of environment and outlook are familiar enough in remote north-east, north and in Central India and have been going on for centuries. No serious problem arises until this process of slow adaptation is interfered with by a development of communication and a sudden increase of contact.

Even excise laws, although in many ways to the benefit of primitive tribes, may operate as a hardship and would be found excessively severe if the very proper restrictions on distilling were extended to PACHWAI and TARI made for household consumption and forming a very important part of the diet of tribes that cannot grow sugar and are too poor to buy it. For three months in the hot weather the Marias of Chanda live almost exclusively on a very mildly alcoholic beverage, much as the Angami Naga does to a less degree in Nagaland. The prohibition of distilling itself may be a hardship, as for the Gond who must offer to his god liquor distilled by the family of worshippers, but this is probably one of those that must be borne in the interests of the community, like the game laws that prevent a Kachha Naga or a Kuki from offering game at the grave of the dead during the close season.

Conflict of Contact

The rapid opening up of communications involving contact at many points and often the practical settlement of tribal country, entirely alters the aspect of any gradual changes that may have been taking place. Generally speaking it substitute conflict for contact. Not necessarily, that is, a conflict of arms but of culture and of material interest. Attempts to develop minerals, forests, or land for intensive cultivation can only be made at the expense of the tribe whose isolation is thus invaded.

The customs which regulate the ownership, or transfer of land among primitive tribes are generally at variance with those observed by more sophisticated communities and in the conflict between the two, the tribal custom is normally superseded by a code which is neither valued nor understood by the tribe and in the application of which the tribe is deprived of its property, generally in the name of law, either by alienation to foreigners or by transforming the trusteeship of a tribal chief into absolute ownership of a kind quite foreign to the customs of the tribe. This has be fallen both the Mundas and other hill tribes.

Application of Alien law

A similar application of alien law also usually disturbs the tribal custom of debt. Tribal customs of debt are frequently, perhaps normally, stated in terms of extravagant usury. Such terms however represent less the real customs observed in practice than the ideal which the lender considers ought to be the return and in point of fact they are qualified for very important considerations. In the first place there is commonly no law of limitation and thus borrower may not expect to repay before the next generation while the lender is very often so placed that there is a moral compulsion to lend under certain circumstances even if no return is expected in his lifetime. Thus it is often the custom for a chief to lend paddy to the most indigent and unprofitable of his villagers in times of scarcity though he knows repayment to be extremely unlikely.

In any case when repayment does take place there is normally a settlement by accommodation between both parties which bears little relation to the payment due on a strict interpretation of the law of usury as formally stated by the tribe. It is only natural that tribesmen whose views of debt are dictated by this sort of vague custom are perfectly ready to subscribe without demur to the most flagrantly usurious agreements exacted by foreign money-lenders who intend to invoke a foreign code to compel repayment on the letter of the agreement and at the time when it suits them to do so instead of at such time as the debtor finds himself in a position to pay.

Similarly the criminal law of a civilised community is often entirely at variance with what is felt to be just and proper by tribal custom. Afforestation again is a frequent grievance, and in forests which were common property under a tribal regime it becomes a punishable offence to exercise what the tribe regards as an inalienable right. But this land has by the great majority of hill tribes been regarded for many generations as their most valuable real property. Such an action would in some tribes have been almost enough to cause a rebellion by itself. In the Tamil Nadu again the same attitude has been taken towards *jhum*, there called *podu* and has been carried to the extent of the prohibition of cultivation, twice bringing the Sawara tribe to the verge of open rebellion.

Primitive system of agriculture are frequently extremely wasteful of forest land and may in hill country prove damaging to adjoining plains on account of denudation, the too rapid escape of rain and consequent enundation below. At the same time wasteful cultivation of this kind is very often the only known means of subsistence.

Again the exploitation of minerals not only involve the taking up of tribal land but generally the introduction of an alien population, usually of an extremely mixed character and not infrequently exceptionally dissolute. This impinges on tribal life in a number of disconcerting ways. Even the invasion of missionaries is liable to produce as much evil as good, if not more, for their conduct and objects are generally in extreme conflict with tribal religion and with taboos of all kinds, and their point of view, readily comprehensible to an alien administration which understands the tribal position very vaguely if at all and backed as it so often is by influentially vocal societies at a distance, is much more likely to obtain the support of the authority than taboos which are on the face of them unreasonable to all except those to whom they are the most vitally important things in life.

A similar misunderstanding of the tribal point of view is apt to arise in the case of many customs, and it may be enough to mention that of marriage by a form of capture common to both Bhils and Gonds, and although quite familiar to the tribesmen themselves, often capable of being treated by British Courts as cases of abduction. Apart from laws in themselves their manner of application may be extremely severe on people whose methods of dealing with antisocial actions or persons is entirely different.

Rai Bahadur Sarat Chandra Roy said "The British System of administration of justice........... has unintentionally produced certain deplorable effects on the moral character of the aborigines. This complicated system of law, which is........ ... suited to advance people, was naturally not comprehended by the people, the simple aborigines and was not suited to their level of culture. And thus this complicated system of administration of justice has tendered to impair the natural truthfulness and honesty of the people in many cases."

He further said "The British system of law and administration has further tended to impair the social solidarity of the tribes and has weakened the authority of the social heads or Panches and the respect they formerly commanded.

It is easy to see how a combination of anti-tribal forces is likely to create a condition of excessive discomfort in tribal life, the most serious aspect of which is the complete breakdown of the communal organisation. A tribe living in comparative isolation will usually be found to have developed an adaptation to its environment which within certain limits approaches perfection, an adaptation which may have taken many millennia to accomplish and the breakdown of which may be the ruin of the tribe."

Again it is not in its devotional aspect that Hutton was concerned with religion, but in its social, and it cannot be denied but society in India is still largely organised on a basis of caste and religion and social conduct is much influenced by local practices which may not be in themselves religious, but which are subject to religious sanctions. The age of marriage, the practice of remarrige, the occupations of women, the inheritance of property and the maintenance of widows, even diet, to name a few of obvious cases, vary according to the caste and the religious community of the individual tribes.

It cannot also be denied that Bhils and Thakurs, living in isolated groups in Hindu villages are gradually yielding to the influence of association and conforming to the rites of Hindu worship as practised locally. My personal view is that the process of assimilation is very slow, much slower than is commonly believed to be the case, even in areas where individual members of the Aboriginal Tribes have descended into the plains and are brought into contact with all the influence of village life. In India as a whole the tribesmen who changed tribal religion to Hinduism numbered several million.

Still we find very ancient and primitive beliefs continuing under the guise of Hinduism in many tribes. The sanctity of the fig tree for instance is possibly to be associated with the beliefs of the Negrito inhabitants who appear to have formed the earliest population of India. It is probably on account of its milk like sap that the *ficus* is associated with fertility cults in Africa, Italy and New Guinea as well as in Assam and in Southern India and it is generally also connected with the spirits of the dead. This cult appears to be shared by the Andamanese who are an approximately pure Negrito race.

Again the flesh of cattle is tabooed by certain clans among primitive tribes of North-eastern India, who do not appear to have come even remotely under the influence of Hinduism, while on the other hand the cow is regarded as completely tabooed by the Shins of Chilas, who are described by Leitner as a Hindu tribe.

The head-hunting and human sacrifice are intimately associated with agriculture and the line is hard to draw at the point at which a purely magical fertility rites begins to develop into ceremonial of a genuinely religious nature. At any rate the tribal cult ceases to be purely tribal and is identified with some definitely religious festival so that the magical, ceremonial and devotional aspects become merged.

The Hindu rites of the *Shradh* provide for the creation of a new body to house the soul of the deceased. In the tribal religion this cult of the dead is seen in precisely parallel form but at a very much more matter of fact and materialistic stage of the development of the idea. Thus in Mysore the Hasalar tribe redeem the soul with a pig from the magician who has caused the death and domicile it in a pot where it is supplied with food and water. The Nicobarese and some Naga tribes fashion wooden figures on which the skull of the deceased is placed in order that the soul may leave it and enter the wooden figure. It is for a time kept supplied with all worldly necessities. A similar practice must formerly have obtained among the Garos of Meghalaya. Further the Sawara of Ganjam district of Orissa uses a similar but more conventionalised wooden figure to accommodate the soul of his cremated dead during the interval between death and cremation and the time for the erection of a stone for the souls of the dead during the year which is done annually about the time of the sowing of crop. In Madhya Pradesh the Kunbi make an image of eir dead in brass which is kept until the superfluity of such mages necessitates their deposit in the water of some sacred river.

The theory however on which it is based that the soul matter is specially located in the head, may be detected elsewhere. Thus the Andamanese attach special importance to the Jaw and to the skull in mourning and at any rate one case is recorded of their carrying off the cranium of a victim killed in warfare.

One phenomenon of primitive religion which cannot be ignored when writing on Indian tribes is totemism, traces of which are shown by primitive tribes in all parts of India. From Bhils in the west to the Chhakma in the east; from Kanets of the Simla hills to Telugu people of South India, clear traces of totemism are found to survive. The Ao Naga try to influence the rice by planting a root or two in the earth, put in the hollow top of the bamboo and so raised above the rest of the field which is thus induced to grow high.

All these tribal customs, locational practices and life styles, well suited to tribal people. Any departure by way of imposing modern system of law, justice and administration will ruin the colourful tribal people. In the alternative they may retain a sort of emasculated tribal life, deprived of the customs and festivals that gave it meaning and cohesion and fall into that psychical apathy and physical decline which has decimated so many tribal communities elsewhere.

The rapidly approaching extinction of the tribes of Great Andaman has largely been due to diseases imported into the penal settlement and communicated to the Andamanese by convicts.

The use of distilled liquor, of opium and even of mercury (as a drug) is performing a similar disservice for other tribes and is likewise the result of the improved communications which corrupt good manners.

Hence the introduction of anti-tribal forces is definitely likely to create a condition of excessive discomfort in happy tribal life and their old communal organisation. It is likely to proceed at a far greater rate than either the gradual change in physical environment or than the still slower process of adaptation to that change.

CHAPTER III

A PORTRAIT OF ARUNACHAL PRADESH

ARUNACHAL PRADESH is a thinly populated hilly tract laying roughly between the latitudes 26°28'N and 29°30'N and the longitudes 91°30'E and 96°30'E on the north-east extremity of India, comprising roughly 83,578 kilometre square of area, bordering the international boundaries of Bhutan, Tibet, China and Burma. The Pradesh is known to be rich in flora, fauna, power and mineral potential. Previously this region was known as the North East Frontier Agency (NEFA) which was constitutionally a part of the State of Assam.

On the 21st day of January, 1970, NEFA has been made into a Union Territory with its capital at Itanagar situated in Subansiri District. According to 1981 census, the total population of Arunachal Pradesh was 631,839. Compare with the population of India, Arunachal Pradesh contains less than one thousandth part of the population. Arunachal Pradesh largely consist of hilly terrains and are inhabited predominantly by the Scheduled Tribes.

There are nine districts in Arunachal Pradesh, namely :

Area, Population and Headquarters of Districts

District	*Area (Sq. Km.)*	*Population*	*Headquarter*
1. Dibang Valley	13,029	30,978	Anini
2. East Kameng	4,134	42,736	Seppa
3. East Siang	6,512	70,451	Pasighat
4. Lohit	11,402	69,498	Tizu
5. Lower Subansiri	13,010	1,12,650	Ziro
6. Tirap	7,024	1,28,650	Khonsa
7. Upper Subansiri	7,032	39,410	Daporijo
8. West Kameng	9,594	63,302	Bomdila
9. West Siang	12,006	74,164	Along

There is much variation in the population size of the districts. The reason for this is that in the pockets like Apatani valley of Subansiri District where Ziro Circle is situated, large concentration of population has resulted because of facility provided by nature for agricultural pursuit. On the other hand, Kibithoo, Taksing, Singa circles, which are situated right on the international boundary, the facilities for agricultural pursuit are inadequate and therefore population in these circles are sparse. The pattern of customs regulating the ownership and holding of land has also played a part in connection with distribution of population in different regions of Arunachal Pradesh.

Natural Population Regions

In distribution of population, Arunachal Pradesh can be divided into six natural regions. The first two regions are the western parts of Kameng District and Tirap District where there are comparatively large concentration of population. The upper, the middle and the lower belts of the remaining parts of Arunachal Pradesh constitute three distinct regions. The concentrated population pockets on the foot hills constitute the sixth region.

Western Kameng. The western half of Kameng District, mainly inhabited by the Monpa, the Sherdukpen and some other tribes, present a picture of marginal food sufficiency. The hill ranges of this part are around 7000 ft. high above the mean sea level, although some ranges reach the height of 16,000 ft. or so. The valleys are situated at about 5000 ft attitude. Many of the hill slopes are amenable to terracing and the people have developed both dry and wet terraces on them. As a result of this, good crop of rice, buck wheat, barley, maize and smaller grains are grown on the terraces. Because of the suitability of the terrain, the horticultural development, such as growing of apple trees, has gained popularity with the people. The pastures of the high hills are suitable for livestock rearing and the people have traditionally developed many cross breeds of the cattle, such as between yak and cow, methun and cow etc. The sheep rearing is also very popular. Due to all these, large villages have established.

Tirap District. In Tirap District, lying in the South-East part of Arunachal Pradesh, the people sustain largely on shifting cultivation which is locally know as Jhumming. The height of the hill ranges is usually 6000′ or below. Jhumming is practised in most other parts of Arunachal Pradesh. Jhumming consists of clearing of a patch of jungles by cutting and burning and dribbling seeds into the clearing patch with the help of a poker. Usually a mixed crop is grown in the Jhum fields which require weeding at least four times and watching out of the wild animals and birds all the time. After a year or two of cultivation, the Jhum fields are abandoned and new clearings are opened elsewhere. The practice of Jhumming requires an extensive area for sustaining a small population. The villages sustaining up on this type of cultivation are, of necessity, small few, and far between.

However, the customs relating to ownership and holding of land of Tirap District have helped in the development of comparatively large villages. The villages of Tirap District comprise of a definite area which contains the village common land for Jhumming and also for extraction of forest produce. Individuals also hold cultivable land and forests. The common ownership of land has led to concentration of population in the villages and a resultant high density of population.

Eastern Kameng, Subansiri, Siang and Lohit Districts

The people of these districts do practice Jhum cultivation in the same manner as the people of Tirap District do. But the terrain and ownership customs of these areas are different. As regards population, these areas can be divided into three belts—upper, middle and lower.

The Upper Belt. The northern parts of these areas, close to the international border, comprises of high hill ranges cut by rivers flowing down hills in deep and steep gorges. Even for Jhum cultivation these areas are not suitable and people largely sustain themselves with cereal substitutes and forest produce for most parts of the year. Some northern tribes have grown groves of Tasse or wild Sago plants upon which individual ownership prevails. The population of this belt is extremely thin.

The Middle Belt. The middle belt of these areas resembles the conditions of Tirap District and the population is largely concentrated in this belt, in the villages situated at the mid-heights of the hills lining the river valleys. Included in this belt are the heavy population pockets like the Apatani valley of Subansiri District and the Basar bowl of Siang District where well watered permanent paddy fields have been developed. But the ownership and holding of land in these areas are different from those of Tirap District. Here the cultivable land is owned by the individuals. The hunting and fishing areas are also generally owned by individual or by the villages as a whole. In certain areas such as in Lohit District, the clan ownership of the cultivable lands used to be the practice but with the passage of time such ownership has passed on to the individuals. As a result of the individual ownership of land coupled with the Jhum practice, the villages did not develop as tight fit economic and social units to the extent they did in the Western Kameng and in Tirap District.

The Jhum cultivation requires close proximity of the fields to the owners. As the ownership pattern of land had been usually from the hill top to the hill stream, small groups of families live together as close to their lands as possible. As a result of this, the villages of this belt are comparatively smaller and the community effort for the development of terraces are not a very great success. Further, the availability of suitable lands for terracing is not very extensive. As a result, although the density of population is larger in this belt than in the upper belt, the same is much thinner than those of the western part of Kameng District and of Tirap District.

The Lower Belt. This belt adjoins the plains of Assam. The hill are comparatively lower in altitude and those adjoining the Assam plains are broken due to earthquakes and extensive landslides caused by heavy monsoon rains. The rivers have created broad valleys in these areas. Due to heavy rains, the forests are luxuriant in growth and large games inhabit them.

Traditionally the hill tribes did not prefer to live in this belt as they did not like the climate and the protection of the field crops from the wild animals is always a problem. Small settlements, however, existed since long, mostly inhabited by members of the tribes who had to leave their villages in the middle belt due to social reasons.

The density of population in Arunachal Pradesh is 8 persons per square kilometre. The highest concentration of population in Arunachal Pradesh is in Tirap District and the lowest density of population is found in Lohit District where only 3 persons live per square kilometre of area.

Scheduled Tribes

The Scheduled Tribes are different sets of people. They comprise of communities maintaining social customs and rituals which different from what are followed by the population of the greater part of the country. Their habitation are usually located in the deep woods or on high hills which are not easily accessible. In the times now covered by the mist of antiquity, these aboriginal groups of people either lived in these parts or fled from the present populated areas as the result of warfare and other pressing social and political factors. There they survived. But they were great losers economically. The Scheduled Tribes lived away from the larger communities but lost their social and economic prowess all the same. But they maintained their pride as people. Their lives are colourful despite their poverty and backwardness.

The remote and inaccessible habitations of these small communities have enabled them to maintain their fascinating identities. These communities are generally poor because they practice primitive methods of agriculture and also depend upon food gathering from the forests by hunting, fishing or collecting edible roots, fruits and other vegetables. As a result of this, the economic and social attainments of these people are at a low norm and they had to succumb to the status of backward tribes.

According to 1971 census, there were 110 tribes in Arunachal Pradesh. But the census organisation is aware that even this long list may not be covering all the identities of the scheduled tribes. The tribe names may go on varying in number and in content.

Identity. It has been found that the tribes of Arunachal Pradesh are seeking larger identity for themselves outside the confines of their tribe names. As for example, 'Adi' was not returned as a tribe name in 1961 census. But in 1971 census not only 'Adi' appears as a prominent tribe name but quite many tribes were also found to have prefixed 'Adi' to their tribe names like Adi Gallong, Adi Minyong, Adi Padam etc. In 1961, census only the 'Adi Pasi' tribe used 'Adi' as a prefix to their tribe name which also appeared in the same manner in 1971 census. Adoption of the name 'Adi' separately or as a prefix to a tribe name, did not follow the ethnological consideration. As for example, the Gallong and Minyong tribe cannot be said to be having the same ethnological origin. The Gallong speech form is more akin with the Nishang or Nissi speech form than with the Minyong speech form. But Gallong have adopted 'Adi' as prefix and not 'Nishang or Nissi'. This clearly shows that adoption of 'Adi' as a prefix to Gallong is guided by factors other than the ethnological affinity of the Gallongs with the Minyongs or the Padams. I may call this tendency as putative desire of the tribe to find a larger identity for themselves. The constituents of the tribes that show this tendency are : Abor, Adi, Adi Gallong, Adi Minyong, Adi Padam, Adi Pasi, Ashing, Bagi, Bogum, Bokar, Bomdo, Bori, Janbo, Gallong, Karka, Komkar, Kongbo, Libo, Millang, Millang Abor, Muktum, Nonong, Pailibo, Pangi, Pasi, Pongkong, Ramo, Simong, Siram, Tangam, Taram and Yateng.

On the other hand the tribes who were earlier known as Dafla by the plain people comprising of tribe name like Bangni, Dafla, Khrodeng Bangni, Nishang, Nissi, Sulung Bangni, Tagin Bangni, Yanoo Bangni etc. are known to be of the same ethnological origin. These tribes now show a desire to be called as Nissi or Nishang. It is not putative. It bases upon a real ethnological linkage.

Similar are the cases of identity for 'Mishmi and Monpa'. In 1961 census Mishmi was not returned as a tribe name. The tribe names were returned as Idu/Chulikata, Mishmi, Digaru/Taraon Mishmi and Kaman/Miju Mishmi. But in 1971 census the tiribe name Mishmi is also returned which illustrates the desire of the members of these three tribes to seek a larger identity.

Monpa was also returned as a tribe name in 1961 census. The people who are known as Tangsa, are very proud of their sub-tribe or clan identity. They usually return themselves with the names of sub-tribe or clan, although they usually add Tangsa to these names. The following are the constituents of the

Tangsa group of tribes : Bolok, Darko, Haish, Havi, Hotang, Katin, Kemsing, Khalim, Korang, Langkai, Lichi, Lonchang, Longin, Longphi, Longri, Longsang, Lowang, Monglum, Morang, Mossang, Namsang, Ngimong, Phong, Rangai, Rongrang, Sanke, Simsa, Taisen, Tangsa Tikhak, Yongkuk and Yougli.

The above statement points to one fact : The identity of the tribes of Arunachal Pradesh in a fluid condition not only because a definite list of the Scheduled Tribes of Arunachal Pradesh is lacking but also because of the fact that the tribes themselves are yet to deside with what identity they are to emerge.

Scheduled Tribes. The Scheduled Tribes of Arunachal Pradesh are 4,41,167 in number or about 66.6 per cent of the population of the state. The Scheduled Tribes males are 2,09,066 or about 47 per cent of the total male population and females are 2,32,101 or about 53 per cent of the total female population.

The Scheduled Tribes comprise about 79 per cent of the population of Kameng district, 91 per cent of Subansiri, 87 per cent of Siang district, 58 percent of Lohit and 71 per cent of Tirap district. About 81 per cent of the rural population of Arunachal Pradesh belongs to the Scheduled Tribes, whereas the same for the urban population is only 20 per cent.

Distribution. The Scheduled Tribes live in exclusive pockets of the territory upon which they have traditional ownership rights. In fact infringement of this traditional rights had led to many a warfare in the past. The tribes like Monpa, Sherdukpen, Aka, Miji, Khowa etc. are entirely confined to Kameng district and live in compact areas of their own, Nishang, Bangro and Sulung tribes live in the eastern part of Kameng District and also in contiguous Subansiri District. Bangro make an exclusive pocket of their own lying on both the sides of the boundary between Kameng and Subansiri. Sulungs on the other hand live amidst settlements of Miji, Nishang and Bangros, situated more or less close to the northern part of the boundary between these two districts. Nishang or Nissi group of tribes cover the eastern part of Kameng District and the whole of Subansiri District excluding the pockets where the tribes like Apatani, Sulung or Bangro live,

The Nishang territory borders on the territory of Hill Miri and Tagin tribes. Beyond Subansiri to the east, is Siang District, the home of the Adi group of tribes. Some smaller tribes like Momba and Khamba live in the northern part of Siang District. The Padam tribe of the Adi group inhabits also in Lohit District but form a compact pocket of their own on both sides of the border between Siang and Lohit District. Miri or Mishing tribe lives in the plain part of Siang District. Lohit is the home of the Mishmi tribe. In the plains of this district, the tribes like Khampti, Singpho and Deori have settled. Tirap district is the home of Nocte, Wancho and Tangsa tribes.

Traditional Contact. The traditional contacts of the tribes of Arunachal Pradesh was largely with the people of Assam. From the plains of Assam, the tribes traded with their forest produce like cane, poison for arrow tips, dried bamboo shoots, skin and fur, Mishmi Teeta, Rengbeng, Jangphai, musk, oil of horn bills etc. for salt, eri, and Muga silk, utensils and cooking pots, iron and iron implements, ornaments, brass and bronze products, animals for slaughter, rice and paddy and other sundry items. The Arunachal Pradesh tribes took active part in shaping the history of Assam by participating in the affairs of the old royal dynasties of kock and Sootiya kingdoom, with the fall of the koch power the tribes harassed the Ahom power with hostility till a political settlement was made with them with the Ahom king.

The traditional contact of the tribes with Assam came under heavy restriction as the result of "Inner Line" regulation promulgated by the British Government in 1873.

The comparative isolation has led to quite many differences in their socio-economic and demographic characteristics.

Dwelling

Out of total population of 6,31,839 of Arunachal Pradesh, 94 per cent are rural. The rural population of Arunachal Pradesh is less than the rural population of any state.

The Scheduled Tribes comprise the largest section of the rural population. Out of total rural population of 5,36,219, the Scheduled Tribes population living in the rural areas are 3,27,523, that is about 16.7 per cent of the total rural population. According to the 1971 cenus returns, 110 tribes constituted the

Scheduled Tribes population of Arunachal Pradesh. Although there are instances that a few villages are inhabited by more than one tribe or a little tribal group, the common rule is that the different tribes or the tribe groups live in exclusive villages inhabited by the members of one tribe or a tribe group only. It fact most of the tribes do possess a traditional territory of their own and the infringement of the territorial rights of one tribe by another may lead to war.

Therefore the pattern of living in rural Arunachal Pradesh is closely related to the customs and habits that the different tribes follow in their day to day life. In addition to this customary background the terrain and the climate have also come into the play to give checkered appearance to the habitation of the rural areas of Arunachal Pradesh.

Size of the Village. The average size of a village is 151 persons. The largest number of villages are situated in Subansiri District and the least in Tirap District. Subansiri district contains about 32 per cent of the total villages whereas Tirap district contains only 10 per cent of the villages, but these districts contain about 22 per cent of the rural population each. The average size of the villages of Lohit district is the least, being 95 persons and that of Tirap district is 312 persons, the largest average size of the villages amongst the districts of Arunachal Pradesh. Lohit district contains about 21 per cent of the total villages of the state and about 13 per cent of the population.

The average size of the villages in the Subansiri district is 103 persons. Kameng district contains about 17 per cent of the villages and about 22 per cent of the rural population. Siang district contains about 20 per cent of the villages, and about 25 per cent of the rural population with average size of 190 persons.

About 40 per cent of the rural population live in about 81 per cent of the villages of Arunachal Pradesh in diminutive village. About 67 per cent live in about 95 per cent of the villages the category of in small villages. About 83 per cent live in about 98 per cent of the small villages.

The basic reason for the villages of Arunachal Pradesh being Small lies in the agricultural practice. The people of Arunachal Pradesh are used to Jhumming or Shifting cultivation. The customary laws regulating the ownership and use of land are rigid and therefore small groups of families have to remain as close as possible to the agricultural land required to be cleared for Jhumming year after year. If the fields are located far away, then the women and children who are required to work in the Jhum fields, may find it difficult to reach the fields crossing over the turbulent revulets and other natural hazards on the way.

Definition adopted for size of the villages

Population range	*Category*
Less than 200	Diminutive village
200-499	Very small village
500-999	Small village
1000-1999	Medium village
2000-4999	Large village
5000-9999	Very large village
10000	Special village.

The smallness of the villages come in sharp contrast with the comparatively large villages of other hill areas of the region like the Naga inhabited area of Nagaland and Manipur. But in the Naga inhabited areas the villages are large only where the inhabitants rely on permanent terrace cultivation. In other Naga areas the villages are also small where permanent terraced cultivation has not developed. As far example, most of the villages of Zeimei, Liengmei and Rongmei Naga tribes, who still practice shifting cultivation are small in size. Even amongst the single Naga tribe of Tagkhuls, the villages cultivating permanent terraced fields like those situated in the western part of Manipur East District, are much bigger in size than those inhabited by the shifting cultivators belonging to the same tribe situated in the northern and the southern parts of the same district.

No village of the Arunachal Pradesh belongs to the very large or special categories, 11 per cent belongs to the category of medium villages and about 6 per cent can be termed as large villages.

Amongst the district, Lohit and Subansiri show a very great predominance of diminutive villages. About 92 per cent of the villages of Subansiri and about 91 per cent of Lohit are diminutive in size and contains about 63 per cent and 49 per cent of the rural population respectively. These two districts may be bracketed together for the distribution of villages by size although Lohit contains slightly larger percentages of villages and rural population in the bigger villages when compared to Subansiri, Kameng and Siang districts, can also be bracketed in this respect. Kameng district contains about 37 per cent of the rural population as against 35 per cent of Siang comes under diminutive villages. About 24 per cent of the villages of Kameng fall into the category of very small villages and contain about 41 per cent of the rural population of the district.

Siang has about 21 per cent of the total villages as very small that contain about 34 per cent of the rural population. Tirap district differs from the other districts with quite a number of villages and comparatively larger population in the small categories of villages. Only about 54 per cent of the villages of this district falls in the diminutive category of villages that contain only about 17 per cent of the rural population. About 30 per cent of the population lives in 13 per cent of the villages that are small and about 21 per cent of the rural population lives in 5 per cent of the villages that are medium in size. About 1 per cent of the villages of the Tirap districts are large and they contain about 7 per cent of the total rural population of the district.

It is interesting to note that the percentage as well as population of the diminutive villages have decrease and the very small and small villages have increase. It is possibly, amongst other things, the people of Arunachal Pradesh are gradually taking to more permanent ways of cultivation Kameng and Subansiri districts do not contribute to this trend except for the category of very small villages. The sharpest indicator of the change is available in Tirap District where the incidence of diminutive villages have fallen by about 5 per cent and their population by about 10 per cent since 1961 census. Siang and Lohit districts show about 2 per cent drop in the incidence of the diminutive villages. But Siang registered a drop of only about 4 per cent in the population of diminutive villages whereas Lohit has shown a fall of about 8 per cent of population.

Urban areas. No place in Arunachal Pradesh satisfied the necessary criteria to be included in the towns, according to norms, namely (1) declared as town by the Government and

(2) considered suitable to be treated as urban area because of their population, density of population. In 1961 census, the entire Arunachal Pradesh was treated as rural. But the district and sub-divisional headquarters of Arunachal Pradesh were found to be possessing district urban characteristics in 1971. These places were mainly inhabited by government servants and other workers who had migrated from outside. Those districts which recorded a population of 2500 persons were treated as towns in 1971 census. Accordingly Along, Bomdila, Pasighat and Tezu were treated as towns.

Urban Population

The urban population of Arunachal Pradesh is only 3.7 per cent of the total population. The proportion of rural and urban population is approximately 24 : 1. Of the total population of 6,31,839 of Arunachal Pradesh, 441,167 are Scheduled Tribes.

It has been stated that only 4 places in Arunachal Pradesh were treated as urban. Of these two towns belonged to Siang district, one to Kameng district and one to Lohit district.

Literacy. 1981 census reveals that out of the total population of 631,839, persons, there were 1,31,333 literate persons in Arunachal Pradesh—98,211 were males and 33,122 were females. The literacy rate was 20.79 per cent, 28.94 per cent male and 11.32 per cent for female.

Out of the total population of 6,31,839 persons, 4,41,167 persons were Scheduled Tribes.

During one decade, the growth rate of literacy of the Scheduled Tribes population is higher than the growth rate of literacy of the over all population. As against the decadal growth of 58 per cent of literacy for the overall population, the growth rate of the Scheduled Tribes registered an increase of 107 per cent during 1961-71. The growth rate of male literate was 89 per cent as against 315 per cent for female.

Another happy indication is that the female literacy has increased at a very fast rate for all district and the rate of growth of female literacy may improve during the coming decade.

The distribution of Scheduled Tribes literates by educational level has a great significance for Arunachal Pradesh. The total Scheduled Tribes literate of Arunachal Pradesh are only 19202 in number, out of whom 1982 are literates without educational level. About 15,191 or 79 per cent of the Scheduled Tribes literates returned primary as their educational level, whereas 1713 or about 9 per cent of the Scheduled Tribes literates returned their educational level as middle. Matriculation or Higher Secondary level education was found only in 250 persons. Out of whom 240 were males and only 10 were females. Siang district is turning out maximum number of literates at all levels of education.

Religion. Hinduism accounts for the largest number of persons returning a major religion. About 25.0 per cent of the total population had returned Hinduism as their religion i.e. out of total population of 631,839 persons, 1,57959.7 had returned Hinduism. Of these 31,729 persons belong to the Scheduled Tribes of Arunachal Pradesh. The Noctes are the largest group of persons belonging to the Scheduled Tribes of Arunachal Pradesh returning Hinduism as their religion. The Nishang or Nissi or Bangni or Dafla or Yanoo Bangni who can be grouped together in consideration of their ethnological identity, are the next large group of Tribes who follow Hinduism. The group is followed by the Mishmi group of tribes comprising of Digarce/Taroan Mishmi ; Idu/Chulikata Mishmi, Kaman/Miju Mishmi and Mishmi with 4,792 persons returning their religion as Hinduism.

Mishing/Miri, Deori, Mikir and Tangsas are the tribes that had returned as Hindus.

Next to the Hindus come the Buddhists in numerical strength. About 67.5 per cent of the total Buddhists belong to the tribes of Arunachal Pradesh. The Monpa group of tribes comprising of Monpa. But Monpa, Dirang Monpa, Lish Monpa, Panchen Monpa and Tawang Monpa tribes account for nearly 50 per cent Buddhists. The Monpa group of tribes followed by Khamptis and then by the Mombas tribes who also follow Buddhism. Also Singphos and Sherdukpen returned as Buddhists. Next are Kaman/Miju-Mishmi and Khowa also belong to Buddhism. It may be generally stated that the Khamptis, the Singhos and the Mishmis belong to the Hinayana Sect whereas the others belong to the Mahayana Sect of Buddhism.

The Christian are only 0.83 per cent of the total population of

Arunachal Pradesh. Sikhs and Muslim population are 0.27 per cent and 0.18 per cent respectively.

Other religion. Many persons returned as other religion as their religions faith in Arunachal Pradesh. Although their numbers are within hundred but most of these are synonymous with the names of the tribes of Arunachal Pradesh. Many interesting names like Abutani, Bhismak, Donipolo and Deva-dharma, have also come out. These names truely represents the sentiment and the faith of the tribes of Arunachal Pradesh.

The faith of the people of Arunachal Pradesh concede the existence of a benevolent God to be called 'Abutani' or 'Doni-polo' or by dozen other names, who is unique, omni-present and omniscient and the literal meanings of these terms (Abutani—the first created. Donipolo—the sun and the moon) do not convey their actual spiritual connotation, a fact that is so very often missed by the students of the tribal faiths of Arunachal Pradesh.

Activity

Arunachal Pradesh is full of hills and valleys and is entirely rural barring six towns. An overwhelming 94 per cent of the population live in about 3,257 villages. The economy is basically agrarian, characterised mainly by slash and burn methods of shifting cultivation constitute 35.33 per cent of the total population and 72.29 per cent of the total number of workers engaged in different economic activities.

In 1983, about 4 per cent of the total geographical area was brought under agriculture, while about 62 per cent of the area was covered by the extensive forests. Over 70 per cent of the cultivated area was under Jhum and about 30 per cent under settled cultivation wet rice and terraced rain-fed cropping.

Rice is the major grain crop. Other important crops are maize, millets, wheat, barley, pulses, mustard, potato, sugarcane, ginger, chilli, cotton etc. Pineapple, oranges, lemon, lichi, papaya, banana and peach walnut, almond etc. are grown.

Weaving and basketry are the important household industries. The small scale industries, numbering 1086 in 1983, comprise saw, rice and oil mills, fruit preservation, soap and candle manufacturing, units, steel fabrication, wood works etc. Of the twelve medium industries some are forest-based, producing veneers, tea-chesis and plyboards.

The important industries in the medium-scale sector, are the light roofing sheet factory at Pasighat, a fruit processing plant at Nigmoi in West Siang district and a cement plant at Tezu. Exploration of the coal deposit in the Namehik-Namphuk area of the Tirap district has been under taken. Vast deposit of dolomite exists at Rupa in the West Kameng district. The limestone available at Tidding in the Lohit district is also being exploited.

In Arunachal Pradesh, the agriculture is largely confined to the practice of Jhum or Shifting cultivation which involves strenuous preparation of land, done mainly by the menfolk, by cutting a selected patch of Jungle after a number of years or Jhum cycle, burning of the cut jungle, dragging of the unburnt logs to the side of the resultant jungle clearing etc. Jhum kheti literally means "collective farming", and collective farming it is at the level of the village or clan at first and the level of family later. By Jhum Kheti the people use the most abundant and the cheapest factor of production—the hill-land—as extensively as possible by minimum application of the scarce factor of production—the hill labour. In Arunachal Pradesh, the women are economic assets who bear equal responsibility for producing food. That is the reason why her participation in the labour force is so complete ; and she carries a bride price. The children or even the very old people have their pre-set responsibility with regards to Jhum cultivation. It is Jhum cultivation that locks up the children of school going age to the land. It is Jhum cultivation that force some old men and women, sometimes even blinded by age, to toil in the field under a scorching sun or under a pouring rain.

In Arunachal Pradesh about 95 per cent of the Scheduled Tribes workers are cultivatiors. 3 per cent of the workers are engaged in other services and about 1.5 per cent are agricultural labourers. 92 per cent of the male Scheduled Tribes workers are cultivators, whereas 98 per cent of female workers are cultivators.

But for the Urban Scheduled Tribes population the pattern is different. Only 32 per cent of the Urban Scheduled Tribes populations are cultivators. For the males, the urban cultivators are only 18 per cent as against 62 per cent of the females. Nearly 58 per cent of the urban Scheduled Tribes workers (73 per cent males and 25 per cent females) are engaged in other services.

Arunachal Pradesh—the land of the dawn-lit mountains—is the first Indian soil to great the rising sun. But it is, perhaps the last soil of the land to greet the rising trend of development in all spheres, because of its isolation for centuries owing to its hostile environment and topography. Lack of communication is also responsible for the territory's backwardness. Now the innumerable roads built across high mountains and deep gorges have put an end to the centuries old isolation and brought the tribesmen in the mainstream of national life. The territory is now taking to modern agricultural practices and taking steps to tap the immense natural resources in a systematic manner aiming at all round development of the area. Arunachal Pradesh is inhabited by a large number of tribes speaking different dialects. Majority of them profess indigenous faith which called Donyi-Poloism by some of the tribes. Some are Hindus and other tribes are Buddhists. They have glorious cultural heritage, which beckons to the explorers, scientists and historians alike to know it more intimately.

LIFE STYLE—THE AKAS (*Arunachal Pradesh*)

Aka is the name given to a small tribal group inhabitating the Sule-Himalayan region of India towards the Southern area of the Kameng district of Arunachal Pradesh.

The Aka area is bounded on the north by the Miji territory, on the south by the Darrang district of Assam, on the west by the land where the Sherdukpens live and on the east by the Bangni territory. The Mijis are very closely related to the Akas, have many similar beliefs and customs and also intermarry with them.

The region of the Akas is covered with forests and mountainous tracts with a number of streams and rivers. The main rivers of the region are the Bichom (*Humschu*), the Tengapani (*Hudju*) and the Kheyang (*Khuwa*). The names given are the common names of the rivers; the italicized names in brackets are the names of the rivers in the Aka-language.

These rivers are fordable for the greater part of the year. The people make cane suspension—bridges for the rains. Besides these three, there are also some big streams. Bamboo jungles are in abundance. Wild plaintain trees grow almost throughout the area ; broad-leafed forests are also common.

The most common animals are the barking-deer, the porcupine, the monkey, the bear and the panther.

The climate of the region is mildly cold. Rainfall is not very heavy and ranges between 40 to 50 inches in most places.

Aka Village. Villages are situated on the hill-top as well as in the valleys. The altitude of these villages varies from about 3000 to 6000 ft. They are always sited with an eye on the water-source. The settlements are usually made in the places where people can find enough land for Jhum cultivation. Field-huts are built near the Jhum lands and these small habitations become known as *Pam* (Pam is an Assame for temporary huts in fields. It is in popular usage among the Akas as well as other tribes of the region) which gradually grow into independent villages.

There are at present twentyone Aka villages. These are Jamiri, Sakrin, Hushigaon, Buragaon, Dijungania, Karangani, Ramdgania, Pusing, Gijiria, Yayong, Tulu, Tania, Palathari, Samigaon, Raghugaon, Rukhugaon, Morrukha, Kararamu, and Pichang, Chisong and Kichang. (last three are Miri-Aka village).

Most villages do not have more than a score of houses. The population of Aka villages ranges from 120 to 200 people, except in case of Dijungania which has more than 50 houses and a population of about 500 people.

Unlike other Aka settlements, which are homogeneous, Dijungania has a mixed population of Akas, Mijis and Daflas. The Akas have close connections and common interests with Mijis (The Mijis call themselves Dhammai) who have more or less assimilated themselves with Aka society, whereas the Daflas have a distinct existence without any social communion with either of them.

People. The Akas call themselves Hrusso. Aka, is a fact, the name given to them by the plains people. The word 'Aka' denotes 'painted' and it may have been used for them by the people of Assam largely because of their customs of painting their faces profusely, which might have served as a distinctive mark.

The Akas have fair complexions. They have a well-built body, usually a flat nose, conspicuous cheek-bones with black hair and usually brownish to pale blue eyes. Men grow scanty hair on the face as well as over the body. Their stature varies from medium to tall, men being usually taller than women.

The Akas are subdivided into two clans : the *Hazarikhowas* or 'eaters at a thousand hearths' and *Kapaschors* or 'Thieves who lurk amid the cotton plants'. The Akas are divided, according to the earlier records, into two main clans, the *Hazarikhowa* or *Kutsun* and *Kapaschor* or *Kovatsun*, each organised under a Raja or chief. The Hazarikhowas had a right to *Posa* (revenue payment), conceded by the Assamese, while the *Kapaschors* enjoyed no such privilege but managed somehow to extort the contributions from the cultivators. It was to the Hazarikhowas that the Assam Government granted the right of *Posa*. From the records of 1825, it appears that the Hazarikhowas were entitled to receive from each house of their allotted *Khels* 'one portion of a female dress, one bundle of cotton thread and one cotton handkerchief.'

The *Posa* may be explained better as a tribute money paid to the hill-tribes of this frontier for peace. At this time, probably the Kapaschors were not considered a separate clan, for it had been learned that the Hazarikhowas were expected to give a part of their collections to the Kapaschors.

The importance attached to the Akas was due to their situation between the people of the valley of Assam and the powerful and very numerous clans of the Miji tribe, who unlike the former, are reported as not being in the habit of visiting Assam but who purchased silk from the Akas against exorbitant price.

Accounting for a second cause of the importance of the Akas, Hesselmeyer remarks : "although powerless themselves, they know how to make themselves formidable through the influence they manage to exercise over the Mijis, whose countless hosts they would be able without much difficulty to lead any day against any foe."

It has been found in the accounts of Aitchison that the Hazarikhowa received a Posa from the Rajas of Assam and that Kapaschor levied contributions without any such title. He said

"Both tribes are small but on account of their superior civilization. They are much respected and even feared by the surrounding tribe."

Apart from the above two clans of the Akas, there is another sub-division of the tribe commonly known by the name of Miri-Akas, who live on the other side of the Kaya river and nearer to the Bangais. The Miri-Akas, who are known as Khrome, share the common customs, beliefs and practices with the Akas or Hrussos, profess the same religion and in physical features too, they are much alike. The difference if any, lies in their language. The Hrussos speak their own dialect whereas the Miri-Akas speak a dialect known as 'Miri'. They seem to have remained rather unapproached by the early expeditions.

Only casual references occur about the Miri-Akas who have been also mentioned as Angka-Miris in the earlier accounts.

History. The Akas can claim to have played an important role in the history of Arunachal Pradesh.

The Akas, like other hillmen who had a privilege to Posa since the time of Ahom rulers, used to come down every year to collect their petty dues from each house. This often led to some sort of trouble for both the people in the plains as well as the authorities. The Government tried to replace this inconvenient practice of individual collection by a more convenient system of an annual camp payment. The intentions of the proposal were in some cases suspected by the Hrussos. The claim under the new arrangement were fixed at Rs. 175 annually for the Hazarikhowas. The Posa was, however withheld for a number of years when the Kapaschors gave rise to some trouble in 1835 and with which the Hazarikhowas were also alleged to have been associated.

The Kapaschor Akas arranged raid under the leadership of their Tagi Raja and wiped out a British outpost at Balipara in 1835. The energy and daring of Tagi Raja had made him this time the virtual chief of both clans of Akas and also given him influence over the neighbouring Daflas. As a result of this trouble, the Posa payment to the Hazarikhowas was withheld by the Government. Peace was, however, ensured after a treaty with them in 1844. The Kapaschors were also made entitled to an annual Posa of Rs. 520 in 1848.

The boundary line of the Akas was demarcated with their neighbouring people in the west in 1872-73. The Hazarikhowas did not object to this arrangement. The grant of some acres of land in the plains in 1873 further gratified them. The Kapaschors did not, however, agree to the boundary line arrangement between the Bhoreli and Khai Dikrai rivers; they instead pressed their extravagant claims. However, after some time, they gave in and the line was demarcated in 1874-75.

Some trouble arose again in 1883 with the depredations by the Akas in their plains. But they entered into a peace settlement in 1888 with the Government.

In 1925 Captain Nevill wrote about them, 'these Akas are an excellent and most interesting people, they are much more civilized than the Daflas and they are capable of great improvement'. They are a much more enlightened and civilized people than the other hill-tribes. Dr. Elwin remarks: 'The Akas in later years continued to win the respect of those who visited them.

No doubt, the Akas were a warlike people. The Sherdukpens and the Khowas used to pay taxes to them in recognition of their supremacy.

After the peace treaty of 1884, the Akas have given no further trouble. They have given up their warlike traits of tribal feuds. The Akas have now become good agriculturists, keen traders and an industrious people. They also sometimes act as middlemen to Dhammais or Mijis and to other neighbouring people.

Language. The language of the Akas is quite different from their neighbouring tribes, the Daflas, the Miji's, the Mompas and the Sherdukpens. The dialect of the Hrussos even differs basically from the dialect of the Miri-Akas.

Hesselmeyer believed that the "the language of the Akas suggested that it contains more words which could be traced to the valleys south of the Patkoi, joining the Shan and Manipur than words indicating a closer affinity with the Daflas and Abor tribes."

Accordting to the Linguistic Survey of India, the Aka language belongs to the Tibeto-Burman group of languages. It holds that 'the difference between Aka and the other dialects of the group'—which is called the North-Assam Group and puts under it, the Aka, the Dafla, the Abor-Miri and the Mishmi dialects—"is still greater." It may only be said that both the dailects of the Akas, the Hrusso dialect and the Miri-Aka dialects, though they differ mostly among themselves, probably belong to the same common stock of languages—the Tibeto-Burman group.

Domestic life. The social and economic life of the Akas is largely determined by the conditions of their habitat. The hilly tracts do not leave any other alternative to Jumming. The abundance of jungle further provides ample resource to practice the indigenous system. The overall result is that the Akas are still one of the main Jhum cultivators among the tribes of India.

The abundance of bamboo-groves plays a great role in as much as it provides to them the material for house-building. As a result, we find the same type of bamboo houses all over the Aka country. A number of vessels and pots of their daily use are covered from bamboo. Similarly, cane which is also quite common in the forests, furnishes a material of great utility for making various articles of domestic use.

Life amidst the forest habitat has rendered them the possibility of supplementing their food by a number of edible forest produce. It is again the thick forests around them into which they have to move constantly and the urge for defence against the wild life that have made the Akas good archers. And lastly, it is the hard and arduous life in these hills and the struggle, which they have to make against the inhospitable forces of nature, that have cast a deep imprint on the life and thought of the people.

The isolation of these people from their neighbouring tribes has helped them to evolve an independent culture which we will see in undergoing paragraphs.

The domestic life of the Akas starts from the individual household and extends to the community as a whole.

The House. The Aka house is a long structure raised on a platform, about six feet above the ground and divided into two compartments by a partition wall. The space between the platform and the ground serves as a shed for pigs and goats of the household. The house is a work of bamboo and wood, bamboo sheets forming the floor, the wall and the roof and wooden logs serving as the main pillars over which the structure of the house is raised. The roof is usually thatched and often supported by bamboo sheets. The four walls of the house are usually high.

The main entrance to the house is from the front though there are inlets both in the front and at the rear of the house. Just behind the front door, there is the first and the small compartment called *thumona* and built especially for guest. As a part of the social tradition, guest from even distant villages visit their friends and relatives from time to time ; hence the special provision for their lodging in every Aka house, with a view to ensure every possible comfort to them.

Next to this compartment, is a small enclosure, called *memkhowrl*, which serves as the main entrance to the inner big hall. The main hall, known os *uluri*, is a big room, standing behind the above enclosure. It is the only hall practically for all purposes. Almost every room in the house has at least on hearth with an iron-stand known as *aescheperi*. To keep the house warm, fire is kept burning in the hearths.

On one side of the house, there is built a small cell to serve the purpose of store-room where the articles of the household or any other belongings of the family may be kept. This is called the *rin*. On the other side of the hall, a small enclosure is built into the wall to keep fire wood and is known as *Sejourin*. All the rooms are kept completely shut off from dight to keep away the *dim-dam* flies which are a constant nuisance in these areas.

A small granary is built usually near the house and food supplies for the year are kept here. This is called *nechi*. Commonly a small kitchen-garden is attached to the house to grow vegetables.

The houses in Aka villages are not compact, they are generally scattered throughout the village. Only in Dijungania the houses are situated close to each other.

The house is built with the joint labour of the members of the village who help one another in building a house for every household of the community. No remuneration is paid, only a big feast is given to the participants by the owner.

Except a few bamboo jars and vessels, all utensils have to be procured from the plains of Assam. The Akas do not practice pottery. They are able to carve only a few jars out of bamboo for their daily use. One of the common jar is known as *kichhu* which is used extensively for storing *lao-pani* (the local drink) and other drinks. Another type of vessel largely used for bringing water from streams is called *schhou.* Another vessel, serving the same purpose but bigger in size, is known as *mon.* A type of bamboo flask, largely in use for drinking *lao-pani* and the two other drinks, *aarah* and *mingri*, is known as *Schaspoo.*

Metal frying pot is called *Soukhou*; *bela* is a bigger pot used for serving food. The transaction of goods is done through barter system in which they give salt and cloth in exchange for the earthen pot.

Weapons. Akas have various weapons which are of practical use to them in war and peace as well as in their day-to-day tasks. They normally made all such weapons. Generally they use weapons for defensive purposes. They protect themselves against wild animals and also practice hunting. The most important weapon of this kind is the bow and the arrow, known by the name of *tkeri* and *moo* respectively and used in the chase. The bows are usually hung over the shoulders while the arrows are carried in a case of bamboo called *thouvou.* The boys get training in archery from their early age.

Another weapon, originally of war but now of defence, is a kind of crude harpoon, one end of which is barbed with sharp iron nails. It is used by hurling at the target from a distance. It was a popular weapon in the days of tribal feuds.

The most common weapon both of daily practical use and for defence or offence, is the *dao.* It is used for cutting wood and bamboo pieces, clearing shrubs, in making baskets as well as killing large mithun and pigs for sacrifice or feast. It is made from steel. Dao, for which the local term is *wetz*, are like bow and the arrow, of various sizes. The biggest type of *wetz* is known as *wetzpa*, the medium size by *wetfa* and the smallest one is called *wetza.*

Cottage Industries. The Akas are very hard working people. They utilize their leisure hour by engaging themselves in various small industries.

Baskets of different shape and sizes are made by menfolk. Bamboo trees are abundantly available. A basket useful for keeping the fish-catch, is known as *gizu schri* cane basket is used for carrying food while on the move from one place to another.

Weaving is not in practice on a large scale. It is known only to the extent of making colourful bags by the Aka women. It is very limited to the villages of Jamiri and Hushigaon.

Dress. The dress of both Akas men and women is simple. They have to depend upon the plains for their wearing apparel.

Men invariably wear a small garment, hanging below the shoulders and covering the upper half of the body. It is made to fit the body and is known as *shoshiu-ge.* They also wear a kind of long coat known as *pol.*

Women wear a long garment over the body which hangs from the shoulders upto the ankles. It is usually coloured dark red. This is also called *pol.* Both men and women cover the legs with a piece of cloth called *gudu.* It leaves only the feet uncovered. It is worn as a protection against the *dimdam* flies.

Men generally do not wear any head dress. Only in some festive occasions they may put a kind of ring-cap of bamboo, called *musarga,* over the head. They wear a dao with a silver case, across the waist.

There is no particular ceremonial dress. The same dress may be worn on common as well as ceremonial occasions. The difference is that women adorn themselves profusely with ornaments around the neck and the forehead in the latter case. The appearance of men on ceremonial occasions does not charge much. Only on some occasions they may wrap over the shoulders a piece of blanket to distinguish the ceremonial from the normal.

Men usually tie hair in the middle of the head in a knot while women wear it at the back.

Ornaments. The Aka women wear a number of silver ornaments as well as necklaces of beads. The common silver ornaments are *melu*—a flat shaped ornament worn over the chest, *rombin,* the big ear bulbs, *gichli*—the earrings and *gejjul*—the wristlets. Well-to-do women wear a fillet of silver chain-work called *lenchhi.* The women also put on around the neck a number of coloured bead necklaces.

An ancestral necklace, called *aescheri,* is worn invariably by women and often by men. It forms a necessary part of the gifts which a bride's parents give at her marriage.

Tattooing. It is quite common among the Akas. The women lattoo their faces in a pattern of a straight line running from below the forehead to the chin where it bifurcates into two directions. No other part of the body are tattooed.

Tattooing is done generally before puberty. This also means it is done before marriage. A scratch is made on the face, with an idea of the design in which the tattooing is desired by means of a thorn and resin, which is poured into the wound. It leaves a permanent blue-black mark on the face.

Aka art. The most common form of Aka art is their drawings on wood in their house. At the entrance to a house in Karangania village, there are found some crude and simple drawings on a wooden frame. The figures and lines in these drawings are drawn usually with the liquid of ling hong (pine-resin), the essence of which gives black-dye.

These drawings are associated with some socio-religious rites. They serve in a way to declare in explicit but symbolic form the desire of the individual who performs the ceremony to attain heights.

Whenever a fowl is sacrificed in some religious rite, then also similar drawings are made.

Food and Drink. The staple food of the Akas consists mainly of maize, which may often be substituted or supplemented by millets. These cereals are taken in boiled form along with some vegetables which may be locally grown or gathered in the form of plants and tubes from the forests. Some local pulses, such as *Shapoo* and *labenchi* (urad and a pulse similar to it) are also added to the food. Vegetables like sweet potatoes and *kochu* are also taken. Rice is not grown much.

On many occasions the main diet is substantiated by meat, pork or beef, though none of these form their daily diet, except for a few persons who may afford it. In ordinary festivals, a pig or a goat is killed. Fowls are however, sacrificed much more frequently to celebrate most of the socio-religious ceremonies.

The Akas are fond of smoking. It is a common sight to see both men and women with a tobacco-pipe. The pipe is made from bamboo. They also take wild betel. The lips of Aka women are often seen red amidst the black tattoo-marks on the face.

Food Taboos. Whereas men enjoy themselves in feast and festivities without any reservation, women are permitted to take only a few of the non-vegetarian dishes. A number of taboos restrict their food habit. They may take pork and beef but *it* is taboo for them to take fowls, which otherwise provide a favourite dish to the menfolk. Even the permitted dishes for women are further regulated by a number of other impositions : the women are forbidden to take the brain and the legs of a mithun. Both men and women discard the portion of brain, legs and stomach while partaking of pig-flesh.

It is common and a strong belief among them that if a women dares to violate any of these socio-religious impositions, the supernatural agencies may inflict a heavy punishment on her. Such a supernatural punishment would then badly disfigure her and thus soon get wearied of her life.

Milk in any form or any preparations made from it are also tabooed for women. It is for this reason that they evince little interest in tea prepared with milk or even with condensed milk in some of the houses, where the people going down to the plains, have learnt to bring occasionally a few tins of it home.

Drinks. The alcoholic drinks in the tribal communities form an ingredient to the staple food of the people. The meal is supposed to be complete only with the addition of a drink. The staple drink of the Akas is *lao-pani.* It is prepared either from maize or millet. *Lao-pani* is taken three or even more times a day, often along with food. The first bowl of *lao-pani* is taken in the early hours of morning. It may be taken a second time in the afternoon with the meal and a third time in the evening when people may sit together with the family. *Lao-pani,* being a staple drink, is taken without reservation by all, men and women as well as children.

The second alcoholic drink, *Mingri,* is more intoxicating than *lao-pani,* *Aarah* is a distilled drink and is therefore, more expensive. Among the Akas, each house prepares drinks for its own use.

There is an interesting story which relates the discovery of the favourite drink of *Lao-pani.* In the remote past, all the different peoples, Akas. Mijis, Daflas, Mishmis and others, had a common ancestor called *Buslo Aou.* He gave the *fa* herb to an animal called *khulpza dum* (similar to a rat). It had eaten only about half of it when another ancestor, called *Subjou Ache*, snatched it away from its mouth. To determine its effect *Subjou Ache* experimented with it on a dog who gained considerably in health. The experiment was then repeated on a chicken who too grew more fleshy. Observing miraculous results, Sibjou Ache preserved it as an invaluable invigorant and has passed the herb on to his posterity. Since then, the herb has been brought into use by the people to prepare their drink from it.

The people have a strong belief that a drink of *lao-pani* tones up their energy.

Economic Structure. The economic organisation of a people centres round their means of sustenance which include their occupation like agriculture, as well as the subsidiary means of livelihood like the collection of forest produce and fishing and hunting.

Agriculture. the Akas are essentially an agricultural people. Agriculture in the hilly areas of the Aka country naturally demands the Jhum or Shifting type of cultivation. A tract of land is selected every year for agriculture and after the forest growth over it has been removed, it is put to fire. The clearing in the forest thus made to serve as the field for cultivation and the seeds are sown over the ash. Men and women join together to share the toil.

The first phase of agriculture begins with the clearing of forest-land, which may start in the month of January and continued up to the end of March. The implements used are *purje* (common axe) and wetz (dao). The clearing of the forest for Jumming is known as *Vichu* in the Aka dialect. Sowing of seed, which usually takes place in the month of April or May, is a simple job for women. They take the seed in a basket locally known as *biu*, remove a little earth and broadcast the seed on the soil. The common crops are maize and millet. Paddy is grown only on a limited scale in a small area. Besides these, a few pulses are also grown, common among which are *urad* or *mas* and some pulses similar to it. French-beans are also grown in some parts. Vegetables such as potatoes, sweet potatoes and *kochu* are grown in the kitchen gardens. Peas are grown only to a limited extent is some parts. A wild plant, *wenekchi*, which grows edible roots, is also used as food.

Over 70 per cent of the cultivated area is under Jhum and about 30 per cent under settled cultivation--wet rice and terrace rain-fed cropping. Now a days rice is the major grain crop. Other important crops which are grown by the modern Akas—maize, millets, wheat, barley, mustard, sugarcane, ginger, chilli, cotton etc. Pineapple, orange, lemon, papaya, banana, guava, and temperate fruits, such as apple, plum, pear, walnut etc. are also grown. Farmer's training centre at Pasighat are providing training in the scientific methods of agriculture.

Rites. Agriculture is the main source of livelihood for the people and thus to ensure its success some rites are necessary. At the time of sowing a piece of white cloth is tied by the priest to a bamboo pole and is planted in the *pam* or the Jhum-field. A piece of *lingehong* (pine wood) is lighted and the woner is allowed to put the first seed in the field. The priest raises prayer to the diety of agriculture. The sowing starts with the performance of this rites. Similarly at the time of the harvest, the priest is summoned to plant the pennant in the field and to burn the incense. The harvesting of the crop follows only then.

Fishing. It is practised largely as a pastime occupation. The fish are caught on the river banks. It, however does not play any important part in the economy.

Hunting. It too is practised in a limited scale. The weapon of hunting and chase are the common bow and arrow.

Foodgathering. Edible plants and leaves are gathered for about six months of the year to supplement the food supply. A wild plant known as *fumpin* is gathered. The leaves of this plant are prepared as vegetables and used with cereals. Another plant, *pasa*, is also gathered.

Trade. The indigenous method of trade are simple in nature and barter plays an important part. The inter-village trade is practised through the barter system. They exchange the surplus grains for paddy or potatoes.

In their trade with the people in the plains, they have to do essentially in cash. With the money they get in return for their commodities, they purchase things of necessity like cloth, ornaments, utensils.

Household Industries. Weaving and basketry are the important household industries. The small-scale industries, comprise saw, rice and oil mills, fruit preservation, soap and candle units, steel fabrication, wood work etc. There are two industrial estates, one at Itanagar and the other at Deomali.

Recently coal reserve has been found in the Namchik—Namphuk area of the Tirap district. Crude oil reserves has also been found. Limestone is found at Tidding in the Lohit district and dolomite at Rupa in the west kameng district.

The rich hydel potential of Arunachal Pradesh is being chanelised for power generation.

Society. The Akas are a small tribe who know themselves as Hrussos. A sub-division of the tribe is known as Khromes or Miri-Akas and as such distinguished from the farmer. They live rather isolated from the Hrussos but enjoy free social relations with them.

The Aka tribe is further sub-divided into a number of clans organised on the principle of clan-exogamy. The tribe is a compact social group which maintains its solidarity by enforcing certain social laws and regulations, supported by traditions, by which all social contacts outside the tribal group are made impossible to its members. Infiltration of any kind from outside is not allowed in any case.

The first social rule to insure the solidarity of the tribes is the rule of tribal endogamy. It forces the members of the tribe to marry strictly and necessarily within the tribal group. Any lapse from this social rule would result in foreign infiltration and break the very foundation of the tribal solidarity and hence is punishable. It even involves the expulsion of the social culprit from the community by enforcing upon him a social boycott or ex-communication from the village. Any marital relations with the Mompas, Khowas, Daflas and Sherdukpens, the other tribe living in the region, thus envolve heavy punishment by the village council. The only concession in this respect is that of permitted social relations of the Akas with the Mijis. The Akas and the Mijis enjoy today social relations with each other.

The Village Community. The unit of Aka society is the village community. Everything relating to society or having a bearing upon the people in general is decided at the village level. The communal always supersede the individual consideration. Even individual functions like marriage and religious rites call for communal co-operation. The co-operation of the village community is also sought in individual work like house—building. The individual religious festivities concludes with a community feast.

The community is also the centre of the political organisation of the village. Its decision become legally binding upon the local individual. The village community is, in fact the integrating force in the Aka society.

The Clans. The clans are the further sub-division of the tribe. The members. of the clan regarding themselves to be the descendants of a common ancestor and thus avoiding marital relations with the members of their own clan-group. Wherein marriage within tribal group is made compulsory, the members of the different clans of the tribe are required to marry strictly outside their own sub-group. The rule of clan-exogamy is as strict in nature as the rule of tribal endogamy. Tribal endogamy and clan exogamy thus go together in Aka society as in all societies.

Each of the Aka village has its specific clans which are limited to the village boundary. Only three villages Buragaon, Hushigaon and Jamiri have the common clans which freely inter-marry under the normal rules of clan-exogamy.

Clan-exogamy in Aka-society is usually accompanied by village exogamy. The members of the clan, besides being required to marry outside their own clan-group, have also to cast their choice outside the villages. Thus a boy of Chidisow clan of Dijungania, besides avoiding a marriage with a girl of his own clan, has to select his male even outside the Fomusow, Paryusow or Galosow clans of his village and should preferably marry in Karangania or in some other Aka village.

There is no class system known to the Akas. All the clans enjoy an equal social footing and there is no dogma of higher or lower creed associated with any of them. However, the people of the three Aka villages, Buragaon, Hushigaon, and Jamiri, do not freely entertain the idea of marriage relations with the members of Sichisow clan who are permitted to marry only with the members of Jabisow clan.

The Family. The family in the Aka Society in the primary unit of the individual life in the same way as the village community is the unit of the society. The Aka family comprises the husband, the wife and their children. The sons stay with their parents till they attain maturity and are married in their turn, after which they separate from the parental roof to found their individual families. The daughters on marriage go to live with their husbands and become hence onwards the members of their families. The parental family thus eventually splits into individual families in either case and returns to the same stage from where it had started, consisting of the husband and the wife. Joint families are not popular among the Akas.

The sons may not separate from their parents immediately after marriage but such a separation becomes necessary as soon as the first child is born. But at least one of the sons has necessarily to stay back with the parents to look after them. This is more or less a social convention, rather an obligatory duty on their part which is discharged sincerely.

As to who among the sons should be the person to stay with the parents, there is no fixed rule. It is largely a matter of mutual adjustment between the parents and the son and often the personal choice of the former decides the issue. Naturally this son is the eventual successor to the parental properly and the household.

At the time of the separation of the sons from the parental roof, the proper distribution of property among them is made. All the sons get an equal share except the eldest, who may get a little more than his brothers. The ancestral ornaments which are kept reserved for the gir's to be given to them at the time of their marriage. Besides these ornaments, girls do not get any other share in their father's property. Land is not subject to division, partly because it is changeable every year, and partly because it is acquired by one's own toil. House is also not a part to the division as firstly the parents may themselves need it for their shelter and secondly it cannot serve the purpose of all the families.

At the time of parting from the parental roof, each of them, according to his will and capacity, contributes some cloth, utensils, pigs and other things that may be at his disposal at the time. The contribution is usually entrusted to them in the presence of the villagers who may gather there for the community feast given by parting people. This is more or less a social approval sought to effect the division of the family.

The pattern of Society. The Akas have an essentially patriarchal society. The patrilocal residence is combined with patriarchal descent and patrimonial inheritance of property. Since girls go to live with their husbands after marriage, it is only the sons who inherit the family descent as well as the property from their father.

The Slave System. Aka society freely entertains the idea of slavery. The slaves known as *Khulo*, are not a part of society but form a separate class by themselves outside the social structure of the Akas, though living with them in the same village. The slaves are recruited usually from amongst the Sulungs. They may be purchased by the people from their Bangni neighbours against mithun and cloth. The person once recruited as a slave remains a slave for the whole life, marries only a slave girl and the children of the slave inherit slavery from them as a liability.

The *Khulo* have to till the soil, look after the *pam* and the Jhum-field, the cattle and the household and do all such menial jobs as their masters may entrust to them. They are given food and clothing. Now the practice is gradually falling into disuse.

Rani in Aka Society. A special feature of Aka Society is its Rani System.

The two most important Aka villages, Jamiri and Hushigaon, each has a Rani. The Ranis are the descendants of the royal family of the Akas who were ruling the Aka country till a few decades ago. The descent has since then been inherited and it is as the successors to that royal lineage that the Ranis of the two villages are given high social honour to this day, not only in their own villages, but also by the Aka Society in general.

The local term for Rani is *Nugum*. The term *Nugum* is today denotative of wealth position and economic stability. The Rani is supposed to be the patron of her village. She is expected to help the needy people of the village.

She also command a place of respect in the political life of the village. They are invited to all meetings of the village council and their counsel is taken for all important issues of the village.

Individual in Society. Life in the tribal societies is more communal than individual in the sence that an individual has to fulfil a number of obligations towards his society for which he gets the co-operation and assistance of the community even in the discharge of his individual tasks.

Rank and property among the Akas are the two main determinants of an individual status. For the Akas, a person who has the spirit of service and tolerance, is ever-ready to extend his co-operation in matters of social interest, makes good use of his wealth in helping the destitute and yet does not think much of himself, is an ideal individual. As such he is proclaimed unanimously as a Nichleu-Nuggo. The honour bestowed on him also brings fresh responsibilities in its train.

Every Aka village is supposed to have a Nichleu-Nuggo. Now a days the Gaon-Burah of a village, who is head of the local political organisation, normally combine in him the social honour of Nichleu-Nuggo, since it is, after all, the local people of a village who select a person to both these offices, political and social. There may be instances where a Gaon Burah may fail to secure the title of the highest social honour from his community.

Position of Women. Women in Aka Society enjoy a better status than many women in sophisticated societies. An Aka women is not merely a wife who bears children to her husband and does the domestic tasks laid down for her. On the other hand, she is an equal partner to her husband throughout his life. She keeps pace with him in most of his economic pursuits. She works with him in the fields, to clear the forest for cultivation, sows the seed and harvests the crop. She also shares with her husband many socio-religious observances. The institution of polygyny also does not affect her position in any way whenever a man decides to bring home a second woman, he has to first take counsel of his wife and find out if she is willing to accept a helping land. And her opinion remains final.

Marriage. Marriage in Aka Society, is a turning-point in the life history of an individual from where he branches off from the parental roof and founds a new unit. A girl on her marriage abandons her parents' house and goes to live with her husband.

Marriage in Aka Society can take shape either by way of negotiation or by the romantic way of capture. The first is the traditional and more popular system of marriage while the latter too though depending more upon one's tactfulness rather than on mutual negotiations, is a socially approved practice.

The marriage by negotiation is generally initiated from the boy's side. The boy may give an indication of his choice to his parents. They then call the Mugou (village priest) to examine the auspiciousness of the proposal. The Mugou makes his diagnosis by killing a fowl and reading through divination the favourable or unfavourable signs contained therein. If the omen turns hopeful, a go-between is summoned to initiate the marriage proposal on behalf of the boy's family. The go-between or the Mukhou, as he is known, may be a relative of a boy or some elderly person of his village. He travels to the girl's village, meets her parents and tells them about the boy's desire. If the parents of the girl agree to proposal and bride-price, the go-between returns to his village to convey the news to the boy's parents. Often he has to pass between the two parties twice or thrice for the marriage. It is not supposed to be auspicious, if it is settled during the very first visit.

The date of marriage is fixed in consultation with girl's parents. The time of marriage is calculated by counting the number of knots bound with a piece of cane-string. The number of knots indicate the days which are required to pass before the marriage may be celebrated. The first string of knot brought by the negotiator is, however, of only formal importance, since marriage never takes place according to the first plan. The people believe, to do so is to invite a bad omen. So a second piece of string has to be brought from girl's house to know the next and final programme. This date is final.

Ceremony. Around the date of marriage, the marriage party comprising the groom, his parents and relatives and some of the members from village, starts in a procession for the bride's village, where the marriage is to take place. On reaching every hill-top they make a loud shout of 'Ho'. As they arrive at the village entrance, they signal their arrival again by a shout. At this, the people of the bride's house, accompanied by other villagers, come to receive them. They also give a small feast to the guest at the place of the first meeting. After the feast, the members of the groom's party march to the bride's house with their hosts. When they approached the bride's house, their hosts pull out their swords (doas) as a sign of resistance. The groom's party also pretends a similar gesture and there ensues a mock fight. Ultimately allow the groom's party to enter the house.

A big feast is arranged by the host to the guest. Songs and dances continue till late night. On the following day, groom's party have to play host and arranged a feast for bride's people. A mithun is killed.

Later in the day, the elder women of the bride's village dress themselves as men and join the groom's party to joke with them.

On the third day, the girls of the bride's village take a ceremonial liberty to play jokes with the youths in the groom's party. They prepare a blackish paint and paint the faces of the boys at the first opportunity. The boys also return the compliment with equal enthusiasm and black-paint the girl's faces.

On all nights during the marriage-party's stay in the village, dances and songs are arranged regularly. At the conclusion of the three-day ceremony, the marriage party returns to its home. The bride does not accompany the groom to his home soon after the marriage. She has to stay back with her parents for a year after the marriage. The husband may visit her during this period. At the end of the year, the husband accompanied by the Mukhou goes to bring her home. The parents or relatives of the bride may also come to escort her to her husband's place. The bride's people give a feast to them. This will continue for four days. Then they will return, leaving their daughter in her husband's charge. From now, the bride assumes full membership of her husband's family. But now the bride may stay with her husband earlier than one year.

Marriage by Capture. This type of marriage is generally taken by youths when they are not sure about their parent's consent to a marriage proposal of their choice or avoid the traditional marriage system. A boy, who may be in love with some girl of his own or other village, elopes with her to his parental village without giving any notice of the event to her parents. He may or may not have given any indication of his plan to his parents also. After reaching home, he sacrifices a pig and invites the village community to a feast. The local priest ties a thread of sheep-hair, called *fokki*, around the girl's right hand along with the ancestral ornaments *aescheri*. This tying of the thread by the priest gives a stamp of marriage and a kind of social recognition to the marital relationship. Now bride enters her husband's family as a virtual member.

On knowing of the incident and her whereabouts, the parents of the girl come to the groom's house. As they find no other way than to agree quietly to the arrangement already arrived at by their daughter. The only thing within their power now is to put forward their demand of the bride-price to which they are fully entitled. The bride-price may be paid by the groom's parents either immediately or later.

Marriages with one's own cross-cousins are quite popular among the Akas. A cross-cousin is in fact regarded as a preferential mate. Such marriages are permitted with all kinds of cross-cousins. A person can marry his mother's brother's daughter ; similarly, a girl can marry her mother's brother's son. Besides, a boys or a girl can also marry his or her mother's sister's daughter or son.

Direct parallel-cousin marriages with one's father's brother's son or daughter are strictly prohibited.

Polygyny is quite common in Aka Society. A man can marry more than one woman at a time. Along with this consent of the first wife is always necessary which, in fact, not difficult to obtain. The two wives can share the burden of household better than an individual women. Generally the first wife welcomes the proposal with good spirits.

But polyandry is wholly unknown among the Akas.

Levirate is popular in Aka Society. A man usually inherits the widow of his elder brother. He however, cannot inherit the wife of his younger brother. Where both of them do not favour a union, she may be allowed to live with the man of her choice from among the community members, provided the man agrees to pay the bride-price spent on her marriage to her husband's brother.

Another form of marrying one's sister-in-law, known as sororate, is also prevalent among the people. A man may marry his wife's sister, either in the former's life-time or after that. The usage of sororate has, like the levirate, a limitation in the sense that one can marry only the younger sister of his wife and not the elder.

Incest Taboo. Marriage or any kind of extra-marital relation within the restricted group of one's own kindred is regarded as incest in Aka Society. The incest taboo, the violation of which involves heavy penalties, wards off such possibilities. The person indulging in it may even be killed.

Kinship. In Akas a single term of address is used for a number of relationships.

Nium is used for younger sister. A person addresses all his cousins and sisters younger than him in age, as *nium.*

The term of address for one's elder sister, *ama,* is similarly extended to all the girls of the clan why stand in elder relation to the speaker. She addresses all her elder brothers as well as elder men of her clan, as *aiya* and younger to her as *nium.*

Father's elder brother is addressed as *akhi,* this term applies to all men of the clan who stand in order to one's father. Father's younger brother is similarly addressed as *alyou.* Mother's brother is called as *as.*

But *Ain* is the term address for one's own mother and does not imply any other set of relationship. Father is addressed as *au.*

Thumona. The conception of friendship and hospitality are highly developed among the Akas. These are refected in their traditional institution on *Thumona.* The term *Thumona* means three things among the Akas. It means a guest, a guest chamber as well as the institution of visiting one another as guest.

At the time of the guest's departure, he is presented with some gifts by the host . These may be a mithun or an ancestral necklace called *Richaji* or a few silver ornaments like *lenchhi* and *melu.* In return visit, he also pays gifts to his guest.

The institution of *thumona* has a special role to play in the social life of the Akas. It brings the people of the community closer to each other, makes them conscious of common groupism and engenders in them a feeling of greater brotherhood.

Dances and Songs. The Akas have a number of dances and songs for the different socio-religious festivities.

One of the well known dance among the Akas is the *Sadinuktso.* A member from the boy's group comes forward, gives his performance for a short while and recedes. A girl then comes and she also dances all alone. This relation goes on till all the boys and giris of the group have danced. No song is sung with this dance. It is generally performed on marriages, guest entertainment or on the construction of a new house.

The *Chhakou-do,* literally means 'to ask for more'. This dance takes place in community feasts.

Life-cycle. An individual in Aka-Society follows more or less the same traditional pattern of life which has come down from his ancestors.

The Birth of a child is a matter of rejoicing to the family and village. During the pregnancy, rites are performed to appease the deity so that the sufferings and pains in child-birth may be reduced.

The most important ceremony associated with the birth of a child is the binding of the ancestral thread-*fokki*-around the right hand of the child by the *mugou* (the village priest). Generally a feast is arranged by the father for the whole village community.

The ear-initiation ceremony for the child, both for boys and girls, takes place at an early age. The ear lobes of the child are pierced through to put on small bamboo ear-rings called *fusva.* Later on they replace these small ear-rings by some other ear-rings called *rembi.* The girls on maturity replaces these by bigger one known as *fuba timb.*

As the child grows, it gradually learns the traditional games and sports. But the sportive life of children soon gives way to the call of domestic duties soon after reaching the age of nine. Distinction in sex is not much marked by the society until they attain puberty. Both boys and girls up to the age of twelve are known by the name of *angasa.* At the age of adolescence the boys are called *mukhsa* and the girls *memsa.*

The boys attain adolescence around the age of fifteen. Now they begin to adapt themselves to the more manly tasks of the community. The girls on attaining the age of puberty begin to feel shy and avoid the company of the boys.

On her first menstruation, a girl completely shuts herself off from the rest of the world around her. During her first menses, a girl is required to live in a separate hut or apartment specially made for this purpose in every house. She is not allowed to enter the main house nor to come into sight of any adult man. Food is served to her in her own room. She has to live a segregated and restricted life during the period.

On her subsequent menses it is not necessary for the girl to stay in a separate hut. After she washes herself, she is allowed to return to her routine of life.

It is a strong belief among the Aka-Society that if a man takes the food prepared by a women in her monthly period, he will fall down on the ground instantaneously, blood will ooze out from his mouth and nose and he may lose his life. A number of social taboos thus surround a woman during her menstrual period to ward off the evil results.

A man in the Aka society generally MARRIES around the age of twenty. The girls are married between the age of fifteen and twenty.

As an individual grows old, his interest towards life gradually wanes. He now entrusts to his grown-up-sons his work. He has also to effect a proper division of property among his sons. Much of his time is occupied henceforth in the social affairs of the village.

The Akas practice burial. The body is carried to the grave and the *Mugou* performs the mortuary rites on the first as well as the last day of mourning. The ceremonial mourning lasts for ten days. The whole community took part in the mortuary ceremonial. All socio-religious observances remain at a standstill for the family during the period of mourning.

The Akas have a belief in the life hereafter. The soul, according to the Aka belief, after leaving the body goes to dwell in a place known as *Jana*. All souls, good or bad, have to pass through this *Jana* from where they are sorted out by the deities according to their merits or demerits during their life. The Mugou raises his prayer to the gods so that they may bless the soul to rest in peace, otherwise it wanders and troubles the people. As the Akas believe in the transmigration of the soul, the Mvgou also makes his prayer to let the soul take birth again in the same family.

The status and prestige of the Akas in the society are largely determined by his social behaviour.

The social machinery of the Akas thus functions with the co-ordination of the members of the village community, who by their regard for the values of their society have not only helped the tribe to maintain the tribal solidarity but have also in a way helped the tribe to retain its distinctive existence.

Political organisation. The political organisation of a tribal community is the traditional way in which the society recognizes the exercise of authority. This authority may be vested in a single individual acting as the headman of the village or it may be entrusted to a few chosen representative of the village forming a council of elders—as among the Adi groups—the acting on belief of the whole village community whose confidence they may command or in the third alternative, the village community may keep the authority to itself.

The political organisation of the Akas belong to the third and the last type. The unit of political organisation in the Aka Society is the village community is a whole acting in the form of a "village council".

Village Council. The village council or *Melley*, more commonly known by the Assamese word *Raiz* among the Akas, consists of the Gaon Burah (the chief of the village), his two juniors, the *Borah* and the *Gibba* and the members of the village community. It is a convention for all the members of the village to participate in the meetings of the council ; particularly when some important subject has to be discussed. In matters of judgment in fact, it is the consent of the village community in its corporate capacity that largely counts.

The persons of importance in the village council are the *Gaon Burah*, the *Borah* and the *Gibba*, who command an influence in their village by virtue of their position. Besides, this the elder people of the community have also a say in the matter. Respect is usually given to age. Importance is thus attached not so much to wealth or property as to age.

The meeting is generally held in the open ground. In Jamiri village, there is a village platform in front of the Rani's house where the meetings of the local councils are held.

The village council or the *Raiz* is the supreme administrative agency of the village. Its jurisdiction extends from ordinary house-to-house disputes to inter-village conflicts. The cases of theft (which are rare), quarrel or fight, elopement and adultery, murder and vengeance as well as sorcery or witchcraft all fall within its province.

Law. The laws followed by the Melley (the village council) are largely based on customs and conventions. In case of theft a meeting of the village council is convened when it receives a report to this effect. The council then calls an explanation from the suspect. If he admits the charge, yet asserts the righteousness of his act saying that he had to commit the offence in retaliation or reparation of some earlier injury caused to him by the person concerned, the village council finds itself in a fix. Where the culprit admits the fault but fails to assign any sound reason for its commitment, he has to pay some compensation to the person whom he may have caused harm or discomfort. He may also be required to take a pledge before the council for not committing the act in future.

If a married woman elopes with some man and if her husband lodges a fomal complaint before the village community, a meeting of the council has to be summoned. The lover is called upon to pay the amount of bride-price incurred on her marriage to her husband along with some additional amount in the form of penalty, if he wants to keep her. But if he fails to abide by the arrangement made by the council, he has to restore her to her husband.

Where a woman runs away with a man of some other village, though of her own community, over which the local village, council have no legal control, an intermediary has to be sent immediately to that village, to formally demand her back or in the alternative, to recover the bride-price from her lover as demanded by her husband. If none of these demands are met with, the village council may decide upon some stern action, even to the extent of raiding the village of her shelter in order to bring her back by force and to punish her lover. Cases of extra-marital relations and adultery are also strictly punishable by the village council.

In case of murder, full opportunity is given to the culprit to argue his case and convince the members of the council of his innocence or of the justification of his act. If the criminal succeeds in convincing the council in his favour, no punishment may be meted out to him.

Even when the indictment against an assasin is established on evidence, he may be required, at worst, to pay some penalty to the victim's family who has sustained a loss by his action,

Besides this penalty, the culprit has also to give a feast to the whole village community, to soothe the antagonism between the two parties in dispute.

If the culprit fails to pay the penalty demanded or if he is intransient he may be handed over to the family of the victim which may then keep him as a captive till he agrees to pay the penalty. Normally the loss of a person is always considered to be compensated by remunerative penalties. Capital punishment, though not wholly unknown to the Akas, is enforced only in the last resort.

The ordeal. To the Akas the most common way of practising the ordeal is to ask the suspect to put his hands into boiling water. This happens usually in case of murder or practice of black-magic where the charge against the suspect seems to be almost established by evidence but where he still pretends innocence.

Where a case of suspected black magic is brought to the notice of the village council, and where the suspect denies the charges, it may arrange an ordeal to decide the case. The village council calls for the chief priest or Mugou to conduct it. The Mugou performs some ceremonial rites and prays to the god to award full justice to the sufferers and to punish the sorcerer heavily if he has practised sorcery.

Water is boiled in a vessel with the head of a snake or a piece of skin of tiger or panther in it. The Mugou in the midst of religious rites addresses the head of the snake with the words : 'ye ? as thou bitest the human beings guilty of some act, cast thine sting to this man if he has really committed the offence'. The culprit is then asked to put his hands into the boiling water which might have been poisoned in either of the above ways. If the culprit can bring himself out of the ordeal triumphantly, without injury to his hands, which may perhaps happen only by some miracle coming to his rescue, he proves himself innocent of the crime with which he is charged and is set free from the clutches of tribal law. If, however, on the other hand, burns appear on his hand, he is supposed to have succumbed to the ordeal and thus is proved guilty of the charge beyond doubt. He is required to abide by the decision of the council which may require him to pay some adequate compensation to the sufferer. But in either case he has to give a feast to the village community.

In, so far as the Gaon Burah, though the local term for him in the Aka language is 'Nuggou', which literally means 'bigman', is concerned, he remains a part and parcel of his village community and his interests remain identical with the interests of his society. He, in fact, only co-operates with the administrative organisation of the village, taking himself a lead.

Religion

In the Aka society there is an hierarchy of gods, deities and spirits who rule over mankind. Each of the deities is responsible for a particular phase of human endeavour in the total mass of activities. Some of them are benevolent while others are essentially malevolent in nature.

The higher gods are identified with the four major forces of nature, the sky, the mountain, the earth and the water. Every effort has thus to be made to secure the blessings of of the supernatural power.

The Supreme among the Aka deities is *Teharo*. He is the benign ruler of the human as well as the animal kingdom. To ensure his blessings he is appeased by way of sacrifice from time to time. As the ritual involves the suspension of all outside activities for a definite period, it is performed preferably after the clearings for Jhumming have been made in the month of April-May. On the last day of the ritual, which lasts for two to ten days, the offering is made to the deity. A mithun or a pig is sacrificed along with several fowls. All the villagers are invited to a community feast after the offering.

After the ritual is over, the members of the household performing the ritual begin to observe some taboos. The shuts them indoors for a few days. The duration of the taboo may vary from a week to about a fortnight. After the taboo period is over, other taboos remain in operation. They still cannot enter into any social communion. They cannot accept a drink outside their house or to accept any social invitation from the people of the village as well as from outside.

The cessation of the taboo is celebrated in a special way.

Another important deity, esteemed high in the order, is known as *Aphinchi*. He is the power behind the birth of a child. Aphinchi, has to be propitiated by way of prayers and offerings during the period of pregnancy.

As soon as the child is born, the interests pass into the hands of another deity, known by the name of *Chamrom*. It is he who now onwards takes care of the child. The first propitiation of chamrom is usually made around the first birthday of the child.

The deity looking after the cattle wealth of the people is called *Jinte-Pinte-Murje*. The deity who reigns over the wild life of the forest and protects them is known as *Pamle-gri.*

Another deity who protects the porcupine is known as *Depukiri*. The deity protecting the fish in water is called *Hukir*. Agricultural activity is controlled and guided by a deity called *Wee-Oesche*.

Apart from these deities, there is a deity who, when propitiated rightly, blesses people with material success in life. He is known as *Humisise-Jumiriri*. There is a deity known as *Thamu* who causes bleeding and all other diseases accompanied by bleeding. *Chholemus* is responsible for the diseases of heart and abdomen, *Nams* causes the psychotic diseases connected with greed and lust.

There are the four gods and goddesses. There is thus, the God of the sky, the God of the mountains. the Goddesses of the Earth and the Goddesses of the River.

The God of the sky is called *Netz Au* (Netz=sky, Au= father). He reigns above and guides all human activities. *Phu Au* (phu=mountain) the symbol of natural prowess, is the mountain God. The earth and rivers are the mother goddesses, *No Ain* (no=earth, Ain=mother) being the goddess of the earth and Hu Ain (Hu=water) the Goddess of the River. To remain satisfied these natural powers need offerings like the deties from time to time. The offerings to the four supernatural powers can be made in a joint religious ceremony.

Immediately after the ritual, a taboo suspends all outside activities for a period of about ten days. The people of the house are not allowed to come out as long as this taboo remains in operation. They get relieved of the taboo by a secondary small ceremonial involving the offerings of pigs.

Apart from the four gods and goddesses who reign in the universe, there is a fifth god whose kingdom is under the earth.

He is the god *Sikchi.* The propitiation for *Sikchi* usually follows in the rainy season, around the month of June or July.

A god-couple essentially looks after the welfare of the womenfolk. They are the god *Brango* and the goddess *Sikchi-Isinsa.* Since they dwell together they are addressed jointly as *Brango-Sikchi-Isinsa.*

The last in the hierarchical order of the venerated powers are the spirit of the departed souls, particularly those that are supposed to have left the world in a state of material attachment or with some unfulfilled or suppressed craving. In all worship of the spirit the underlying feeling is that of awe. The spirits are known as *chigje.*

Whenever it is felt that a *chigje* is causing some trouble to the house, the priest is called for counsel and to raise prayers to the spirit to withdraw its evil influence and thus save the people from imperilment. The ritual is perfoımed by offering pigs and fowls.

The Mugou is the medium between the people and their gods, deities and spirits. Due to his vast social and religious duties, the Mugou in indispensable for the village people.

The religious life of the Akas is thus interwoven around the ritual-complex which is based on the fundamental desire to appease the supernatural powers controlling the destiny of man.

Magic. Magic is generally interpreted as the ability to produce marvellous results or miracles with the aid of spirits or some supernatural agencies. Among most of the tribal communities the imitative magic is common. The popular method of magic among the Akas is called *Shizou.* A man who has a quarrel with some person and is overwhelmed with a feeling of revenge and if he is a little versed in magical knowledge, may take resort to this form of magic. He may slaughter a dog and take out its blood. He sprinkles the blood upon his enemy without being detected or throw a few drops of blood into his enemy's house or burn them in his enemy's hearth. If the magic bears results, the person is supposed to either lose his life.

Another common type is *Fukhu-Sisto-Chasra* magic. The man searches for teeth of any of the wild animals such as tiger panther, bear and snake. The magician may put the teeth over the footprints of the person on whom he wishes to aim his black magic. It is supposed that the species of the animal whose teeth may have been used would kill the person.

The black magic of the Akas may thus be practised to serve various ends. The magic is regarded as anti-social by the Aka Society. The belief among the Akas is that the magical practices hamper free and sound living of an individual in society. It is considered a state in the back and therefore highly deplorable.

The strong attitude of the society against magic also suggests that the Akas have full faith in its efficacy and in its power to produce miraculous effect. Though it is no longer an approved practice, the elaborate theory of magic is known to the people to this day. It is thus possible that in the past magic may have had an important place in the Aka Society.

LIFE STYLE—THE ADIS (ARUNACHAL PRADESH)

According to Mr. O. Ering who is well informed about the history of Adis, visited the foothill areas in and around Pasighat in the early part of the 19th century where they ultimately established their settlements. The Adis practised Jhum (shifting) cultivation in the area now comprising the town, Pasighat, also started banana plantation on an extensive scale. In course of time the place became full of banana plants all around and people started calling the place as PAKLEK PIGO or the port or ghat of plantains.

Before the Adis came down to the foothills their principal trade connections were with Tibet. But as they migrated to areas further and further south their trade flowed more and more across the Brahmaputra.

After their settlement at Pasighat the Adis progressively come into closer and closer contact with the people of the Brahmaputra valley.

Settlement. A good number of Adis live in Mirmir village bordering Passighat town. They always take part in the social and cultural activities in the town. hence their youth organisations and the institution of *Kebang* are very interesting.

The Moshup. In common with some other tribes of India the Adis have also the bachelor's dormitory called the *Moshup* (also known as Dare). It is not only the sleeping house and the training centre for the young men but it is the most important community centre for the village. Important village festivals and feast and *Kebangs* (meeting of the villagers for taking decisions on different matters) are held in this house. Guests are also generally received in the *Moshup* where they can also sleep in the night. It is the place of gossip and killing time for the old and disabled who can even sleep in the night. This is indeed the "hall of audience and debate" for the village.

Very rigid rules and discipline are observed in the *Moshup*. While all the members are to collect firewood, water etc. the younger members are incharge of fireplace where they are to light the fire and to keep it burning for the whole night.

In the *Moshup* the youngmen not only learn to value community living but are also inducted into the tribe, is glorious past, mythologies, beliefs about the origin of man, animals, natural phenomena, crops and all other earthly things. They are also taught to revere their customs, festivals, social law and the gods and goddesses.

Rashang. It is the place where the young unmarried girls spend their nights. After taking their night meal—they generally take their dinner very early—they come here and learn their different traditional arts, such as spinning and weaving as also dancing and music. Here they receive youngmen from the *Moshup* and have courtship for finally choosing their husbands.

Kebangs. The system of the three-tier *kebang* obtaining in the Adi society is a unique example of direct democracy in the truest sense of the term and is remarkably similar to the Panchayat System. All important decisions on political and social matters are taken in the Kebang as also the disputes among the members of the community are tried and settled. The names of Kebang are : Bane Kebang, Bango Kebang and Bogum Bokang Kebang. There is also another Kebang called Atek Kebang for settlement of particular cases of disputes.

In Bane Kebang all the male members of the village can take part and express their opinions freely. In the past in this Kebang decisions on waging war against another village or tribe and to make treaties were taken.

The Adis are great speakers—in the Kebang, for hours on end, they will be discussing on issue. When any decision is taken, which is never by vote by general consensus, everybody abides by it.

Atek Kebang sits to try and settle particular cases of disputes. The parties involved in disputes approach the *Gams* (village leader appointed by the government) to sit in a Kebang to try their cases.

The Gams and the people of both the parties collect at a previously fixed place to settle the disputes. Women are not allowed to attend such Kebang unless some women are involved in the particular case concerned. In the past, this Kebang could inflict even capital punishment.

Bango Kebang consists of the Head Gams of a number of villages and it has one secretary and also some funds to manage. It mainly deals with inter-village disputes and development problems.

The Bogum Bokang Kebang is a federal organisation—its jurisdiction extends to the whole district of Siang. In this Kebang assemble representatives of each village and of each Bango. This organisation has also got one president and one secretary and also funds to operate. The date for its sitting is fixed and announced well in advance to enable representatives from remote villages to attend. Their social customs and relations, inter-village and inter-Bango disputes, political and economic changes affecting their life etc. are discussed in this Kebang. The Bogum Bokang adopts resolutions and recommends measures to the government for meeting them.

Cultural Life. Adi village has a rich cultural life. The tribal people are famous for their *Ponung*. That is dancing with the accompaniment of songs. A group of girls dance in a circle holding each other by stretching their hands over each other's shoulders while the leader—usually a man called the *MIRI*—dances and sings in the centre—holding aloft and shaking a sword-like musical instrument called 'Yoksha'. First he sings a line and then it is repeated in chorus by the maidens rhythmically moving in a circle at a low pace. On all important occasions *Ponung* are arranged.

Festivals form an important part of the socio-economic and religious life of the village. In March-April every year the Adis enjoy the *Aaran* festival as their New Year's day celebrations. But they perform their biggest festivals at the time of their *Solung Puja* in the last week of August or the first week of September. This is essentially a manifestation of their fertility cult. In the ancient times, once Doying-Bote (God of Heaven) met *Kine-Nane* (Goddess of wealth and prosperity) and as, being sexually excited was about to have intercourse with her, two demons *Tolel Mone* and *Dudeng Mone* intervened and snatched off his penis and in so doing scattered the divine sperms over different places from where sprouted the paddy plant. Since then men have been growing paddy on the earth. She asked them to offer her Puja in the name of the *Solung* and men have been doing so ever since. *Kine-Nane* also helped men to acquire the Mithun (baffalo) and the pig—the two animals which are sacrificed at the time of the *Solung Puja* to propitiate both *Doying-Bote* and *Kine-Nane*. It is believed that if they are satisfied, the former appears in the form of clouds and rains and the latter in the form of greater fertility of the soil.

It continues for five days. The first day is *Solung-Gidi Dogin*, (the day of preparations). Next day called *Doreph-Longe*, the Mithun is sacrificed. On the third day known as *Binngyat Binam*, the virgin girls go to the paddy fields accompanied by the *Miri* (priest) and offer meat to *Kine-Nane*. They devote the fourth day to the making of bows and arrows and other weapons of war. On the last day the *Miri* is given a ceremonial send off.

An important aspect of this festival is the Solung Abang Sung by the *Miri* every evening. Through the song he relates the stories about the origin of man, animals and plants, the ancestry of the Adis, lives and deeds of the Adi heroes.

Another popular spring festival of the area is the Holi festival. They also celebrate Durga Puja. All these festivals of all India character is due to the cultural contacts with the neighbouring plain people.

CHAPTER IV

A PORTRAIT OF ASSAM

THE ASSAMESE have always lived in isolation in a remote corner of India encircled by the mighty Brahmaputra. Nevertheless affinity of Language and religion bind the Assamese to the rest of the country.

Since Independence the State of Assam has lost territory—the district of Sylhet at partition, the Naga Hill in 1958, Meghalaya (Khasi, Jaintia and Garo Hills district) in 1970 and Mizo Hills and Arunachal Pradesh (NEFA) in 1972.

The state has now been reduced to the Brahmaputra Valley, where Assamese is spoken ; the Barak alley (Cachar) where Bengali enjoys the status of the officially recognised district language ; and connecting Mikir and North Cachar Hills where tribal languages have official local provenance.

In the Brahmaputra and Barak Valleys tribal groups like the Bodos and Kacharis lived by fishing and hunting and spoke Tibeto-Burmese languages till about 2000 years ago when people from Mithila speaking a dialect of the outer Group of Indo-European languages came and settled.

The immigrants brought iron tools to hack down thick semi-tropical evergreen forests and to work the heavy soils of the Brahmaputra Valley. They produced more food and could sustain bigger population than the primitive people. The immigrants therefore multiplied faster. Their language and culture ultimately became the language and culture of the valley.

In the Barak valley the Kacharis continued to hold their own till the 18th century when their king was given a fictitious kshatriya lineage. Immigrants from tne East Bengal overwhelmed the Kachari indigenes, but the area retained its name : Cachar. The people are referred to as Kacharis (with ak), but the district is referred to as Cachar (with a C).

There are sixteen districts in the state of Assam. The majority of the districts are in the plains area. Of the plains district, Cachar is in the Barak valley and other districts are in the Brahmaputra valley. The districts in the plains with their fertile land naturally contain most of the population.

Districts	*Area (sq. km.)*
1. Barpeta	3307.3
2. Cachar	5102.2
3. Darrang	3465.3
4. Dhubri	2745.5
5. Dibrugarh	7023.9
6. Goalpara	2843.8
7. Jorhat	6400.0
8. Kamrup	6648.7
9. Karbi Anglog	10,332.0
10. Karimganj	1839.0
11. Kokrajhar	4716.5
12. Lakhimpur	5646.4
13. Nogaon	5561.0
14. North Cachar Hills	4890.0
15. Sibsagar	2602.9
16. Sonitpur	5255.2

According to 1981 census, the total population of Assam was 198,96,843 person with an area of 78438 sq. km. The density of population in Assam is 254 person per square kilometres.

Dwellings. There are nearly 22,224 inhabited villages in the state. In these villages live the overwhelming majority of the Assamese people. Out of the total population of nearly 20 million people, nearly 85 percent are village dwellers. Only 15 percent are town dwellers.

Of the total of 23,331 villages in Assam, 22,224 are inhabited and remaining 1107 are uninhabited.

The villages of Assam are of various sizes. The majority of the villages are small. The average population of a village in 1971 in Assam was 613.

The most important urban centre and only city of the state is Guwahati. It is an ancient town. Its ancient name was Pragjyotishpur. The first historical account of the town is that by Huen Tsang who visited it about 640 A.D. It is not known when the town changed its name to Guwahati but at the time it was under the Ahoms, it was already known as Guwahati or Goahawtee or place dotted with arecanut trees. The year 1961 saw a phenomenal spurt in the population which rose to 100,707. This gave Guwahati the status of a city for the first time in 1961. The percentage increase in population during the decade was 131 percent. This was due to inclusion of new areas in the municipality, establishment of industries in and around Guwahati and increase in government offices, educational institutions and trade and commerce.

The rural communities are engaged in agriculture. Industry, trade or commerce has very little to do in a village community. Rural life is therefore simple and the villages are bound by traditions and social customs. In urban areas most of the people are engaged in non-agricultural activities like industry, trade and commerce and service. An urbanite unlike his rural counter part is less conservation and quick to adopt new ideas and ways of life. The surplus population of the rural areas are attracted by the opportunities of employment offered by the towns and cities. There is therefore a constant flow of people from rural to urban areas.

Dependency. The Dependency ratio of workers in India is 92 and for Assam is 107. In other words for every 100 persons who can work and produce there is roughly an equal number of old persons and children who cannot work but depend on them. This the working population of Assam has to carry a heavy burden. The very high dependency ratio is mainly due to the high proportion of young people of the age group of 0-14 in population. Nearly 42 percent of population is below 15 years of age. This high proportion of young in the population of Assam in particular and India in general is the result of high birth rates in our country. This is an obstacle to economic development.

Literacy. Assam occupies the twelfth rank among the states so far as general literacy rate is concerned. The percentage of literacy is 28.7 percent. The growth rate of literacy during the decade. 1961-71 is 23 per cent for the country. The literacy in Assam has made little progress during the last ten years. The growth rate of 4.9 per cent has been the lowest in Assam. It is true that there has been an increase of literate persons of the order of about 13 lakh persons during the last decade but it could not make any impact on the proportion of literate persons to the total population which has increased only marginally from 27.4 per cent in 1961 to 28.7 percent in 1971.

The menfolk are much more literate than the womenfolk. 37 per cent of the males are literate as against only 19 per cent among the females. The actual numbers of male and female literates are 29 lakhs and 14 lakhs respectively. Thus out of every ten men four are literate. But out of every ten women only two are literate. If we look at the growth of literacy during the decade 1961-71 we notice that the literacy rate among males has declined from 37.7 per cent to 37.2 per cent during the decade. The proportion of literates among women has increased from 15.6 per cent to 19.3 per cent in the same period.

It will be interesting to find out how many can read and write among children and adults separately. We find that only 33 per cent children of school going age can read and write. Among the adults 67 per cent are literate. Ten years back the figures were 36 per cent for school going age group and 64 per cent for the adults. This shows that during the last decade although literacy has gone up slightly among the adults, it has declined in the young age group.

But there is a wide gulf between the rural and urban literacy. While in urban areas every six persons out of every ten are literate, in the villages only three persons out of every ten are literate, If we further break up these populations into males and females we find that 34 per cent of the rural males are literate as against only 16.5 per cent among the rural females. In the urban areas, however, the men and women are much more literate. The urban males have a general literacy rate of 65 per cent and the females 51 per cent.

We have already noticed that villagers have a lower level of literacy than the town people. This is reflected in the individual districts also. Sibsagar district tumbles to the fifth position while North Cachar Hills holds the first place.

Religion. The religious composition of Assam is slightly different from the all-India pattern. Hindus in Assam account for 71 per cent of the total population of the state, the Islam only 24 per cent. The religion next in numerical importance is Christianity with 4.5 per cent. Sikhism, Buddhism and Jainism each account for less than 1 per cent of Assam's total population.

Scheduled Tribes. There are numerous tribal communities in different parts of our country many of whom still maintain their primitive culture. As they remained away from the main stream of society, they became backward socially and economically in comparison with the rest of the population.

The total scheduled tribe population in Assam according to the 1971 census was 1919947. This constitute nearly 15 per cent of the total population of Assam. During the decade 1961-71 the population belonging to these tribes experienced a net increase of 35 per cent.

The Hills districts are predominantly inhabited by scheduled tribes, the proportions ranging from 55 per cent in Mikir Hills up to the 69 per cent in North Cachar Hills. In none of the plains districts the proportion exceeds 14 per cent. The plains districts with more than 10 per cent of their population belonging to the scheduled tribes are Goalpara, Lakhimpur, Darrang and Kamrup. While Cachar shows the lowest figure of 0.9 per cent. If we however, consider the absolute numbers, we find that more than two thirds of the scheduled tribe population live in the plains districts.

There are 23 scheduled tribes in Assam according to the scheduled castes and scheduled tribes list (modification) order 1956. Boro-Barokachari is the numerically strongest tribes in the state. Next come Miri and then Mizo. Other tribes among the first eight numerically strongest tribes are Kachari including Sonowal, Mikir, Rabha, Lalung and Dimasa (Kachari).

The literacy rate of the scheduled Tribe is 26.03 per cent as against the literacy rate stightly higher of the general population of Assam. The proportions of workers among the scheduled tribe population is 28 per cent. The proportion of workers engaged in agriculture is much higher, nearly 92 per cent.

The following are the scheduled tribes of Assam :—

1. Chakma
2. Dimasa (Kachari)
3. Garo
4. Hajong
5. Hmar
6. Khasi and Jaintia (including Khasi, Synteng or Pnar, War, Bhoi or Lyngngam)
7. Any Kuki Tribe including—

    1. Biate or Biete
    2. Changsan
    3. Choggloi
    4. Doungel
    5. Gamalhou
    6. Gangte
    7. Guite
    8. Hanneng
    9. Haokip or Haupit
    10. Haolai
    11. Hengna
    12. Hongsungh
    13. Hrangkhawl or Rangkhol
    14. Jongbe
    15. Khawehung
    16. Khawathlang of Khothalong
    17. Khelma
    18. Kholhou
    19. Kipgen
    20. Kuki
    21. Lengthang
    22. Lhangum
    23. Lhoujem
    24. Lhouvun
    25. Lupheng
    26. Mangjel
    27. Misao
    28. Riang
    29. Sairhem
    30. Selnam

31. Singson
32. Sitlhou
33. Sukte
34. Thado
35. Thangngen
36. Uibub
37. Vaiphei

8. Lakher
9. Man
10. Mizo (Lushai) Tribes
11. Mikir
12. Any Naga Tribes
13. Pawi
14. Synteng
15. Barmans in Cachar
16. Boro Kachari
17. Deori
18. Hojai
19. Kachari including Sonwal
20. Lalung
21. Meeh
22. Miri
23. Rabha.

Activities. Of the total population of Assam 198,96,843 persons, nearly 34.7 per cent are workers and remaining are non-workers. In other words majority of the persons are dependents.

Nearly 49 per cent of menfolk are workers. Only 5 per cent of total owner are workers. This however does not mean that most of women do not make any contribution to the economy. We know that there are many women, particularly in the rural areas, who work in the fields or participate in household industries in addition to their household work.

If we consider the rural and urban areas separately we notice that the proportion of workers in the urban population is slightly higher than the proportion in rural population. 30.4 per cent of the urban people are workers against 28.15 per cent in the rural population.

As regards male and female workers, the proportions of workers among men are much higher than those among women in every district. 49 per cent of the male population are workers for the whole state. In the plains districts the proportions vary between 46 per cent and 51 per cent. In the hills districts the figure ranges between 51 per cent and 57 per cent.

In the hill districts where shifting cultivation is the rule, the womenfolk participate in cultivation in much greater measure than their counterparts in the plains districts. The proportion of female workers is high in the hills. The highest proportion is in North Cachar Hills district, nearly 24 per cent. The districts, with the lowest percentage of women workers are Goalpara, Kamrup and Nowgong. Lakhimpur and Sibsagar districts show a comparatively higher percentage of women workers, nearly 8 per cent. This is perhaps due to the presence of large number of women among the tea plantation workers in these districts.

As is to be expected agricultural workers predominate in the state. The cultivators alone form 57 per cent of the total working population. If we add the agricultural labourers to the cultivators the percentage of workers in agriculture rises to 66 per cent. After agriculture, the next highest proportion of workers is in Livestock, forestry, fishing, hunting, plantation, orchards and allied activities, nearly 10.5 per cent. Then comes other services.

In the rural areas, as is to be expected, the largest proportion of workers are made up of cultivators and agricultural labour. These two categories together constitute over 73 per cent of the workers in the rural areas. Workers in Livestock, forestry, plantations etc. and in other services account for 11 per cent and 8 per cent of the rural workers respectively. The remaining categories of workers represent only small proportions ranging from less than one per cent to 3 per cent of the rural workers.

LIFE STYLE—KACHARI PEOPLE

Assam State of India, has multiracial and linguistic groups of people with different cultures of whom the Boro Kacharis or the Bodos from a very important section of these groups and are believed to be among the earliest settler of Assam. At one time they built a powerful kingdom with capital at Dimapur and then at Maibong and Khaspur. They spread over the Brahmaputra Valley, North-Bengal and Bangladesh and constitute a very important group of Indo-Mogoloid people of the east. Those who live in scattered hamlets along the foothills of the Himalayas in the North-East as well as in scattered areas of the Brahamaputra Valley, have now been mixed up with the neighbouring peoples. But they still call themselves 'Boro or Bodo' although they are otherwise known as 'Kacharis' in the Assam Valley. A Section of this tribe who have gradually become Hindus speaking Assamese and considering their status to be higher than that of the Kacharis who are known as the Koches. In the Brahmaputra Valley, the greatest concentration of this tribe is in the districts of Gopalpara, Kamrup, Darrang and Nowgong. They also skirted the southern bend of the Brahmaputra and occupied the Garo Hills where the Garos still show close affinity with them. South of the Garos Hills, they spread in northern Mymensingh where the semi-Bengalized Hajong tribe shows that it is of Bado origin. In the borders of North Cachar Hills and Dimapur, there are two distinct groups known as Dimasas and Meches who also call themselves Bodos or Kacharis. In the range of hills south of Surma Valley there are the Tipperah whose language is a branch of the ancient Bodo.

Attempts were made to find out the local belief about their origin, but most of the villagers practically knew nothing about it although some of them were of the opinion that they are the direct descendants of Hirimba, a wife of Bhima. Such mythological origins are however common among Hindu India.

Sri M.M. Brahma, research scholar of the Tribal Culture and Folklore Research Department of the Gauhati University in his collection of the 'Folk-songs of the Bodos' remarked that "In so far as the Bodo language is concerned, there is little doubt that the language is very rich in vocabulary and in specially noted for its phonological peculiarity". Though the language is widely current not only in Assam but also in some parts of West Bengal, there is no Bodo alphabet as such. In an article 'Boro Lipi' (Boro alphabet) by Shri Gahin Basumatari published in the issue of Asom Bani dated November 22, 1963 it is stated that in the Brahmaputra Valley the Boro Kacharis use both the Assamese as well as the Roman alphabets in Bodo literature. Since times immemorial, the Bodos living in the districts of Goalpara, Darrang and Kamrup have composed Bodo songs, poems and dramas in the Assamese alphabet and the first Bodo journal, the 'Bibar', was also published in the Assemese alphabet in 1923. Due to the interaction of cultures, it is found that words of both Assamese and Boro languages are found in either language. The Kachari Rajas, during their reign, took immense interest in the growth and development of Assamese literature. Dr. S.K. Bhuyan, in his 'Kachari Buranji' thoroughly, discussed this point and, according to him, one king of Cachar was the patron of Madhab Kandali who translated the Ramayana into Assamese.

The majority of the people of this community are bilingual in the sense that they use their own Bodo dialect in speaking among themselves while Assamese is used as the medium of expression with the neighbouring Assamese people.

Race and Physical Appearance

Considering the linguistic affinities of the Kacharis with the Garos as well as the tribes known under different names as Dhimal, Chutiya, Koch, Rabha, Mech etc. many authors opine the possibility of existence of some ethnological relationship between these tribes, but without thorough anthropometric data it is difficult to say to what extent such racial affinities exist among them. Some scholars like Prof. S.K. Chatterjee include the Bodos under the Indo-Mongoloid Stock, while Haddon finds the Dolichocephalic Platyrrhine (Pre-dravidian) racial elements in the tribe. In physique, the men and women are as a rule medium-statured and well built, strong and healthy.

Religion, Caste and Community

The villagers generally call themselves Hindus, although one section is under the influence of the Brahma Samaj—a reformist cult. The Brahma Samajis have adopted a new mode of worshipping the deities and all the religious parts connected with their social occasions are performed according to the Hindu rites. The main annual festival amongst this Brahma group is the 'mahalaya'. They perform the religious ceremonies through the observance of the 'homa ceremony' and frequent offerings are made to fire through the enchanting of 'slokas' from the religious scripts. The other non-Brahmas who also call themselves Hindus still owe allegiance to their traditional tribal deities and still annually perform the Kherai and Garja' community worships. They believe in the existence and active interference in the affairs of men of certain invisible spiritual beings, considered as evil spirits which cause one's sickness and other natural calamities and are for the most part influenced by malevolent motives, the ill effects of which towards mankind is overcome by frequent offerings of rice, plantain, pigs, goats, poultry, etc. to the household deity. Bathau Bodo or Mainao, also perform of the Kherai puja or the garja puja. There is of course a tendancy among them to identify the tribal deities with the Hindu gods and goddesses through a process of syncretism and hence Bathau is being frequently identified with Siva and Mainao with Lakshmi—a typical symptom of the influence of Brahminism.

Language

The language of the people is Kachari and the speakers of this language consist of Boros, Bodos, Garos, Hajongs, Koches, Lalungs, Meches, Rabhas, Chutiyas, and Tipperahs. In the Census Report of 1961, this language is grouped under the Tibeto-Burman family which is a branch of the Sino-Tibetan or Tibeto-Chinese family according to the Linguistic Survey of India.

As the plains tribals live along with the Assamese people and nowhere are they in big concentrations, it has become necessity for them to learn Assamese and they do speak Assamese while conversing with their neighbours. But among themselves they speak their own language. With independence and a new realization of their selfhood, the Kachari people are now definitely trying to re-discover their personality as well as their old traditional customs, manner and beliefs. The 1961 Census has revealed that the number of speakers of Boro is 280,343 apart from the Dimasa, Kachari, Lalung and Rabha speakers who number 32,077 ; 64,421 ; 10,576 and 38,308 respectively. Compared with the figures of the 1951 Census and earlier Censuses, these figures do not fail to show that the plains tribals are now all out to re-discover themselves. The Kacharis are now having primary schools in their own mother tongue and they are also clamouring for higher secondary schools and high schools with Kacharis as the medium of instruction in areas where they are in concentrations.

In the sphere of their community life, the villagers form what looks like one large joint family where people commonly share their pleasures and pains, joys and sorrows. Mutual co-operation and help, both in individual and common cases, are exchanged whenever occasions demands, either in social or economic life. They are deeply attached to their social and religious customs and usages. When the young folk sing and dance, in which respect they are very rich, they forget all the worries of life. The followers of the Brahma religion also still maintains the tie of relationship with those who are yet to come under the same canopy of their religious principle and inter-change of marriages is still prevalent between the two groups.

The people are peace-loving and easy going. Any dispute among themselves is still settled by the 'Gaonbora' and they need hardly refer any case to the Kachari Samaj—a bigger organisation which controls the entire judiciary of the tribal population with its own jurisprudence. But the wind of change has started blowing, and sooner or later the naive people of this beautiful hill, will be cast into the mainstream of social, political and economic upheaval. May its people withstand the stress and strain of the change-over and may they preserve for ever what is good and distinctive in their tradition.

DIMASA KACHARI HISTORY AND ORIGIN

The Mongoloid people of India, speaking various languages and dialects of the Sino-Tibetan language family appears to have started to come to India through the Eastern and Northern gate of the country from over 3,000 years ago. The basic Mongloid element which gives the tone to the population of Assam is very largely a contribution of the Bodo tribe (Chatterjee 1959). According to Chatterjee (1959) the Bodos at one time had formed a solid block of a Mongoloid people throughout the whole of North Bihar, North Bengal, East Bengal, and the Brahamputra valley, with extensions in the Cachar Hills, the

Garo Hills and in the Tripura Hills. Local Austric and Dravidian elements were in possibility absorbed by the Bodos.

In Mahabharata (which dates back to the middle of the 10th cent. B.C.) mention has been made of Bhagadatta—a powerful king—who came with his host of Kirata and Cina troops and took part in the battle of Mahabharata as an alley of Kauravas. Kirata appears to be the name by which the Aryan speakers knew the Indo-Mongoloid. The Bodo (Bara) Tribes are linguistically connected with the Nagas, where as the Naga have always remained isolated, but the Bodos spread over the whole of the Brahmaputra valley and North Bengal as well as East Bengal, forming a solid block of Indo-Mongoloid (Kirata) people in Eastern India (Chatterjee, 1951).

In the Puranas, mention has been made of the ancient dynasty of Assam consisting of Hinduised Bodos, as belonging to the family of Narakasura, of which Bhagadatta was a branch, and appear to have ruled over Assam, right down to the middle of the lst millennium A.D. (Chatterjee, 1959). We do not have any direct evidence of happenings in Assam from the time of Mahabharata right down to the time of Bhaskar-Varman (7th cent. A.D.) According to Chatterjee (1959) the Bodos have kept up their tribal identity by maintaining their language which has dispersed in several detached pockets in Kachar (both hills and plains) and in Chutiya area to the north of Brahmaputra and in Central and Western districts of Assam as well as in the North and East Bengal, where they are found as Rabhas, Mechs, Rajbansis and Garos (within the Garo Hills), as well as Hajongs and as Tipras in Tripura. Thus it would appear from the foregoing account that the inhabitance of Kachar (of hills and plains) are of Bodo origin as evidenced linguistically.

According to Endle (1911, p. 4) that the people known to us Kacharis and to themselves as Bada (Bara) were in earlier days the dominant race in Assam. By Bada or Bara he implies the Bodo race as evidenced from his monumental work on the Kacharis (1911). Endle divided the Kachari group into two broad groups.

(1) Northern group
(2) Southern group as follows, where the Brahmaputra was taken roughly as the dividing line.

Name	*Area of Habitation*
I. Northern Groups	
1. Bara (Kachari)	Western Darrang Kachari Duars and in North Kamrup.
2. Rabha (Tolata)	Goalpara.
3. Mech (mes)	Do.
4. Dhimal	North-east Bengal
5. Koch	On Northern Frontier from Jalpaiguri to North-west Darrang.
6. Solanimiyas	Only in Mangaldai sub-division.
7. Mahaliyas	Western Darrang.
Phulgariyas	All slightly
Saraniyas	Hinduised Kacharis
II. Southern Groups	
1. Di-ma-sa "Big-water folk"	North Cachar Hills
2. Hojais	Do and Nowgong
3. Lalungs	South-west Nowgong and adjoining districts.
4. Garos	On Garo Hills and at foot of same.
5. Haijongs	On plains adjoining southern slope the Garos Hills.
6. Hill Tippera (Tripura) People	

According to Allen (1905, p. 23) the Kacharis or Bara (mispronounced Bodo) as they call themselves, belong to the great Bodo tribe, whose original habitat was somewhere between the upper waters of the Yang tse-kiang and Haang-ho and they gradually spread in successive waves of immigration over the greater part of Assam. Kacharis who had ruled in different parts of Assam from time immemorial to the middle of the 19th century A.D. are traditionally known as Karatas (Nath, 1959) Kacharis of North Cachar Hills are known as Dimasa Kacharis (Allen 1905).

Dimasa Kachari is a Scheduled tribe of Assam as given in the President's Scheduled Castes and Scheduled Tribes list modification order, 1956.

Allen (1905) has given the following account for the separation of the Bodo and Dimasa, but according to him no trace of the story has been found amongst the Kacharis of Darrang. "Long ago the Dimasa fought against a powerful tribe and were beaten in pitched battle. They were compelled to give ground, but after a time further retreat was debarred by a wide and deep river. In despair the king resolved to fight again on the fillowing day, out in the night a god appeared to him and told him that the next morning the army could cross the river if they entered it at a spot where they saw a heron standing on the bank. No one, however, was to look back while the movement was in progress. The dream proved true......A heron was seen standing on the bank, and the king and a great portion of his people crossed in safety. A man then turned to see whether his son was following, when the waters suddenly rose and swept away those who were in the river bed and prevented the others from crossing. The Dimasa were those who succeeded in reaching the further bank of safety."

Allen (1903) stated that this legend account for the separation of the Bodo and the Dimasa find no place among the Kacharis of Goalpara (Kacharis of Goalpara are known as Mech). Thus one tribe style themselves as Bara and the other Dimara, Though both use languages of Bodo origin. According to Allen (1903, p. 45) the Mech tribe is believed to be absolutely indentical with the Kacharis. But the Dimasa Kacharis of the N.C. Hills does not support the views expressed by Allen (1903) in total, but they have not denied that the Mechs are also a branch of Kacharis which got separated in distant part, but how and when is not known, probably lost in the mist of the history.

Allen (1905, p. 90) stated that the Totlas are superior section of the Kacharis, and occupy an intermediate position between the Kacharis and the Koch. Kacharis when they are converted to Hinduism, were generally incorporated into the ranks of the Koch caste in lower Assam (Assam District Gazetteers, Vol. VIII, 1905, pp. 86-87). According to Allen (1905, p. 76) the Kacharis at Nowgong are divided into two sections, these who live in the Barbhangha, Dhing and Khatoalgaon near the Brahamaputra are said to be Bodos a kin to the Kacharis of Darrang, while those in the valley of Kapiti are Dimasa. The former are known as Jharuas, or Chaidvaria, Kacharis the latter as Hojais....There are no subdivisions amongst the Jharuas, but the Hojais are said to be divided into endogamous clans as Rabha, Ramsa, Kheremia Thengal, Sonwal and Jaladha."

The Kacharis may perhaps be described as the earliest known aboriginal inhabitants of the Brahmaputra Valley. They are identical with the people called Mech in Goalpara and North Bengal. These are the names given to them by outsiders. In the Brahmaputra Valley the Kacharis call themselves Bodo or Bodo fisa (sons of Bodo). According to Endle (1911) the Kacharis became widely separated as the Western (Bara) and Southern (Dimasa) a corruption of Dima fisa or "sons of the great river". They were known to the Ahomes Dimisa, clearly a corruption of Dimasa, so that this name must have been in use when they were still in the Dhansiri Valley (Gait, 1953). According to Endle (1911, p. 4) "It is indeed not all unlikely that the people known to us as Kacharias and to themselves as Bada (Bara) were in earlier days the dominant race in Assam;......have left traces of this domination in the nomenclature of some of the physical features of the country, e.g. the Kachari word for water (di : doi) apparently forms the first syllable of the names of many of the chief rivers of the province, such as, Diputa, Dihong, Dibong, Dibru, Dihing, Dimy, Desang, Diku etc. and to these may be added Dikrang, Dipu, Digaru etc., all near Sadiya, the earliest known centre of Chutiya (Kachari) power and civilization."

"The origin of the word Kachari (the first is short in Assamese and long in Bengali) is difficult to trace, but it may be mentioned that, according to the Limbu legend of creation given by Risley in the Tribes and Castes of Bengal, one of the two progenitors of the human race settled in the Kachar country, which is the name given by the Nepalese to the tract at the foot of the Hills between the Brahmaputra and Kosi Rivers ; and there became the father of the Koch, Mech and Dhimal tribes, or the head-quarters of a powerful Mech dynasty, the member of the tribe in Assam may well have been called Khacharis or Kacharis. The Kacharis are believed to very closely allied to the Koches, and also, so far at least as language is concerned, to the Chutiyas, Lalungs and Morans of the Brahmaputra valley, and to the Garos and Tipperas of the Southern hills. Having regard to their wide distribution, and to the extent of the country over which Bodo languages of a very uniform type are still and current, it seems not improbable that at one time the major part of Assam and North East Bengal formed a great Bodo Kingdom" (Gait, p. 1963).

Ahom, a branch of the Shan race, crossed the Patkoi (Patkai) range to the South-east of Assam in the early years of the 13th century A.D. (1228 A.D.) under the leadership of Sukapha who was compelled to leave his ancestral kingdom of Nara as he had no prospect of sovereignty there. The Ahoms ruled in Assam from A.D. 1228 to 1826 A.D. till it passed into the hands of the British by the Treaty of Yanadaboo (Bhuyan, p. XVIII, 1933). According to Hem Barua (1926) the Ahoms are a great Mongoloid race of Hukwang (Hukawang) valley, who migrated into Assam in the 13th century, through the Patkoi range.

According to Anderson (c.f. Endle, p. XVI) the Dimasa, Great-River-Folk (di-means "rivers" or "water"), were driven out of the valley of the great river Brahmaputra in historical times, and finally became rullers of what is now known as the Cachar District.

There are no written records of Kachari rule, and the traditions current amongst the people, consist of title more than long lists of kings, on the accuracy of which it is impossible to rely. According to Fisher the Kacharis of North Cachar believe that they once ruled in Kamrupa, and their royal family traced its descent from Rajas of that country, of the line of Hatsungtsa. How long this kingdom existed, it is now impossible to say ; but what is known with some degree of certainty is, that they were engaged in a prolonged struggle with the Ahoms, a section of the great Shan (Tai) race, who crossed the Patkai Hills from the south and east about A.D. 1228 and subdued the Morans, Borahis and other Kachari tribes living near the Northern slopes of these hills (Endle, 1911, p. 6).

According to Barman (unpublished manuscript 1968), originally, this eastern region of Bharata was termed as Kachchha Desha, indicating land of Runn or narrow sea gulf, and the people of this region used to be termed as Kachchari, meaning the inhabitants of the land, called Kachcha.

The Ahoms gradually subdued the Kacharis who drove their opponents to take refuge in or about Dimapur on the Dhansiri at the foot of the Naga Hills. In Dimapur the Kacharis were in comparative security and they appeared to have attained a high degree of material civilization evidenced from the architecture and archaeological remains though not fully excavated of the Kachari kingdom.

This section of the Kacharis are known as the Dimasas. According to Barman (1966), "Hidimba-pur" (pronounced as Hihimbapur) was the real name of this capital and kingdom. Reference is there in the Mahabharata, that Bhima, the second of the Pandava brothers, married the demon princess, Hidinba (Hirhimbaa), sister of the local potentate of terrible ways, then called Rakshasa...The ruling family of the Kachchharis, since the days of antiquity, therefore, assumed the distinction of Hidimbba-chha, meaning the progency of Hidimbbaa, then generic mother. This term, Hidimbas-chha, got distorted into Dimabaachha, and then into Dimachha or Dimasa in the later phase."

The Dimasa Kacharis could not live in peace and prosperity for a long time because their ancient foes, Ahom, followed them up to their new capital Dimapur, and about the middle of the 16th century the Ahoms succeeded in capturing and sacking Dimapur itself. The Kachari Raja thereupon removed his capital to Maibong which is at a considerable distance from Dimapur (Maibong literary means "much paddy"). At Maibong the Kachari dynasty would seem to have maintained itself for some two centuries (Endle 1911). According to Endle (1911), under pressure of an attack by the Jaintia Raja the Kachari sovereign withdrew from Maibong to Khaspur in Kachar (circa 1750 A.D.) There they seem to have come more and more under Hindu Influence, until about 1790 the Raja of that period, Krishna Chandra, and his brother Govinda Chandra made a public profession of Brahminism. They were both placed for a time inside the body of a large copper image of cow, and on emerging thence were declared by the Brahmins to be Hindus of the Kshatriya caste, Bhima of Mahabharata fame being assigned to them as a mythological ancestor. Hence to this day the Darrang Kacharis sometimes speak of themselves as "Bhim-ni-sa" i.e., children of Bhim, though as a rule they seem to attach little or no value to this highly imaginative ancestry.

According to Endle (1911, p. 7), the region of the last Kachari King, Goind Chandra, was little better than one continuous flight from place to place through the constant attacks of the Burmese, who finally compelled the unhappy monarch to take refuge in the adjoining British district of Sylhet. He was, indeed, reinstated, in power by the aid of the East India Company's troops in 1826, but was murdered some four years later, when his kingdom became part of the British dominions. His commander-in-chief, one Tula Ram, was allowed to remain in possession of a portion of the sub-division now known as North Cachar, a region show in old maps of Assam as "Tula Ram Senapati's country", But on the death of this chieftain in 1854, this remaining portion of the old Kachari Raj was formally annexed to the district of Nowgong.

As regards this last mentioned migration, i.e. from Maibong to Khaspur about A.D. 1750, and the conversion to Hinduism which soon followed it, it would seem that the movement was only a very limited and restricted one, confined indeed very largely to the Raja and the members of his court. The great majority of his people remained in the hill country, where to this day they retain their language, religion, customs etc. to a great extent" (Endle, 1911).

Even to this day they are sticking fairly rigidly to their old customs and practices unlike the Ahoms.

Population

The Dimasa section of the Kachari people are mainly concentrated in the United Mikir and North Cachar Hills. The district covers an area of 5891.7 sq. miles and has a population (1951) of 165444 in which the Dimasa number 14,714. It is larger than any autonomous hill district of Assam and it shows the lowest density barring the Arunachal Pradesh being only 28 per sq. mile.

The earlier census figures of the Dimasa Kachari population is as follows :

1931	—	14,680
1941	—	15,971
1951	—	14,714
1961	—	68,718
1981	—	1,37,434

The total number of Dimasa in Assam, according to the Census of 1981 is 1,37,434.

Population trend of Dimasa Kachari/Kacharis from 1911

Year	*Male*	*Female*	*Total*
1911			228,528
1921*	105,364	101,902	207,266
1931	7,439	7,241	14,680
1941			15,971
1951			14,714
1961	36,575	32,143	68,718

*In 1921 Census (p. 99) figures on Dimasa Kachari are not given as such but as Kacharis as a whole, further Kacharis were divided into Hindu and Ammist and the poled value have been presented here.

Population of Dismasa Kachari

State/District		*Persons*	*Males*	*Females*
Assam	R	68,405	36,359	32,046
(Hills)	U	313	216	97
Garo Hills	R	1,309	615	694
	U	11	7	4
U.K. &	R	17	14	3
J. Hills	U	83	69	14
U.M. & N.C.	R	67,069	35,725	31,344
Hills	U	213	140	75
Mizo	R	10	5	5
Hills	U	4	—	4

R = Rural ; U = Urban

The table above shows the distribution of the Dimasa Kachari in the State of Assam, Meghalaya, Mizoram and in the different hill districts of Assam.

Physical Appearance

Endle (1911, p. 1) has given a brief outline of the physical characteristics of the Kacharis as such in general, the same is given as follows. "They are certainly not a tall or handsome race and in general appearance bear some resemblance to the Nepali, being as a rule shorter and stouter than the people of the North-west India, though well fitted to bear up against physical fatigue and Hardships. In face and figure they show a distinct approximation to what is known as the Mongolian type, i.e., they have square set faces, projecting cheek bones, with almond shaped eyes, and scanty beard and moustache, the last-mentioned being often wanting altogether." The mean stature of Dimasa Kacharis is 163.9 cms.

The Dimasa Kacharis are short to medium statured people. The mean stature of the Dimasa Kacharis is 163.9 and which is close to the mean value of 1630.5=5.9 observed among the Kacharis (c.f. Gupta and Dutta, 1966).

Majority of the Dimasa Kacharis are of medium brown colour with low waves in hair form. They have a shallow to medium nasal root with normal wings in most of the cases. As far as the Mongoloid characteristic like eipcanthic folds and eye-slits are considered, they suggest more of the non-mongoloid features as evidenced from the frequency distribution of those characters.

The appearance of the non-mongoloid features in the Dimasa Kacharis may be due to their mixing in the biological sense with the plains people of Assam through centuries.

They have round to broad faces with prominent chins. Majority of them do not show prognathism and they have medium lips with prominent cheeks.

ECONOMY

Agriculture

Land is one of the most important economic resources of the people, their livelihood, mainly depend on cultivation. The lands may be classified into the following categories, (1) uncultivable land, (2) cultivable land and (3) land under forest.

The lands which are used for homestead purposes, playground, footpaths etc. are included in the non-agricultural lands, uncultivable land signifies the barren land area which are unfit for cultivation and the land under forest indicates the area which is covered with jungle trees and which is not included in the net areas cultivated. In addition to this there is another type of land known as cultivable but it left fallow for the present time.

The jhum land in a village is restricted to a particular area for a village in consultation with the Sarthe or the 'gaonbora'. of a village. If any disagreement arise about selection of the Jhuming site among the villagers, the gaonbora refers the case to the District Council, whose decision in consultation with gaonbora is taken as final. Individual plots with in the selected area for jhuming may be demarcated by the individuals in consultation with the gaonbora. There is no restriction as to the size of the land allotted to different individuals, it depends upon the ability or capacity of a family to cultivate. A family or a person loses the right of occupation or cultivation if they leave the village or shift to another village for the purpose of permanently settling there which is under the jurisdiction of another 'gaonbora'. When the old plot is exhausted and the person wants to shift to a new plot for cultivation then they have to get the permission of the gaonbora. Sometime a temporary dwelling is constructed near the jhuming site only to stay during the operational session, if the jhum land is at a fair distance from the house.

The village people obtain the fuel from the felled trees while clearing the forest for jhuming, which they may also store for future utilization. If needs arise the people have the right to cut trees either for construction purposes or for fuel from the unclassed state forest i.e. the forest areas near the village which is not reserved. This area is forest in name only, since unrestricted jhuming has virtually eaten up all most all the forest trees rendering the whole area covered with only bamboos and grasses with a few scattered trees here and there. Reserved forests where the people have no right to utilize the forest material. The forest reserved of the district are potentially very rich which give a very good revenue to the district particularly for the bamboo trees. The evergreen forest are the home of various kinds of wild animals such as elephants, wild buffaloes, tigers, bears, deers etc. The menace of the wild animals in the villages are not an uncommon sight. Rabits are a great pest in the jhum fields and the villagers are always for on the look out for the rabbits holes and alway's try to scare the rabbits. Various kinds of poisonous as well as non-poisonous snakes abound in the jungle, and the villagers have to tread with an open eye while moving through the jungles. Monkeys often assail the jhum fields in company. Varieties of birds break the silence of the forest with their sweet melodies.

The forest is chiefly infested with the different species of bamboo, cinnamon, sal, deodar and many other trees for valuable timber. The wild plantain trees abound in the forests and form a ready source of food for elephants, monkeys and the like.

Livestock Rearing

The secondary occupation of the Dimasa Kacharis is the rearing of livestock, Poultry, goats and pigs are commonly reared either for their food and commercial purposes or for ceremonial and sacrificial importance. Milch and drought cattle are kept for milk and for ploughing the fields respectively, Deer and wild pigs are frequently caught, sometimes by the use of large nets, enclosing a considerable extent of grass land in which some keen eye has detected the presence of the much prized game. The net gradually encloses the prey which comes within the reach of the man or the party, hunting, and then the dao speedily brings an end of the animal.

Fishing and Implements

Fishing by the Dimasa Kacharis is a very favourite pastime as well as an occupation. On certain prearranged dates men as well as women of the village, some of not all, in a group go to fishing in the nearby streams. The day for fishing is fixed by mutual consultation. The fishing implements used are of a very simple nature and are commonly prepared from materials which are indigenous. The river water being shallow, the nets are rarely employed for fishing. Zakhi and Palha are the two implements commonly used for fishing, the former being employed chiefly, but no exclusively, by women. Both implements made of spilt bamboo fastened together with cane. The Zakhi is a triangular basket, open at one end, the three triangular sides closing to a point at the other end. This is attached to a bamboo handle some three or four feet in length. By holding the bamboo handle one enters the stream which is usually very shallow, and lowers the basket to the bottom, keeping the open and in front of the person and then quickly lift the basket and examines the content, and if any fish is found trapped, it is rapidly transferred to the fish basket. Palha is the other fishing implement. It is made of spilt bamboo fastened together by cane strips and is about 4½ feet in height and about 3 feet in diameter at the base. The upper portion is drawn somewhat closely together, leaving an open space at the top sufficient to allow the admission of a man's hand, the whole structure being quite light and easily manipulated by one hand. With this in hand the fisherman quitely enters the shallow water at any likely spot and places the basket closely clutching the ground, and the fish so enclosed are then withdrawn by the hand through the opening in the upper part of the instrument.

Another instrument used by the Kacharis in catching fish is a small, pointed spearhead attached to a light bamboo. With this fishes like eels are caught by spearing. This instrument have become obsolete even in interior villages, instead rod and line has become popular particularly in urban folks more so those who are having white collar jobs.

Cottage Industry

One of the important household industries amount the Dimasas is the culture of the eri silk-worm and the manufacturer of the eri cloth. They also manufacture muga cloth.

The loom employed for weaving the eri silk is simple tension loom and is made from the material available in the village. The loom is unlike the loin loom. The loom is usually kept under a thatched cover which protects the weaver from the scorching sun. The weaving is always done by the lady of the house or by one of her daughters. The cloth which they weave are mainly for their personal use and if there is any surplus they sell it in the market. But this does not happen very often as almost all the households are having their own looms. Among Dimasa women weaving is a must ; a women who does not know the art of weaving is looked down upon in the society. With the exception of weaving which is done by the females, the bamboo and cane works are done by the males only the black smithy are done by their Bengalee or Assamese neighbours. Bamboo and cane works are taken up by the males mostly for their personal use than for sale. The person knowing the art of basketry makes bamboo or cane baskets of various kinds according to the use of which they are put. For example, baskets for carrying and storing paddy or food grains or for keeping cloths and ornaments etc. ; cane tables, chairs, murrah (low-stool) are also made by them, particularly those who are living in the urban areas.

Jhuming Cultivation

After the allotment of the jhum land to the individuals of the village of plot is put to cultivations, trees are felled and jungle is cleared. The felling of the trees are allowed to dry until March when they are set on fire. Tillage and spreading of the ash, obtained from burning the trees, is then done with the help of the hoe.

Agricultural Implements

In the interior villages, the agricultural implements are invariably of very simple type and the manner they use is the dried and decomposed leaves and burnt up ashes. The important agricultural equipments are the following—the axe (rowa), the spade and sickle another dao. All these are obtained from the market or are prepared when ordered by blacksmiths, particularly in the interior villages who usually do not get readymade things for use.

Paddy Cultivation

Paddy is then sown with the first rains in April-May. Everything regarding cultivation like, clearing, slashing, burning, tillage, sowing and harvesting are done by individual families and some time with the help of daily wage labourers. Joint participation at the family or the clan level is not found, except in harvesting where friends and relatives extend their helping hands. Paddy is sown in April or May and is harvested in

Nov.-Dec. In addition to paddy other crops like maize, millet, mustard etc. are also sown along with paddy as side lines in the holes so made for the purpose by hoes. Thus the sowing is over, before the first rains and the harvesting is done in the ensuing cold weather. The ears of paddy are cut with the help of a sickle. The sheaves, on getting dry are collected and thrashed on the spot by beating against some stone.

Wet Cultivation

Those Dimasa Kacharis who are much influenced by their Bengali or Assamese neighhours who are having plain lands for cultivation and adequate water supply for their fields from near by streams take to wet cultivation if they can afford it. In wet cultivation the soil is made into a thick paste by means of a hoe or in some cases those who can afford to use bullocks for ploughing. Weeding and transplantation in done generally by women. Sometimes no transplantation is done, where the water is not adequate, and some time plants which are blown off by the wind is cerefully re-planted. Sometimes a watch house is also constructed in the field so that the owner or any one of his family may stay to watch the crops and keep the animals and birds away from the field, particularly before harvesting.

Source of Income

The only source of the income of the whole village under discussion is cultivation. The majority of the households in the village, fall within the annual income group of Rs. 301-600, comes to be 28 households. The second largest number of households, i.e., 16 households are in the income group of Rs. 601-900, while 7 households are in the income group of Rs. 901-1200 and only 6 households are in the income group of Rs. 1201 and above. The villager takes to other jobs other than cultivation, like some unskilled jobs in the Public Works Dept. or Government hospitals or some other offices, but such services are only taken up when the agricultural operations are over.

The expenditure incurred by each household in the village for paying revenue is Rs. 3 to be paid to the District Council. Among the higher income groups the expenditures comparatively higher than that in the lower income groups. Households which fall in the higher income groups like the above Rs. 1200 usually spend a large amount on food and other necessities like furniture etc. The economic condition of the households are fairly goods since the village is free from poverty and there is none living in acute want and poverty of much economic distress.

SOCIAL STRUCTURE

Religion

Though the Dimasa Kacharis claim themselves to be the followers of Hinduism their religion can hardly be regarded as covered within the fold of Hinduism. It appears as if their religion is an outcome of the reactionary forces of their traditional types of religion, commonly known as animistic and Hinduism. The general conversion of the Kachari people into Hinduism took place in the latter part of the eighteenth century. The Ahoms succeeded in capturing and sacking Dimapur about the middle of the sixteenth century, there upon the Kachari Raja removed his capital to Maibong, where the dynasty seemed to have maintained itself for some two centuries, and finally when attached by the Jaintia Raja the Kachari Kingdom was shifted from Maibong to Khaspur in Kachar in circa 1750 A.D. It is during this period that the Kacharis were more and more under the Hindu influence until about 1790 the Raja of that period, Krishna Chandra and his brother Govinda Chandra made a public profession of Brahminism. It is said that they were both placed for a time inside the body of a large copper model of a cow and in emerging from there, were declared by the Bahmins to be Hindus of the Kshatriya caste, and Bhima of Mahabharata fame was assigned to them as a mythological ancestor (Endle 1911, p. 6).

The conversion to Hinduism was formerly limited only to the members of the Royal family and the great majority of the Dimasa people retained their language, religion, customs etc. to a great extent intact. But as the time passed more and more people were influenced by Hinduism, particularly the Barman Kacharis who are residing in the plains of Cachar. But Hinduism in its strict sense is not found among the Dimasas.

The Dimasas have many gods and godesses, of which there is one supreme called Madai. Under him there are many other

Madais, some are family deites and some are evil spirits. The progenitor of these family deities or madais is known as 'Airekhidima', who is supposed to have the form of a big female bird. According to traditional beliefs, the bird (airekhidima) after looking for a suitable place for her nest at last came to the banyan tree and built her nest on it. In the cource of time the bird laid seven eggs. The first one to come out of these eggs was 'Braisibrai'. It was then followed in succession by 'Aloomaja' (also known is 'Dooraja'), 'Naiphuraja' 'Waraja', 'Morangraja' and 'Hamaido', when the last egg was not yet matured and hamaido being impatient kicked at it. The egg broke and the liquid content fell hither and thither on the land and water and thus turned to evil spirits or madais. These Madais or evil spirits trouble to the people and hence they were deprived of being treated as deities. 'Braisibrai' being the eldest one is worshipped as a common god by all the Dimasa Kacharis and the last one 'Itamaido', because of his misdeed was not worshipped as an ancestral god. The remaining madais became the family deity or nokhoni-madais and are worshipped as such by the Dimasa Kacharis annually but there is no fixed time, for it depends upon the wish of the family members.

Community worship is done periodically at an interval of three or more years when 'maisingba' or sacrifice of animal is offered to a presiding deity, at a 'Madaikho' gods house or temple. These are located in certain fixed places, some of the clans combine to form a big circle and each such circle has one Madaikho. As the clans are spread over cast areas so they have to get toghether whenever such ceremony takes place. Before the community deity, goats which are completely black are sacrificed in addition to pigs, fowl, pigeons eggs etc.

There is no authorised priestly clan among the Dimasa Kacharis. In common Hojai represents the priest. In one village there may be 2 or 3 priests but in other villages there may not be any priest. In such cases, a priest is borrowed from the nearby village. The following are the office beaters who deal with the religious practises.

I	Dainya	Perform the Sacrificial ceremony,
II	Janthi	Assistant
III	Gisia	Highest Priest

IV Phatri	Through him god speaks or through him comes the divine utterances.

In early days all these offices were hereditary but now except the Gisia others are not hereditary. They can lead a married life but all have strictly to follow a good and devout life. They should not partake food from other's hands. These offices bearers may be classified on the basis of the food they take.

(a) Misham : i.e. those who take all the food or takes food without restriction.
(b) Gathar : i.e. those who do not take pork, crab, snail and vegetable like Bairethai and Yaulaisa.

All these officials perform religious ceremonies during the community worship.

For worshiping in the family level only two categories of the priest perform the religious functions, they are ;

(a) Hojai	Priest
(b) Barowa	Assistant

These officials are not hereditary and any one who knows the art of worshipping became Hojai, and to them there is no restriction for eating. The deities are not represented by any figure or object but by small mounds of earth and these are known as Habom.

Among the family deities, the 'nokhone madai' is the most important. The performance of the ceremony is different from that performed in the community level. Here the priest sacrifices the animals besides performing the duties of prayer and rites. This ceremony is usually performed just before the sowing season for bringing about the prosperity of the whole family. Another performance known as 'madaima daimba' is performed for the well being of an individual in the family.

Community worship is generally held at the times of femine which brings successive failure of crops due to drought etc. A meeting of the village priests and elderman takes place and the date and place is fixed where such ceremonies are to be performed and the representatives of the respective village bring their animals and birds to be sacrificed.

Society

A number of community development blocks have been established covering almost every village in the state, there are also other organizations for social reform and welfare, working among the Dimasa Kachari. The 'Dimaraju' organization look after the welfare of the Dimasa. There are branches of this organisation throughout the North Cachar district in all important places like :—

Barakhola	Jaipur	Tungpreng	Haflong
Maibong	Sheoratal	Diphu	Dhenashri
Hojai	Haoraghat	Dimapur	Lamding
Lanka	Bikrampur	Dhalai	Thaligram

There is a good number of members in all these centres ranging from 12 to 107 persons. The Assam Tribal Welfare works have also organized some primary schools in the villages where the tribal children get free education.

Since the Dimasa Kacharis are not much influenced by Christianity so there is no missionary welfare organization working in the Dimasa Kachari Villages.

Social Structure

The Dimasa Kacharis have been influenced by their Assamese and Bengalee neighbours particularly those who are living in the plains. Much of their old customs of their social organization has survived even in the present day administrative change. The routine administration of each village is run by the village council, particularly by the village head man the 'gaonbora'.

The jhum land in the village is distributed by the 'gaonbora' whose voice in this matter is final. If any disagreement comes then only the case goes to the District Council. The 'Gaonbora' is elected by the village people, who are usually elderly person and commands respect of the villagers. The District Council is simply an approving authority and has no say in the election of the 'gaonbora'. The District Council recognizes the functions and duties of the 'gaonbora' and does not interfere with the customary rights and privileges of the community.

There is no authorised priestly clan among the Dimasa Kacharis. In common Hojai represents the priest. Gisia is considered to be the highest priest and only for 4 or 5 villages combined may have one Gisia and all the religious ceremonies are performed under his supervision. In early days the religious offices were hereditary but now except the Gisia—the highest priest, others are not hereditary. Gisia—Commands respect from all the village people as well as from distant villages which does not have any Gisia of their own, but they take the services of the Gisia from other villages. The other offices of the priestly clans are not hereditary and any one who knows the art of worshipping becomes Hoaji.

It is the duty of the 'gaonbora' to summon the members of the village council to a sitting and it is he who puts forward proposals relating to the affairs of the village and the members discuss the matters and give their verdict. The 'goanbora' can only preside over the village council but cannot take any decision of his own without the consent of the members of the village council. The village council plays an important role in regulating the social, economic and religious life of the community, though its power has been somewhat curbed with the establishment of the District Council and all important matters like theft, murder, disputes over land (which cannot be settled by the village council still occupies an important place in the social organisation and still retains much of its traditional powers in deciding various matters affecting the community as a whole.

CEREMONY AND BELIEFS

Birth of a Child

The Dimasa Kacharis believe that the birth of a child is at Gods hand. A pregnant women is always looked upon with care and is not allowed to do any heavy work. She is exempted from doing work in the field and is also exempted from carrying fire wood and other such things, but is allowed to do light household chores. Delivery of a child is generally and preferably done by an experienced elderly women among the relatives. In return the dhai is paid in cash or kind. When the child is about to be born the expectant mother is made to lie on a mat on the floor and the attendant dhai keeps watch over her. Then all the things like piece of cloth, sharp bamboo split, thread etc. are kept ready for the delivery of a child. When the child is born the dhai cuts off the naval cord with sharp split bamboo and a piece of cloth is tied around it. After she has given birth to a child she is kept in isolation. This confineness lasts till the performance of the 'dausthaiba' ceremony which is usually dries up and comes out by itself. This ceremony is done so as to be free from the bondage of debt incurred during the delivery from the relatives and friends.

In this ceremony a pair of chickens are sacrificed and the killed animal is given to the 'dhai' by the parents. Before the delivery the women are given normal diets as is taken by the other members of the households. While after the delivery she is given Muru i.e. boiled vegetables. In addition as a substitute of milk she is given the juice of Mishage, a plant leaf, which is a good substitute for milk.

Name Giving Ceremony

The naming ceremony of the child is also performed by the 'hajaijig'. The child's name is usually selected by its parents or and grandparents according to their likings. This ceremony is known as Nanabasinjiriba and in this the horoscope of the child is prepared and then one chicken is sacrificed and the boy is presented with Thali, Bati, clothes and jewellery etc. Not all are able to perform their ceremony, particularly the poorer sections, and it is not obligatory so only those who can afford it perform this ceremony. A feast is held on this occasion in which friends and their relatives are invited and zu and pork or other meat with the exception of beef are supplied to the invited guests.

Until about a month before the mother is held unclean and is subjected to certain restrictions in social and religious matters. That is, she is not allowed to approach the domestic altar in which her relatives offer rituals and offerings to the gods. This period of ceremonial uncleanliness is usually terminated by the use of the holy water (dithat) by the priest (jonthai), which is sprinkled on the mother as well as at the different places and corners of the house. Then only the mother is considered from the social and religious limitations and is at full liberty to resume all her social and religious duties.

The child is fed with the mother's milk until the end of the suckling period which usually lasts about seven to eight months when the child is old enough to be fed with rice. On approaching the end of the suckling period the child is generally given rice masticated by the mother. When the child's teething period is over and the teeth have come out, normal diet, that is, that which adults take, is given. The mother generally carries the child at her back, while at work, when the child attains an age of 3 or 4 months. The child is allowed to crawl on the floor all by itself until it learns to stand.

The Dimasa Kacharis who are living in the urban areas or those who are living near the urban centres take the help of the hospital during delivery and everything goes according to the routine of the hospital authorities.

Marriage

Marriage among the Dimasa Kachari is strictly monogamous. Marriage within one's sengfong or jaddi is not permissible and they strictly follow the rules laid down by their traditional customs. Marriage outside the community is looked down by the society and the parents out of disgrace, may drive the boy or girl away from their home. Seduction is rare and if at all it occurs the girl's parents have to give their girl away in marriage. Illegitimacy and adultry is very rare and if at all any such case is detected it is usually tried by the village council and the guilty pair is tried publicly thus subjecting them to the jeers and scorn of the neighbour. They are released only when the fine imposed by them is paid. The amount of the fine varies from Rs. 50 to Rs. 100 depending on the case and the decision of the Council and the amount is given to the injured husband or wife.

A younger brother may marry his elder brother's widow, but an elder brother cannot marry the widow of his younger brother. Marriage with one's wife's younger sister (after the death of the former) is permitted but not the elder. Child marriage is not found and the above rules are strictly enforced and any breach of them renders liable to be outcast from the society.

Generally the boy's father will go to the girl's parents for formal negotiations though only after ascertain the wishes of the boy. In absence of the father a close relative like an uncle will represent for the marriage negotiations. The marriage negotiatons are done in a sort of set pattern of phrases. When the proposal is accepted of the girl's father receives a basket (made of cane and leaf) full of salt weighing about a seer (½ £). This is known as 'Saudidang Singbha'. If the girl's father does not accept the proposal even at the later stage, then the salt has to be returned to the boy's father and the engagement is broken. After the formal engagement the girl's father seeks approval from the clan members and conveys the same to the boy's father who comes after for finalization of the marriage. At this time the boy's father goes to the girl's father with two or three gourds of rice beer accompanied by some of the close relatives for finalizing the marriage day. This is known as Laotai langba, i.e., taking of gourd. Then after sometime again a meeting is held between both parties and on this occasion the price of the bride known as Kalti is fixed. The account of the Kalti varies from Rs. 50 to Rs. 200, according to the economic position of the bridegroom's father as well as his position in the society. The number of animals to be sacrificed during the marriage as well as the quantity of rice beer, is finally decided and settled along with the Kalti. The proposal being thus finalized, the date of the marriage is set according to the conveniences of both parties. The Kalti is paid on the date set for the marriage. Thus the actual marriage ceremony takes place usually after five or six months from the first day of negotiations. According to the Dimasa Kacharis the following days of the week are not suspicious, as Saturday, Tuesday, Sunday and the birth day of the daughter or son. The marriage ceremony is held at the bride's house. If the groom is of a distant village then the groom's party reaches a day earlier than the actual marriage day, as it is on this day that the bride's price is given. The arrangement for the staying accommodation of the groom's party is done by the friend's and relatives of both parties. The marriage ceremony is completed before the end of the afternoon. Both the parties assemble together in some open space in the village or if the house of the bridge is fairly large enough with a big country yard, then the ceremony is held at the bride's house.

In this ceremony the members of both the parties varying from about 200 to 300 members sit in the open space on either side facing each other. The sitting arrangement is so made that the 'Khunang' or village Headman sits at centre, the groom's party sit on the right hand side, the bride's party on the left and the invitees in the front. When this is done, the bridegroom is summoned to bow and touches him on his head and blesses him. The groom moves towards each of the relatives and members of the other side under a cover, usually, a big umbrella or a big canopy, held by his six, or seven friends. When the blessing by the elder members is over then the 'Sampradans' ceremony takes place. In this the elder members of both the parties have verbal fights. Which is followed in a traditional way, over the eligibility of the boy or the girl in the marriage, in which the groom's party will invariably win and the girl's father will offer his daughter in marriage.

In the earlier days the bride does not come to the courtyard before the public, but now in families who are influenced by the urban way of life, particularly their neighbour, the Bengalese and the Assamese, come out in the court along with the relatives and friends during the Sampradan' Ceremony. Thereafter the bridegroom accompanied by the girl's relatives goes to the house of his father-in-law leaving the guest behind to feast merrily. The bridegroom spends that night in the outer chamber (nokhung) apart from the bride. He is admitted the following day into the inner chamber (noshing), to live with his newly wedded wife. On the third day after marriage, the bridegroom with his bride and relatives and friends return to the parent's house. This is known as 'phira phoiba' or the visit of the daughter-in-law. After staying for some time he along with his wife again return to his father-in-law's house to stay with him as long as he desires which usually lasts for about a year. This period of staying with his father-in-law is known as 'min-ha-bha'. During this period the newly wedded couple help the bride's parents in jhuming and other domestic work. The groom stays in his in-law's house until he is able to build his own house and start a life at their own accord.

Divorce

A man may divorce his wife on any reasonable grounds but he will not get back the Kalti paid by him on the day of marriage

If the wife commits adultry and she is divorced she should return the 'Kalti' to the injured husband. She has also to pay to the husband Rs. 40 to Rs. 50 as a fine and all present given to her must also be given back. Should the husband commit adultry the wife may divorce him and he will not be entitled to get back the 'Kalti' as well as the presents which he has given to the wife either on the day of marriage or during their stay as husband and wife. If the husband and wife agree for separation the 'Kalti' is not returnable but may be kept with the wife or her parents. The children invariably belong to the wife if the husband does not come to claim them. In all cases of divorce both the parties are free to remarry and all the ceremonies are performed as in the case of the first marriage. The decision of divorce always comes through the 'Khumang' whose decision is final and when he announces it publicly then only the legality is valid. The only act performed by the husband or the wife for divorce is the tearing of a betel leaf into two pieces, indicating thereby that their married life is severed for ever.

Death

The Dimasa Kacharis always cremate the dead body except in cases where a person has died of unnatural death as well as in the case of a child's death. The body of a child less than two months old or where no erruption of tooth has taken place, their burial is the usual practise, but where in a child is having at least one tooth the body is qualified for cremation. A woman dying in child-birth is buried and no feast is held and friends and relatives generally do not assemble except the close elderly relatives who attend the burial and all the personal belongings of the woman are thrown out in the jungle or burnt. The belief behind this practice is that if any one takes it the same fate will befall on the person. Dimasa Kacharis believe that all deceased persons go after death to the place called, Habson, i.e., the place above the earth. And people who have done good deeds during their life are able to go to Dambra or the heaven.

When a person dies the relatives of the deceased inform close friends and relatives, who flock to the house of the deceased. The ceremony starts with the killing of a fowl. The dead body is then washed and dressed in clean cloths by any elderly man or woman of the family depending on the sex of the deceased and then the body is put on a mat on the floor. The dead body is placed to lie flat with the head towards the west. Then the friends and relatives who have flocked to the deceased house console and sympathize the bereaved family and pay their last respect to the deceased person by placing a gift like a piece of cloth or money by the side of the dead body, depending on the ability of the person. When all the guests have seen the dead body it is taken on a bief (doli) to the cremation ground (mankulungling) which is generally situated on the bank of a river or stream. Seven layers of dried wood are raised to form the funeral pyre (thairik) and over this pyre the corpse is placed and fire is lighted by a male relative of the father's side. In case the body does not burn well it is stated that the cause is due to the absence of some relative or friend. In such cases any of the male relatives standing there throws some grass and states the reason of the relative's absence. This practice is known as 'dohongsuba' (throwing sungrass) which is usually done when two thirds of the body is burnt. When the body has been thoroughly burnt the bones and ashes are collected and thrown into the nearby stream except the frontal bone (tain) which is retained and placed in the memorial house (Mangkilong) which is erected on the cremation ground preferable on the spot of cremation. The structure is made of bamboo and looks like a small temple. The bone so placed in Mangkilong is allowed to remain there until the shradha ceremony takes place. The date of the 'shradha' ceremony is set by the relatives, which must be over before the harvest or the Bihu festival. Until the 'Shradha' ceremony (maimutharba) is over the family is considered to be in mourning and throughout the period meal has to be offered after the name of the deceased person at Mangkilong or if the structure has not been erected then the meal to the deceased person may be given in the house on a plaintain leaf. On maimutharba ceremony the memorial house a Mangkilong is burnt and friends and relatives who took part in the cremation of the dead body are given a feast. On this occasion only rice beer is served. Burning of the Mangkilong is performed on the day set for 'shradha'. While returning from the cremation ground every individual has to dip their big toe in a half open bamboo pipe where water is kept. 'Shradha' is usually held with great pomp and the ceremony and it lasts for two days. Animals like pigs and fowl are killed and rice beer is prepared and all these are served to the invitees. Thus with the end of the shradha the death ceremony or the purification ceremony is over.

On the death of the husband, a wife takes off all her ornaments and remains in mourning, until the next harvest festival. For the first three days after death she is not allowed to take rice. Similarly, on the death of one's wife, a widower remains in mourning until the harvest festival. On the death of parents, children are not allowed to eat until the following night. During the period of mourning neither widow nor widower can remarry.

FAMILY AND COMMUNITY RELATIONSHIP

Family

The Dimasa Kachari family is ordinarily of simple type, that is a nuclear family consisting of husband, wife and unmarried children. The system of residence can hardly be called patrilocal (Ghosh : 1964) as the husband often settles in his wife's village after marriage. This tradition has been operative from olden times, as it is found that out of ten inter-village marriages (Ghosh : 1964) which took place from the age-group of 40-60 years, five bridegrooms whose parents have already died, frequently prefers to live in his wife's place. When an inter-village marriage takes place and if the man decides to shift to his wife's village, he first lives with his mother until he can build a new house of his own. When marriage within the village takes place, the newly wed man prefers to build his hut by the side of his wife's fathers' hut.

The family type among the Dimasa Kacharis is usually composed of the parents and their unmarried children. Thus the households are normally small, this is because of their system of residence, where the family can never be extended either vertically or laterally as the sons become separate from the parents after marriage. Thus the Dimasa family splits up when the sons and daughters get married. Generally, within a year a man should be able to set up a new house of his own. Though the splitting of the family takes place, nevertheless, due to the characteristic residence pattern among the Dimasa Kachari, the process of proliferation thus always goes as most of the families in one village are related to each other by some ties of kinship.

In order to understand the nature of the residential arrangements, it is necessary to examine their rules of discent as both are intimately related.

Clan and Kinship

The Dimasa follow a characteristic lineage system, which is quite different from that of other neighbouring tribes like the Mikir and the Nagas. The male children reckon their descent along the father's line or Sengfong. This is their primary affiliation ; but they also feel related to the mother's clan or Jaddi which is the secondary affiliation and is avoided in marriage. Similarly the female children reckon descent along their mother's line or Jaddi, but they feel secondarily related to the father's clan Sengfong until marriage. After marriage a women is adopted formally into the husband's clan and the secondarily attached to her husband's Sengfong. The secondary clan affiliation entails certain duties for both men and women towards both respective clan members. Thus among the Dimasa Kachari the choice of mates are regulated specifically by means of clans instead of otherwise as is observed among the Hindus where marriage is avoided in one's gotra as well as with members of one's kin-group. Thus Sengfong and Jaddis plays a very important part in the regulation of the Dimasa Kachari marriage system. The son and son's son all belong to the Father's Sengfong while the daughter and son's daughter's daughter belong to their respective mother's Jaddi. Thus all the sons of all the brother's follow the same Sengfong while the daughters differ in jaddi. Thus patrilineal and matrilineal forms of descent are present among the Dimasa Kacharis. The patriclan and the old rules of primary and secondary relationship to the clans is more or less strictly maintained with regard to marriage. Ghosh (1965) reported cases in the village of Hajadisa (Mikir Hills) where the rule of avoiding the patriclan had been broken in 16 out of total of 44 marriages, while there was not a single case of breach of the rule regarding avoidance of the matriclan for the same purpose. In all the 16 out of total of 44 marriages, while there was not a single case of breach of the rule regarding avoidance of the matri-clan for the same purpose. In all the 16 cases of the breach of the custom of exogamy the guilty persons were fined and then allowed to remain as husband and wife. But the usual rule as laid by the age old tradition regarding the breach of the custom of exogamy is punishable by excommunication,

In case of the other 4 villages in North Cachar Hills District, no case of breach was observed at all in regard to either the Sengfong or the Jaddi.

Due to their system of residence, the family among the Dimasa can never be extended, either vertically or laterally as the sons become separate from the parents after marriage, thus the family tends to split up. When marriage within the village takes place, it has been found (Ghosh, 1964) that the newly-wed man prefers to build his hut by the side of his wife's hut. After marriage a man may live about a year in the wife's house this being known as minhabba. But it is found that many people have settled in their wives villages though they were at liberty to construct houses in their father's village.

The patri-clans and matri-clans among the Dimasa people are widely dispersed. Each clan has its distinctive names ; though totem-like names are used to designate clans, but totemism in its true sense is not found among the Dimasa Kachari. Thus the objects which have given names to the clan are not regarded as totems, as they are merely names.

There are 42 patri-clans and 42 matri-clans in all. It is said that there were only 7 Sengfongs (Ghosh 1965) when Dimapur was the capital of the Kacharis Kingdom. It became 12 in number when the capital was shifted to Maibong and lastly because 42 at Khaspur. Up to Dimapur period (middle of 16th cent.), there is no evidence of Jaddia. According to Dimasa Kacharis the creation of the Jaddis by the Kachari king in all probability of Maibans, was done to prevent the Kachari men from marrying the women of other communities like Kuki Naga etc., who were found around the Kachari Kingdom.

The clans have no hierarchial demarcation, all of them (42 Sengfongs and 42 Jaddis) enjoy equal status. Out of these, following 4 Sengfongs and 4 Jaddis are called danga, that is those who lived near the king and took a leading part in all royal activities.

Sengfongs : Riae, Khemprai, Phonglosa, and Seingyung.
Jaddis : Mairungma, Saidima, Miungma, and Banglaima.

A short List of Sengfongs and Jaddis among the Dimasa Kacharis are given below

	Sengfongs	*Meaning*	*Jaddis*
1.	Naidingsa	Son of Scout	Gachauna
2.	Nabingsa	Son of Angler	Rajama
3.	Seingyunsa	Son of Big sword	Saidima
4.	Khempraisa	—	Miungma
5.	Adosa	—	Madarma
6.	Daudungsa	Son of a kind of Bird	Buguma
7.	Maibangsa	Plenty of paddy	Longmaisajilu
8.	Keras	—	Anumajilu
9.	Parbasa/Girisa	Bill or mountain	
10.	Laobangdisa	—	
11.	Diphusa	Name of a river	
12.	Jrambusa	—	
13.	Mitherfansa	—	
14.	Baderbagia	—	
15.	Monisa	—	
16.	Swurungfansa	—	

Inter-Community Relationship

The Dimasa Kacharis who are staying in the urban areas may engage in services of barbers, washerman, tailors and shoe makers from other communities, but the Dimasas are far away from the urban centres in the interior villages never allow persons other than their community members. Untouchability is absent and they do not forbid any one who belong to another community to interdine with them or take water from the same wells though this is observed only in urban areas or among those who are educated. Inter-marriage with other communities like Burman Kachari, Mech Kacharis are permissible since they are having the Sengfong and the Jaddis like Dimasa Kacharis.

The tribal ways of the Dimasa Kacharis are still persistent among the people living in the hills than those living in the plains. The Dimasa Kacharis who are surrounded by the

Assamese and the Bengali neighbours in the plains and their long experience and steady contact with the plains people has resulted in certain changes in their customs and manners as compared to the Hill Dimasa Kacharis.

Dipali Ghosh (1965) observed that "the Dimasa have recently developed a tendency to conceal the presence of their matri-clans and matrilineal descent of their women from outsiders. Nowadays girls are being sent to school and they are being given the surname of their father (which is that of his Sengfong) as in the case of their Assamese or Bengali classmates."

Marriage is not prohibited between the Burmans of Cachar District and the Hills Dimasa of the North Cachar Hills as both of them observe the rules relating to Sengfong and Jaddi. In contrast to the Dimasa Kachari, the Boro Kachari have no concept of matri-clan or Jaddi. So no marriage takes place between the Dimasa and Boro.

The dress has also been influenced by their neighbours in so far as the Dimasa Kachari males of the plains or the educated Dimasa Kacharis are concerned. Most of the males who have come in contact with the plains people have substituted their traditional cloth for dhoti, pants and shirts. While those in the interior hills still retain much of their traditional dress. Most of the people have changed from jhuming to wet cultivation possible due to the influence of their Assamese or Bengalee neighbours. Even if they are aware of it they are not in a position to follow the wet system due to the condition of the terrain. The Dimasa Kacharis who are living in the urban areas or in the plains are more educated than the hill people, possible this may not be due to the fact that there is lack of proper facilities in the urban areas rather this may be due to an urge to get educated which may be the effect of their Bengalee and Assamese neighbours, a competitive attitude, which is a healthy sign of a community. Another fact is that the Dimasa Kacharis of the hills are reluctant to accept the change of their social customs, while their brothern in the plains are apt to adopt change according to the needs of the time.

Different Segments of the Community

The people generally known to us as Kacharis, as they call themselves Boro or Bodo (Endle, 1911, p. XV). There were once a very powerful and wide spread race in the whole of Assam. Through the passage of the centuries this large and powerful group of Bodos gradually broke up into a number of segments, in different geographical regions of Assam, and they can only be linked with the common language. According to Endle (1911, p. XVII), no one who has heard members of the five branches of the Bodo race speaks their respective languages can fail to recognize that they belong to the same linguistic group.

The Kachari or Bodo group comprises the following groups within the folds, as based on the account given by Endle (1911) and Gait (1961).

Bara (Kachari)
Rabha (Totala)
Mech (Mes)
Koch
Sonwal Kachari
Garo
Hajong
Dimasa
Hojais
Lalungs

All these tribes are the branches of the great Bodo race. Most of these tribes have been influenced in varying degrees by the venner of Hinduism. Each group is strictly endogamous though there are instances where marriage has taken place among Dimasa Kachari and Burman Kachari or Mech Kachari. Such alliances are as a rule not looked upon with favour and they are generally outcasts from the society but peace may set-in by providing feast to the fallow-villager or by paying the fine imposed by the village elders, but even in that case the couple has to stay in the outskirts of the village.

DWELLING, DRESS AND FOOD

Dwelling

The Dimasa Kachari generally reside in the clearing patches of the forest, in the hills and the factors which determine the location of the Dimasa village in the nearness of the cultivating plot and the source of water. In the hills the villages are demarcated not by fencing around but the natural objects like ditch, small streams, or hillocks, which marks the limit of a village. Villages are kept apart from one another in isolated blocks on the foot of the hills nearby a stream or a river for the convenience of cultivation. This is also evidenced from the name of some of the Dimasa villages as Majadisa ; Northdisa : Nablaidisa ; Didambra The word disa or di in the Dimasa language means river. A Kachari village in the hills is much more compact as the houses being built more closely together than their brethren in the plains or the Assamese. Even in a compact village the arrangement of houses are dispersed in such a manner so as to provide space for rearing of livestocks and for the kitchen garden for each of the houses. The houses in the Kachari village are not clustered clan-wise (Sengfong-Jaddis) but according to the convenience of the individuals.

In former times the Gaonbora belonging to a particular sengfong was generally surrounded by the people on his sengfong in the majority thus forming a clustering of a particular sangfong. Each house, with its granary and other out buildings, is surrounded by a ditch and fence. The fencing is usually done by ekra reeds, jungle grass or split bamboo etc. The ditch, some three or four feet in depth, surrounds the whole homestead and the earth (mud) taken from it is used in erecting a mud wall some 2 or 3 feet in height very close to the dwelling house. But those villages which are having some urban influence have fencing around the house with open spaces in between the fence and the dwelling unit, which is utilized for rearing poultry or for kitchen gardens. Houses are generally large and the shape of the house looks rectangular and the structure as a whole is raised about 2 feet from the ground, supported by stout wooden posts. The whole structure of the house including the side walls is made up of split bamboo finely woven and knitted together so firmly that no plastering of the sort is necessary. But those who are rich or those villagers in the vicinity of the urban areas who can afford this prepare mud plastered houses.

The roof of the house has slopes on either side thatched with sun-grass (Shan, Bengali ; Thiri Dimasa term) which is generally replaced after three or four years, when it gets rotted or damaged by natural processes. The floor of the house is dark except for the scanty light that creeps in through the openings in the split bamboo wall. Generally, there is no window or chimney, the main door and the tiny slits in the bamboo walls serve as source of ventilation. The house are of rectangular type varying in length from 35-45 and with breadth of about 20 and is usually divided into two rooms by a partition. The outer room is called Nokhung and inner room is called Noshing. The outer Nokhung is used by the males of the household and is also meant for the outsiders or guest. There are only two doors, one connecting Nokhung to the outside which serves as the entrance to the house and the other door connects Nokhung with Noshing which is meant for the family. The hearth is placed at one corner of Noshing almost touching the side wall. The household equipment is generally kept in the inner room.

Given below is a list of household equipments of a Dimasa Kachari house :—

Bengali	*Dimasa Kachari*
Kalshi	Damsura
	Dik
Kalshi (earthen)	Ara
Thala	Kopra
Hatha	Khuku
Bati (of Bell metal)	Bela
Bamboo Pipe for strong water	Diphong
Axe	Rowa
Small stool	
Bamboo baskets	Khamplai
Clothes	Zapsi
Cereals	Maikho

It may be noted that the people from other Sengfong are not allowed to touch the Maikho. Almost all the household equipments are of brass or bell metal and are made by the Bengali smiths, which may be obtained from the nearby market.

Household goods are of simple variety meant for the purpose of utility rather than for decoration. There are baskets of various shapes and sizes and bearing different uses. They are generallyfor used storing cereals, clothes and other articles of daily use. Bamboo pipe each with a node on one end and an opening on the other are used for carrying water and for storing spices.

Dress

The dress of both males and females is simple. The males commonly put on short Dhoti (Gamcha) and shirts, particularly those who are residing near by the urban areas. In the interior villages the upper part of the body is convened by a rectangular sheet of cloth like Gamcha called Rimchan and is worn like a whichcross belt, the border of which is embroidered in various colours.

The Dhoti (Gainthou) is short and is wrapped round the loin unlike the Bengalese-Assamese. The males sometime wear a turban (Sidaupha) more so in festive occasions which generally has a length of about 20 arm-lengths or about 7 yards and in width about a yard in length. Boys generally put on shirts and pants instead of Dhoti particularly those who are living near the urban centres. Those who are living in town almost always wear the European dress which has become the fashion of the day. Women put on a short patticoat called righ fastened around the waist by means of a belt made of cotton cloth. Another cloth known as Rizamphain is used to cover the upper part of the body which is tied under the arms and is drawn tight over the breast. Over and above the clothes is placed Rikhausa a sort of veil which covers the head and the face and is hung on either side of the shoulder covering the breast. But this is not generally in use except in marriage and other religious ceremonies. Their ceremonial dress is similar to the types described earlier except that they are multicoloured and looks gorgeous.

Women generally keep long hair, and tie it in a knob behind the head. Males cut their hair short and seldom care to comb. They comb hairs with their fingers which usually perform the functions of the comb. Though the Dimasas staying in the urban areas or those who have experience of the urban life or influenced by the plains people like Assamese or Bengalese out their hair in the fashion of the plains people. Nails are trimmed with a knife and the teeth are cleaned with a piece of jungle tree or sometimes only with the fingers along with some tooth powder if available ; while those who are staying in the urban areas and are enlightened, use tooth paste for cleaning the teeth.

Footwear is seldom used both among the males and females particularly in the villages away from the urban centres. The Dimasas who are living in the urban centres, particularly those who are office goers use modern footwear.

On ceremonial occasions both males and females will generally put on their traditional dress except in a few cases, especially among the youths who are much influenced by the urban ways of life. The priest or Hojai, put on the common dress i.e., Gainthou or Rimchau and the turban Sidaupha, these are the common dress put on by the priest but they are always worn clean that is which are not used earlier on ordinary occasions and are set apart for only ceremonial purposes. Those who can afford to put on a new dress, do so.

The Dimasa Kacharis are very fond of ornaments. Women of prepubertal age put on a nose ring (Khamauthai) and necklace of beads shells (Lick). Rangbarsa is another necklace made of silver beads which are matched with Pearl beads. The thread is also made of silver.

Women of post-pubertal age wear Khadu in hand which is made up of pure silver and is fairly heavy and weighs up to 15-20 tolas. Khadu is also worn in anklets but it slightly varies from that worn in hand in that it remains open at one side instead of forming a complete ring.

Ornaments are rarely worn by men even in the interior villages. In earlier times men used to wear an ear-ring of copper called Khirik. As no ear ornaments are worn by the males so there is no ear-piercing ceremony. No tattooing is done among the Dimasa Kacharis.

Food

Their staple food is rice and they eat all kinds of meat with the exception of the beef. The following type of rice is generally taken by the Dimasas as—Maisa—common rice (Maima and Maisa—larger and smaller grains) ; maizu—used for the preparation of Zu ; Bairing—a special variety known as 'Biron chaul' in Bengalis.

Meat is taken either roasted or cooked or after it is thoroughly dried in the sun. Dry fish is mostly preferable which they store in small baskets. The following are the common vegetables and fruits which they usually take—sweet pumpkin, corn, gourd, snake gourd and different types of vegetable leaves. Curry is prepared using Khar (Soda) and oil. Only mustard oil is used. Naphalam is an indigenous product and is prepared from a fish (Punti in Bengali) and mixed with Khar, salt and chilly, and is kept for 2 or 3 months. According to them it is very nourishing and is almost always taken along with the rice. There is, however, one common article of food, which no orthodox old fashioned Kachari will ever touch, i.e., milk. Usually no cows are found in the village as they consider them to be an unclean animal. But presently this prejudice against the use of milk seems to be passing aways.

All the members of the family eat together in the same house. Meal is generally taken three times a day, in the morning in the afternoon and in the evening. Rice, beer or 'Zou' is their favourite drink and figures prominently in the observance of their ceremonies and festivals. Outsiders and strangers are also offered with this for the sake of courtesy.

An essential ingredient in the preparation of this most popular form of refreshment is the condiment known as emao which is usually composed of at least three or four distinct elements. To a definite proportion of (1) husked rice is added (2) the jack-tree leaf and Dhetai (a jungle plant) (3) another jungle plant-poison fern. All these ingredients are vigorously pounded together into a powder which is then sieved for at least two times. The powder so prepared is then mixed with water and is made into a paste, these are then left for drying for some weeks and are made into small discs after that they are kept covered for the some time by the rice straw. They are then exposed in the hot sun for another four or five days, so as to become thoroughly dry. Finally they are kept suspended over a fire place in an earthenware water-vessel and from there they are taken out when required for. The adult people smoke and consume betel with areca-nut, the latter is more common and is consumed by both the sexes.

Recording of Time

The Dimasas generally record the end of the night with the cock's crow. In the interior villages the time or the period after day is known by the position of the sun or when going on a journey the time is generally recorded by the time taken for the eating of a piece of betel nut which generally takes fifteen minutes for each place. The periods of the day and night are as follows :

Dawn	Naiju —
Morning	Phoron
Ascending Sun (9th 10 a.m.)	Saindaphuba
Midday	Sainjew
Descending Sun (1 to 4 p.m.)	Sainjerkheraba
Evening (5-6 p.m.)	Sainblee
Dusk (6-8 p.m.)	Sarifon
Night	Flar
Midnight to Dawn	Hakjer

Measure of Weight

The recording of space and weight by the Kachari is done according to their Bengalee or Assamese neighbours. The use of Seers, Feet etc. are common even in the interior villages. The type of weights and measures used before the pre-British days could not be ascertained but all are of the opinion that they used some different types of measures other than what they are presently using, as for example, in some of the interior villages even now they are using the unit—'mai'.

1 Mai = 4 Seer (approximately)

Measured by means of a bamboo basket 12 Mai—1 Bain (48 Seers).

VILLAGE LIFE AND RECREATION

Sanitation

Dimasa Kacharis villages are not compact, because they build their homes on the foot of the hills, on a large open space. Almost every Dimasa Kachari house is having space for the sizes of the domestic animal and for homestead gardens. Generally pigs, goats, poultry are kept in a separate enclosure adjacent to the main house. Those who are rich and can afford, build the sheds for the domestic animal a little away but within the boundary of the individual house. Owing to the keeping of their domestic animals very close to their houses, and as rubbish is thrown all around the areas surrounding the home, it always remains very dirty and smelly. As there is no common place for throwing the rubbish so it gets accumulated all around and the pigs and dogs act as Scavengers. Although this makes the whole atmosphere foul smelling, the people are used to such things and they seem not to be bothered by this, thus sanitation in the real sense of the term is totally absent in the villages. There is no drainage, system and foul water finds its way to the villages streets. Sometimes such drain water accumulates in the ditch and serves as the bathing pool for the domesticated animals.

There is no lavatory or latrine and the nearby jungle offers a good place for this, and where dogs and pigs would swarm for their food and serve as scavengers. The Dimasa Kacharis who are living in the rural areas are having lavatory or latrine at one corner of their house away from the main rooms. The village people generally do not care to clean their clothes, but only doing this on festive occasions while those who are rich usually take to new clothing. The common people who are having urban influence wash their clothes with soaps. But the poorer sections put on the same clothes every day until it is in such a condition that it cannot be worn by the person any more due to its torn nature. In any case, even the poorer section of the Dimasa Kachari apparently looks much clearer than their neighbours the Semis and the Mikirs. They clean their face and feet and soothe away their fatigue and wearness at the nearby stream or well while coming from their hard days work in the fields.

Cooking utensils and dishes are washed after every meal. There houses are dark and one cannot see what is inside unless he is accustomed to the darkness. Doorways and in some cases windows or the opening in the walls serve as source of ventilation and as there is no chimney the smoke hovers like a cloud in the ceiling of the house until it is forced out of the wind through some opening.

The common diseases are dysentry, boils, malaria, and other skin diseases. Some of the Dimasa Kachari names for the common diseases are as follows :

Small Pox	—	Linthai
Cholera	—	Murkhi
Ordinary Fever	—	Limba
Dysentry	—	Kamri

In the villages far away from the urban centres, they do not rely much on the modern medicine, but rely on their indigenous medical herbs with which they treat all kinds of diseases, which they can diagnose. There is no particular medicine man but the old and experienced person gives medicine some times voluntarily to the diseased person. The villages near the urban centres are using the modern medicines and are getting all the modern medical facilities in the Municipal hospitals, while in the interior villages, where facilities of the modern medicine are not available, they use the indigenous medicine and worship and propitiate the god Madaikho. The proportion is done by Hojai and the family has simply to bring the materials for the desired propitiation.

Recreation

The Dimasa Kacharis who are staying in the villages and are agriculturists, work in their fields from morning until evening and relax themselves only after coming from the fields. The men and women sit around the hearth snapping stories and gossiping about the fields and crops and the prospects of the coming harvest, thus removing the fatigue due to the days work. When they meet with friends and relatives the inevitable subject of crops always comes up for discussion amongst them apart from some family matters or other matters. Some time they sing in chorus while working in the fields or sing simple melodies while thrashing the orps, which seems to dispel the fatigue due to the hard labour and weariness from the body and mind. Though they have to undergo through the rigours of nature mind. Though they have to undergo through the rigours of nature which makes their life hard, yet their hearts are full with hope and joy and they are satisfied with what they have. They are the children of the nature and find music in the winds, streams and woods which fill their mind with much delight.

Games

The little boys and girls in the village do not play any specific game, to them, games are like climbing trees, or throwing stones, or other similar activities with which they remain engaged and thus spend the day until feel tired and go to their homes..The grown up boys and girls play some of them modern games borrowed from outside, generally learned through the school mates or from the plains people. Hide and seek is played generally by girls. Football is a favourite game among the boys especially those who are staying in the urban areas. Sometimes teams are formed among themselves for friendly matches for a tournament in a competition. Indoor games like carrom, ludo, and cards etc. are also played by both young and old. Those who have received some education read newspapers, story books etc. or sometime listen to the radio or transister if available, in a neighbour's home or if possessed by them.

The housewives and elderly women are hard pressed with their household chores such as fetching water, cooking, cleaning and washing etc. and whatever little time they get to spare as leisure time they spend in gossiping or visiting friends and relatives. The young men frequently go during their leisure time for shooting some wild game or fishing in the nearby ponds. The village young men particularly those who are staying in the interior villages generally spend their leisure time in dancing or singing or playing on the drums or discuss problems which they come across in their day-to-day life and exchange their experiences.

LANGUAGE

The Dimasa Kacharis speak the Kachari languages, which is followed by the other sections of the Kacharis like Burman Kachari, Mech Kachari, Sanwal Kachari etc. Sir George

Grierson (Linguistic Survey of India, Vol. III, Part II) classed the Kachari language in the Naga-Bodo group. In 1921 Census there were 259,587 Bodo, Mech and Plains Kachari speakers, (p. 58) while Dimas speakers (p. 59) were 11,040 persons of which 5519 were males and 5,521 were females. In 1931 Census (pp. 228-29) Bara, Bodo or Plains Kacharis were 282,582 of which 143,544 were males and 139,038 were females. While the Dimasa of Hill Kacharis numbered 14680 of which 7439 persons were males and 7241 were females.

The total number of Dimasa Kacharis who have stated their mother-tongue as Dimasa Kachari is given below :

(Census of India : Assam : Vol. III, Part V.A., pp. 370-381).

	Total Speakers		
Tribe	*Males*	*Females*	*Mother Tongue*
Dimasa	2,323	1,920	Assamese
Kachari	6,641	5,460	Bangali
	31	61	Bodo/Boro
	10,874	9,490	Dimasa
	—	45	Garo
	6	—	Haijong/Haijong
	8,604	7,482	Kachari
	8,087	7,683	Mikir
	1	1	Naga-Unspecified
	8	—	Rabha

The table above shows that the Dimasa Kacharis who had reported Dimasa to be their mother-tongue are maximum in number, the next in descending order comes Kachari and Mikirs respectively. Thus it is evident that the Dimasa Kacharis have reported different languages as their mother-tongues. Majority of the Dimasa Kacharis belong to the Dimasa, Kachari, Mikir Bengalee and Assamese language group.

There are a few publications like magazines and books in the Dimasa language with the Bengali script. Some of them are translations of famous Bengali books like Naukabilas.

A list of the few books are given as follows :

1. Jamyani Rajthai
2. Malsokhruni Malsothsothai Ranghha Dihahaihe
3. Dimasa

The literacy percentage of Dimasa Kachari is 8.89 per cent while the literacy percentage of Dimasa Kachari is 29.57 per cent among the Scheduled Tribes of Assam and 0.66 per cent when the total population of the state is taken.

LIFE STYLE—THE MIKIR (ASSAM)

The Mikir tribes are scattered over the Golaghat subdivision of the Sibsagar district, Nowgong, Kamrup, Khasi Hills and North Cachar Hills but their main habitat are the hills named after them. Mikir is a name given to the tribe by the Assamese. They call themselves *Arleng*, which means man. We find other tribes of this region also calling themselves just man e.g. *Singhpho* (=man), Boro (=man) are the names of two other tribes and so are *Achik-mande* (=hill man), Mizo (hill man), the names respectively of the Garos and the Lushais. Apparently each tribe considered the members of his own race alone to be human.

The Mikir Hills are of much lower elevation than the neighbouring Khasi or Naga Hills. The climate of the hills and the contiguous plains inhabited by the Mikirs is not salubrious like that of the Khasi and Jaintia Hills. Till recently it was highly malarious and infested by Kala-azar. The percentage of leprosy cases is also the highest there in the state. The climatic disadvantages find themselves reflected in the physical appearance of the people. One does not find among the Mikirs that fair skin and rosy cheeks that greet you in the neighbouring Angami Naga and Jaintia lands. There features resemble more those of the tribal elements among the Assamese than Tibeto-Burman races inhabiting the hills. The complexion generally is yellowish brown with a sprinkling of the quite fair. The men are comparatively tall, the average height being 5′ 4″. As with the Garos facial hair is scanty, a very thin growth over the upper lip of men being only an apology for a moustache. Although not robust like the Nagas, the Mikirs are a hardy people, capable of prolonged, arduous labour. They make good porters and can carry heavy loads over several miles at a stretch. The load is carried on the back, tied with a bamboo or cane strap (tump-line) passing over the forehead.

The Mikir dress is elegant. The men put on a long striped coat (choi) without sleeves and with fringes covering the lower part of the body up to the knees. They wear a short Dhoti called *Rikong*, sometimes of silk. On the head they wear a *pagri* (*Pohu*). In cold weather they cover themselves like the Assamese with a wrapper or *bor-kapor* of eri-silk which is warm.

The women wear a petticoat (*Pini*) fastened round the waist with an ornamental belt (*Vankok*) exactly like the Lakhers of the Lushai Hills. The upper part of the body is covered with a wrapper (*Jiso*) passing under the arms and drawn tight over the breasts. Both men and women draw their hair back which is tied in a knot above the rape.

The women insert a silver tube (*Kadengchinro*) in the ear-lobes, which is a Mikir version of the Assamese *thuria*. Ear-rings of gold and silver (*no-rik*) are suspended from the upper part of the ears. Necklaces (*lek*), rings (*arnam*) bracelets (*roi*) of gold and silver are worn in Khasi-fashion. Feathers of the horn-bill (bhimraj) adorn the head of both men and women on festive occasion. The weapons used are the *dao* (nok-jar), the spear (chir) and the bow (lop-thali) made of bamboo.

Mikir men do not tattoo any part of their body but the womenfolk, on attaining puberty, wear a tattoo-line made with indigo, running perpendicularly down the forehead, the nose, the upper lip and the chin. It is said that this practice started during the Burmese invasion of Assam and was intended to protect young girls from the invaders.

The original home of Mikirs is not known. According to some of their legends they came from somewhere in South-east Asia but these are too vague to be worthy of credence. They do not claim kinship with any other tribe in Assam. There are strong affinities of languages with the Kukis and of customs with the Nagas, but yet they form a distinctly separate tribe which cannot be grouped with any of the other Tibeto-Burman races inhabiting the mountainous region between Burma and Assam.

The principal characteristic which marks the Mikirs out from the other tribes is their pacific nature. While their neighbours—Nagas, Kukis, Kacharis and Syntengs—had been indulging for centuries in internecine feuds among themselves, the Mikirs preferred to remain aloof, pursuing their peaceful vocations of agriculture, hunting (animals and birds) and fishing. Furthermore, unlike the other tribes, which after some generations, tend to break up into sub-tribes, the Mikirs have maintained their homogeneity in spite of their migration from their original habitat to widely separated areas.

Whatever might be their ancient origin, in recent times, the Mikirs resided in strength in the North-Cachar Hills, where raids by the Angami and Kaccha Nagas from the east and of the Kukis from the south-east apparently drove them away to the Jaintia Hills. There, harassed again by the Synteng Chiefs, they sought the protection of the Ahoms, then ruling over the plains of Assam and since then they have been living peacefully in the region allocated to them.

The Mikirs, as compared with other hill-tribes of Assam, are rather backward, especially in education. This is ascribed to the fact that Christian missionaries have not been able to make much headway among the Mikirs, because of the proximity of their habitat to the plains. In fact, many of the Mikirs living in the plains have become undistinguishable from the Assamese. They have also become bilingual, speaking Assamese generally and Mikir at home. This process of assimilation can be seen at work even amongst the hill-Mikirs and if politics and proselytisation do not pull actively in the opposite direction the complete assimilation of the Mikirs, like many a tribes before them, is a matter of time.

Domestic Life. Unlike other neighbours, except the Kukis, the Mikirs build their houses on piles, the floor several feeta bove the ground. Houses are built of split, flattened out bamboo, the roof being thatched with sun-grass. The house is divided into separate compartments. A partition (*arpong*) running longitudinally divides it into two main parts. The one on the left is called *Kut*, where paddy is stored and the family also sleep. There is also a fire-place in it. The other part is called *Kam* which is meant for guests. The *Kut* has only one door, while the *Kam* has a door in front and another at the back. There are two fire-places in the *Kam*. In this room, on a platform or *Chang* called *tibung*, at a level higher than the floor, they keep their water-*chungas* (bamboo-tubes). There is a verandah at the front (*hongkup*) and another at the back (Pang-hongkup) beyond which there is an unroofed platform

(Pang). On the left hand side of the *Kut* a portion with its floor at a lower level is partitioned off for the fowl and goats (vorai). *Dam-tak* in the kut is where the family sleep and the paddy is stored. Behind the fire-place in the middle of the *Kut* is the *dam-buk* where the grown up children sleep. *Theng-poi-rai* is the place for storing fire-wood. In large houses a space is provided for guests to spend the night (*hong-phasla*). The platform of the house is reached by the *don-don* at the night.

The furniture of the house generally consists of a raised platform of split bamboo which serves as bed, a block of wood (inghoi) corresponds to the Assamese *pira* or low stool. Baskets of bamboo serve the purpose of wardrobes, in which paddy, household goods and clothes are kept. Joints of bamboo (Lang bong, Assamese *Chunga*) are used as containers for water as well as ornaments and other valuables of the family.

Crops, Food and Drink. The main crop of the Mikirs is rice. Cultivation, as in other hill areas, is done according to the Jhumming System. In addition they grow sizeable quantities of maize, cotton, yarns and castor plant, the last especially for feeding the cri silk worms.

As all over Assam, the women weave their own and family's requirements of cloth on rough wooden looms. The cotton or cri thread is dyed with indigo, which is grown in almost every house.

Every village has a blacksmith's workshop, which is more or less an institution coming down from antiquity. He makes *daos* and knives, spears and fishing hooks. Pottery is made without the potter's wheel, like the Khasis. The Mikirs made their own gold and silver ornaments also but these industries are dying out because of the tendency to purchase ready-made cheap and tawdry foreign stuff.

Rice is the staple food with which the Mikirs eat the meat of fowl, goats and pigs. They are fond of eating eggs, but the finest delicacy is the crysalis of the cri silk worm. Fish which is available in plenty, is almost a daily dish, especially dried and smoked fish. Like the other hill-tribes they do not drink milk, rice-beer (*morpo*) being drunk on any pretext whatsoever at any time of the day. Opium was freely consumed till it was prohibited by law. Smuggled opium is still used and this is one of the main causes of the emasculation of the Mikirs. Tobacco is smoked and also chewed. So is betel-nut, distance being measured as by the Assamese, by the time required to chew a pan.

The most important institution associated with agriculture, social and almost all other activities is the *maro* or *terang*, the youngmen's club (Assamese-deka-chang).

In the olden days, the village youths, from the age of twelve to twenty, lived together in the *maro*. Of late the Gaonburha's (village headman) house has more or less replaced the *maro*, of which the Nagas and the Mizos have their equivalents in the *Morungs* and *Zawlbuks* (the latter have almost disappeared completely). The young men's clubs where the younger boys had to serve and obey the older boys instilled into the youth discipline, respect for and obedience, to elders, a spirit of service to the community and a number of other admirable qualities.

The *maros* have or at least had a regular hierarchy of office bearers. The chief boy is called *Kleng-Sarpo*. Next comes the *Kleng-dum*, the Sodor-kethe, the *Sodor-so*, *Sangho-kerai*, the *barlon* (carrier of the measuring rod), *Cheng-brup-pi* and *Cheng-brup-so* (chief and assistant drummers), *phankri* (attendant on the chief), *moton aree* and *moton arvi*, *langbong-po* (water carrier), *arphek-po* (broom carrier) and the *Chinhak-po* (carrier of the basket of tools).

The village youths (*Risomar*) work in the fields together, a portion being allotted to each house. Work is enforced by penalties. In the olden days shirkers were said to have been burnt alive ; now-a-days of course, such drastic punishment cannot be meted out. Nevertheless severe beatings are often given to shirkers. The boys of the *maro* are in great demand for social services, especially tasks and ceremonies connected with the dead. Dancing and singing are practised is these clubs, which keep old usages and custom alive. The Mikirs especially the youths, are very fond of hunting and fishing. They hunt with dogs and spears and traps. Fishing is sometimes done with rod and line, but mainly with traps and baskets as in other tribal people.

Social Organisations. The Mikirs are divided into three sections, namely, *Chingthong*, *Ronghang*, and *Amri*. The Chingthongs live in the Mikir Hills portion of the Golaghat and

North Cachar Hills, the Ronghangs in the plains of Nowgong district and the Amris in the Khasi and Jaintia Hills and the Kamrup districts. Each of the three sections has within it some *Kurs* (clan—a word borrowed from the Khasis) and observe the same rules of exogamy. There are five major kurs or groups : (1) Ingty (2) Terang (3) Teron (4) Timung (5) Inghi. The Ingty tribe is again divided into five groups : (1) Hencheck (2) Kiling (3) Kathar, (4) Ingleng and (5) Taro. The Terangs are divided into eleven groups, the Terons into six and the Timungs and Inghis into thirty each.

The children belong to the father's kur and marriage within a kur is strictly prohibited, all members of a kur being supposed to be brothers and sisters. They can however marry their first cousins on the mother's side and also maternal uncle's daughters. Mikir names of men are Sardoks, Bura, Mon, Pator, Dili and Long and of women Kareng, Kache, Kaban and Kajir. The prefix Ka to the women's name had evidently been borrowed from the Khasis.

Customs. Child marriage is practically unknown. A boy marries from the age of 16 and a girl from the age of 14. The most usual age for boys is 18 or 19 years and for girls 15 years. If a young boy likes a girl he sends his father or both the parents to the girl's father and leaves a betrothal ring or bracelet with the girl. Sometimes a gourd of rice-beer is taken and accepted. If, after the acceptance, the girl gets married to another boy, the village council fines the girl's family.

The length of engagement is not uniform. If the girl and the boy are of age, it does not last long. After a day has been fixed for the marriage, both the families prepare beer and strong drinks. If the bridegroom is rich, he provides drinks to the whole party. If the bridegroom's party has to go through difficult villages he has to give a gourd of beer to each village it passes through on his way to the bride's house. When they arrive at the bride's house, they sit down there and the bridegroom's party offers one gourd of beer and one bottle of strong drink to the bride's father then conversation starts. The bride's father asks the bridegroom's party why they have come and why the presents have been offered. The bridegroom's father replies : "your sister (bridegroom's mother) has become old and cannot work, so we have brought our son to marry your daughter." The reply from the bride's father is as follows : "My daughter is unworthy and she does not know weaving or any other household work." The bridegroom's father then replies, "Never mind, we will teach her those things ourselves." After these verbal exchanges, the bride's father asks his wife to enquire of the daughter if she is agreeable. According to Mikir custom, unless the girl gives her consent, the beer and drinks cannot be touched. If the girl agrees and the consent is given, the beer and drinks are taken by the two fathers. It happens sometimes that they have to sit and wait the whole night before the girl's consent can be obtained. During this wait the people of the village also take part in these formalities, singing, "we cannot send our daughter to your house or to the boy's party", to which they receive the reply, "we cannot leave our boy to stay with you", and so on and so forth. When consent is finally obtained and beer and drinks are finished the bride prepares a bed inside the house for the bridegroom. If the boy feels shy, he can send his garments to the bed instead of going himself. Next day the girl goes with her husband to her new home along with her parents. Her parents are entertained with food and drink and they return home the following day. If the girl is the heiress or only daughter, she does not go out of her house. It is the boy who then has to come to the father-in-law's house. This kind of marriage is known as *Akemen* ; it is rare.

Generally, Mikirs are monogamous. No one is allowed to marry two wives. There are however, cases of rich persons marrying more than one wife. Divorce is very rare but permissible if there is no offspring or if the girl goes home after marriage and refuses to return to her husband. In the second case, the husband has to take a gourd of beer to his wife's parents house and declare himself free. After divorce both parties are free to marry again. Widow marriage is also allowed.

Inheritance. The sons inherit property, The wife and daughters get nothing. If there is no son, the nearest relatives of his own kur inherits. If the deceased has no son or brother, the widow can retain the property, provided she marries a man of the same kur as her husband's. The widow can always retain her personal property. It is the eldest son who gets the major share of the property. Very, often, the property is divided by the father before death. The sons generally live together even after the father's death and support the widowed mother.

Religious Beliefs. The Christianity has not been able to make as much head way among the Mikirs as among the other hill-tribes. The Mikirs have no idols, temple or shrines. There gods are innumerable and they worship them in different ways at different times and at different places. Arnam Kethe, which means the 'Great God', is one of the household gods. This god gets a sacrifice once in three years, if there is no occasion to worship him often. Though he is called the 'Great God' he had no authority over other gods. His appropriate offering is a pig. If a man is sick, the diviner declares that the Arnam Kethe wishes to join the household. A ceremony is performed but no offerings are made at that time. After three years or earlier, if there is any sickness in the family, a pig is killed and a feast with rice-beer and wine is given to the villagers.

Another god's name is Peng. He is also a household god. The proper offering to him is a goat which is given yearly. Maize, rice and a gourd of rice-beer are placed for him above the verandah of the house along with the first fruit of the harvest. Another god is Hemphy Arnam. People play to him for deliverence from sickness. Rek Anglong is also a household god, but he is worshipped in the fields. The sacrifice to him is a fowl. The god Arnam Paro is entitled to 100 shares of rice. He is worshipped either with a white goat or a white fowl.

All natural objects of striking or imposing character, such as the sun and the moon, are regarded as divine objects, but are not specifically propitiated. Localities with impressive mountains, waterfalls, deep pools in rivers, great boulders etc. have each assigned to them gods which are supposed to be interested in the affairs of men and have to be placated by sacrifice. These local divinities of the jungle are worshipped chiefly to avert mischief either by tigers or by terrible plagues. Trees or animals are not worshipped.

The Mikirs believe in reincarnation. They generally name their children after their dead relatives, because it is believed that the dead come back to the world.

Divination and Witchcraft. Prolonged sickness is generally ascribed to witchcraft or a spell cast by some one, who may be a man or a demon. The services of a *Sung-Kelang-abang* or *lodet* corresponding to the Assamese, *mongoloti* or diviner, are then requisitioned to find out the author of the spell divination is made, as by Assamese *mongolotis*, with the help of rice or *cowries*. As in the case of some other hill-tribes, divination is sometimes made by breaking an egg. Another mode is to use the *nok-jir*, a long-handled *dao*. It is held upright in the hand and the names of probable enemies or displeased gods or demons are pronounced, accompanied by the recitation of a charm (mantra). When the right name is pronounced, the *dao* shakes and thus the guilt is fixed. If the cause of sickness is a god or demon, he is propitiated. If it is a man, necessary rites are performed to exercise the evil spirit employed by the person practising witchcraft to do harm. Such persons are tried by the *me* or village council. The *San-Kelang-abang* is a superior kind of diviner who is believed to be inspired or to work under divine power. The *lodet* or *lodet-pi* is the ordinary diviner. The general term for both is *Uche* (feminine *Uche-pi*).

Oaths. The Mikirs do not have ordeals of the kind practised by the Garos and other tribes. Oaths and imprecations are resorted to instead. Earth is put on the head of a person who says, "May I be like this dust" ; or the scrapings from a tiger's tooth are put in water which is drunk and the oath pronounced, "May the tiger devour me". Such oaths are taken to attest the truth of evidence given or of the denial of an accusation.

Funeral Ceremony. The funeral ceremony is very elaborate, costly and most important of all the ceremonies performed by the Mikirs. These ceremonies are obligatory in the event of the birth of a still-born child also. Persons dying of smallpox or cholera are buried immediately but the funeral service is performed later on after digging up the bones which are then duly cremated. The dead body is kept in the house for one day but if a regular funeral service is held, it may lie there for more than a weak or 12 days. The body lies in the *Kut*. During this period the cooking of the family is done in the *Kam*. The dead man's wife or any major close relative of the dead person must go across a stream or a creek to cook and eat. No one during this period can stay in the house. If the deceased is a rich man, beer is prepared in the house ; rice is husked and a convenient day is fixed for the funeral service. If the house is not big enough, the villagers build and add a platform to it, attached to the platform in the front. From the day of death each household in the village gives a man to sleep in the dead man's house every night when sufficient rice and beer required for the function lasting for four or five days have been prepared, the young men of the village are called out about eight in the evening. They come with their drums and beat them in front of the house and some of them dance in pairs holding in their left hand a shield and in the right hand a stick. They go round twice in a circle and then holding each others hands dance round and round. This dance is called *chomang kan*. After an hour is spent in this way, they go back to the village headman's house to sleep.

Next morning, they come without beat of drum and dance the same dance again. After some time they go back to their own houses. The following day they come again and repeat the performance. Next morning a fowl is killed and roasted. The third and the last night is their great dance-night and before that night during day-time the young people have to work hand to get ready stout bamboo poles to which the corpse is to be slung, a *banjar* i.e. a long bamboo ornamented with early shavings and projecting arms and a shorter bamboo stick similarly ornamented and tipped with leaves. The men have to go to the village burning place and prepare a *machang* or platform there with logs for burning the body. A skilled old women is then called to prepare the necessaries while an assistant beats a drum. Then comes a young girl who is supposed to be the bearer of the corpse although she does not actually carry it but carries on her back only a gourd for holding beer. This girl must belong to the dead man's mother's clan.

If the family can afford, a goat is now killed for the dead. About mid-night the villagers armed with torches and drums assemble in the house. Each contingent is welcomed with drum beating and joins in the concert. All the young boys and girls are dressed in their best. The *Kleng Sarpo* (leader of the village young men) calls the young people to touch the beer. They are not allowed to taste it yet. After touching the beer they start dancing. All present join the dance in a circle, holding each other's hands. Young girls join the dance by holding the coat of the boys and the boys hold the belt of the girls. The girls cover their head with a black scarf and wear a petticoat with red strips. Just before cock-crow, seven young men go up to the platform. One of them goes inside the *Kam* and dances there while the other six wait at the door. After a quarter of an hour they return to the circle of dancers. At dawn they go up and dance in the *Kam* again till sunrise.

As soon as day light comes the circle breaks up and the drum-beaters go round and round and dance for 10 to 20 times, playing a different tune each time. At that point a pig is brought near the dancers and tied up for killing. The young people in successive parties recount over the tied-up pig the history of the deceased and his family. The pig is then killed and cut up for the young boys and men engaged in the funeral service. Those people have to cook and eat the meat. A small portion of the meat is cooked by a selected old woman for the dead man and this portion is put in the plate of the dead and carried up to the body. An old experienced man then performs certain rites over the dead body. The cooked meat and rice are then distributed to the young girls also. The young boys are provided with rice, beer, salt, chillies and green vegetables from the dead man's house for their entertainment. After they have been fed, two or three of the young people pick up a cock from anywhere on the road, take it to the burning place, kill it and eat it there. A small pig is killed by the young lads where they dance and the head and a leg are sent to the young boys on the road side. The blood of this pig is caught in a bamboo tube. The old women has by now got the food ready. The woman and the girl then proceed to the burning place. An old man enters the house and wraps the dead body with the dead man's clothes and they tie it to a bamboo. Thereafter, beating the drum they all march in a procession to the burning place. The dead body is placed on the pyre and it is lighted. The women who knew the deceased start singing his life story and telling the others how and where he is going to see his dead relations. Dancing by the young lads continue on the cremation ground till the body is fully burnt. The bones that remain unburnt are tied up in a cloth and buried. The old woman now places the food she prepared on a flat stone over the grave and the ceremony comes to an end.

Festivals. The Mikir observe several festivals. The one known as *Ringker*, is an annual compulsory village festival. It is held in the beginning of the cultivating season, i.e. in June. At this festival they sacrifice a goat or a fowl, whichever they can afford. There is no music or dancing at *ringker*. At the time of harvest there is no sacrifice but all the villagers help one another in reaping the crop and bringing it home, after which they feast together on rice-beer and dried fish which are saved up from a long time before for this occasion. No animal is killed at this feast as they believe that if an animal is killed at that time the paddy they bring home would be small in quantity.

LIFE STYLE—KUKIS (ASSAM)

'Kuki' is a vague term applied by the people of the plains not only to the tribes of the Chin-Lushai-kuki group but to hill-men generally who cannot be distinctly labelled as a Khasi or a Garo or a Mikir etc. The tribe never calls itself by that name which they regard as one contemptuously used by plainsmen.

Kuki is a generic term covering a number of tribes, sub-tribes and clans with varying customs and manners, with certain common characteristics which mark them off from other tribes of the region such as the Nagas. From the similarities in language, customs and social organisations, there can be little doubt that the Kukis, Lushais and Chins originally lived in the same land (Chin hills of Burma) and are related to one another. Out of a hundred words picked up at random about fifty would be found to be identical in the three languages. Physically, the

Kukis are smaller in stature and frailer in constitution than the Lushais and the Chins, their style of doing the hair particularly with a bun at the nape giving them an effeminate appearance. Women tie the hair into a knot above the forehead like Pawi men.

The Kuki population in North Cachar Hills is about eight thousands of which half are Hmars, a Kuki tribe, who are now claiming to be a separate, independent race embracing most of the Kuki clans. From linguistic and other similarities there can be no question, however, that the Hmars are a sub-tribe of the Kuki-Chin-Lushai group. In fact the Hmars living in the Mizo district have now become completely assimilated to the Lushais of Mizos. This fact would become clearer from the history.

History. According to their legends the kukis originally belonged to a place called Sinlung in South Western China. Some natural calamity compelled them to migrate to the shan country to the north-east of Assam from where the Ahoms had also come. After they had lived happily in that country for many generations, a great famine forced them to go in search of new land down the Chindwin Valley to the China Hills.

They called their new habitat chinlung after their original home sinlung. There is a common practice among the Chin, Lushai and Kuki tribes (who are or at least were till recently, nomads) to call their new settlements by the name of their former ones with the result that in North Cachar Hills many villages have the same name as villages in the Lushai Hills such as Biate, Thiak, Khawbung, Zote, Darngawn etc.

From Chin Hills the Kukis moved in search of more fertile lands into the Lushai Hills. When the more vigorous Lushai tribes started making the same movement from Burma into Assam, the Kukis were gradually driven towards the lower and hotter northern region of the present Mizoram and came to be known as Hmars (Hmar = north). Towards the end of the eighteenth century, the Hmars, consisting of two tribes, namely the Rangkhols and the Bietes, either under pressure from two other Kuki tribes, namely the Jansens (more correctly changsens) and the Thadous or perhaps because their nomadic impulse had not spent itself, moved across the plains of Cachar and settled down in the North Cachar Hills and came to be known there as the 'Old Kukis'. Later on the Jansens and Thadous were similarly compelled by the Lushais to follow the Ranghols and Bietes to seek shelter in the North Cachar Hills, where they came to be known as the 'New Kukis'. This second migration took place in 1851-52. The Hmars claim to be a separate tribe independent of the Kukis tribe, but those of them left behind in the Lushai Hills, have become more or less completely assimilated with the Lushais. Lushai being the general name covering all the tribes living in the Mizoram except the Lakhers and the Pawis who are also undergoing slowly the process of assimilation.

The term Lushai is derived from Lusei, the tribe which under the thangnur and the sailo chiefs became the most powerful of all the tribes and held sway all over the Mizoram.

The Kukis are a populous tribe, scattered over Chin Hills, Lushai Hills, Tripura, Cachar, Manipur, Nagaland, Khasi and Jaintia Hills and the North Cachar Hills. Although the four Kuki tribes inhabiting the North Cachar Hills mentioned above are included in the generic term Kuki, there are marked difference between the Rangkhols and the Jansens. The former have democratic tradition. Their villages are administered by a group of village officials, the *kalim* or headman, the *kabur* or assistant headman and their subordinates *chapia-kalim* and *chapia kabur*. These offices are not hereditary and an aspirant for the headmanship has to start at the bottom of the official hierarchy. The Jansens, on the other hand, are ruled by hereditary chiefs, whose authority, like that of the Lushai Chiefs, was almost unlimited before the British occupation.

The classification given above of the 'Old Kukis' and the 'New Kukis' may not be the last word on the subject. I have seen the Jansen Kukis who are definite about belonging to the Old Kukis and not the New Kuki group. In the Mizoram, the Rangkhols (called there Hrangchals) and the Bietes are two of many clans collectively called Hmars, i.e. north from the position of their villages with reference to those of the Lushais. Amongst themselves these two sub-tribes are called Khawchak and Khawthang i.e. Eastern and Western.

The principal Kuki clans are Biete, Changsen (Jansen), Thadous, Khelma, Hrangkhol, Sakachep, Vaipheii, Linthang, Thangin, Lurhim and lastly the Hmars. As customs, manners, religious practices etc. vary from sub-tribe to sub-tribe and clan to clan, it is not possible to give a composite picture of the Kukis as a single group.

CHAPTER V

A PORTRAIT OF MANIPUR

IF YOU LOOK at the map of India you will find that Manipur is a small state nestled in between Assam and Burma. If we rank all the Indian States in order of population size according to the 1981 census, Manipur occupies the nineteenth position.

Population. The area of Manipur is predominantly hilly. The total area of the state is 22.3 sq. km. Out of this about 20,720 sq. km. comprise the hilly region. You may now imagine how there has been concentration of the states' population in district regions. The state has been divided into six districts.

District	*Area (sq. km.)*	*Population*
1. Manipur Central	2238	929,077
2. Manipur East	4544	82,946
3. Manipur North	3271	155,421
4. Manipur South	4570	134,776
5. Manipur West	4391	62,289
6. Tengnoupal	3313	56,444

The last four districts are entirely hilly areas while Manipur Central district comprises the plain or the Central Valley of Manipur and three hilly sub-divisions of Chandel, Chakpikarong and Tengnoupal. Now Tengnoupal sub-division has been raised to the status of a district. Naturally the bulk of the population of the state is found in Manipur Central and Tengnoupal districts. The second most populous district is Manipur North. And the least populous district is Manipur West.

We have very often seen that some areas are comparatively more thickly populated than the others. Thus the number of persons living in the same size of land-area varies from place to place. In the language of the census, this land-people ratio is called the density of population. The average density of population of Manipur is 64 persons per sq. km.

It will be seen that density of population is higher in plain areas. Manipur West, Manipur South and Manipur East are entirely hilly regions with highly inadequate transport system till today. The Manipur Central district comprises the entire portion of the fertile valley of Manipur.

Housing : Like food and clothing, a house is a basic need of human beings. Due to cultural and socio-economic factors, the types of houses, the material of the walls and roofs and even the shapes of the houses differ from place to place.

The number of households with two rooms each is the highest in all districts except Manipur South where the number of household with one room is the highest.

Dwellings : A village or town is recognised as the basic area of habitation. For all demographic sociological studies of population it is customary to bifurcate the same into rural and urban. In our country the rural population is extremely enormous. Like the rest of the country, the areas of Manipur are predominantly rural. The rural life of Manipur is still simple though the influence of the towns is increasingly felt. The rural area of Manipur covers 22,310.1 sq. km. and as such as 86.81 per cent of total population live in villages. There are nearly 1993 villages in Manipur, out of which 1949 villages are inhabited.

Except Manipur Central and Tengnoupal districts, the other four districts of Manipur are hilly region. The villages in these four districts are thinly populated and the large majority of the villages in these districts have less than 200 persons each.

It is well known that towns serve as centres for the spread of knowledge, education and technology and influence the growth of socio-economic life of the areas around.

Manipur is among the less urbanised state of India. Imphal, the capital of Manipur, is one of the major commercial centres east of Calcutta. The present industrial status of Imphal is partly associated with the cultural background of the people and the type of industry that we find in Imphal is mostly collage in nature. The people of Manipur, especially the women folk are good at their looms and the handloom products which carry the cultural genius of the women folk need little description. It may be mentioned here that the completion of multipurpose Loktak Project of Manipur has extremely minimised the shortage of electricity and hence many small and medium sized industries have come up. This means urban oriented immigration of the ruralities and Imphal will become more thickly populated than before as a result of increase in the volume of trade and commercial activities.

Education. The ability to read and write makes a man literate. The rate of literacy in any state does not remain the same in different periods of time.

In the year 1941 the total population of Manipur was 512,069 persons. The total literate population was 24,905 persons only consisting of 23,242 males and 1663 females. Thus the proportion of literates to total population was 4.86 per cent in 1941. The proportion of female literate to total female population was miserably poor with 0.63 per cent only. And the proportion of male literates to total male population stood at 9.33 per cent. After one decade, that is in 1951, the total literate population was 65,895 persons and their proportion to the total population was 11.41 per cent.

In 1961 census we find a different picture. In the said year, the literacy rate rose to 30.42 per cent with 2,37,276 persons out of total population of 7,80,037 being literate. In 1971, 3,53,090 persons were returned as literates and their percentage to the total population is 32.91. The increase of 2.49 per cent from 1961 or a growth rate of literacy rate of 8.19 per cent is a poor performance.

In 1981, 587,618 persons were returned as literates and their percentage to the total population was 41.35. The increase of 8.44 in one decade is appreciable.

These figures clearly indicates that the growth rate of literacy in Manipur is encouraging.

In the foregoing paragraphs we have seen a general picture of literacy rate in the state.

The proportion of literate population to the total population is highest in Manipur South district with 34.68 per cent. This is closely followed by Manipur Central district with 34.64 per cent and Manipur East district with 34.10 per cent. These three districts have literacy rates above the state average.

In all districts, the number of literate males is more than the number of literate females.

Rural Literacy : Almost three-fourths of the rural population of Manipur are illiterates. This is not however an exceptional case. Manipur with 29.83 per cent of rural literacy fares much better than other major Indian States. Manipur has higher rural literacy rate than the country's figure (23.74) per cent.

Urban Literacy : Out of six districts in Manipur, only two districts namely Manipur Central and Manipur South have urban areas. In Tengnoupal district there is only one urban area namely Churachandpur. The performance of males and females in these districts in the field of literacy is worth noting. Out of 66,973 males population in the urban areas of Manipur Central district there are 44,022 males returned as literate. The proportion of the literate urban males to the total urban male population is 65.73 per cent. The corresponding percentage in Manipur South district is 66.88, where 2990 out of 4471 urban males are found literate. It clearly indicates that the literacy rates in the urban areas of Manipur are fairly satisfactory. With 56.90 per cent Imphal leads the other towns in literacy Churachandpur stands second with 56.66 per cent and Nambol third with 53.91 per cent.

There is a surprising change as regards female literacy. Imphal does not enjoy number one position in female literacy. Churachandpur leads the rest with 45.88 per cent of female population being literate and Imphal stands second with 43.89 per cent and the third position goes to Nambol with 42.29 per cent. Lamlai with 20.92 per cent of its female population being literate comes last.

Language : Almost every ethnic group in the country has a language of its own. In Manipur the total population of speakers of languages specified in schedule VIII to the constitution is very small. For the country as a whole Hindi has the largest number of speakers and Bengali comes next. But in Manipur, Bengali tops the list followed by Hindi.

Manipuri/Meithei which is the mother tongue of more than 63 per cent of the total population is undoubtedly the lingua-franca of the state. Manipuri/Maithei is understood by almost every inhabitant of the state. Manipuri/Methei which is the predominant language in the state maintains the same position in both the rural and urban areas also.

Religion : We cannot ignore the significance of religion in the life and culture of any people throughout the world. Religion is an important social variable having a bearing on the demographic, cultural, health and economic characteristics of the population.

India is a land of many religions. However, the number of the followers of Hinduism is the highest. The population of the Hindus is very great with 82.72 per cent of the total population.

The population of Manipur is predominantly Hindu. Hinduism had been the state religion during the days of the early Manipur kings. Still more than 50 per cent of the total population of Manipur are Hindus. The Christians come second with 26.03 per cent. Besides the Hindus and the Christian, other religious communities like the Muslims, Sikhs, Jains etc. comprise the minor communities so far as their population size is concerned. The Muslims account for only 6.61 per cent. The population of either the Jains or the Sikhs is below 1500. Each represents less than 0.14 per cent of the total population.

It may be mentioned here that Manipur has a long tribal belt where the people are still following the traditional religion of their forefathers and they represent more than 7 per cent of the total population of the state."

According to 1981 census, the proportion of Hindus in both the rural and urban areas of the Manipur is highest. Christianity comes next and Islam third. The proportion of the Hindu population in the urban area is higher than in the rural area.

The highest proportion of Hindu population is found in the urban areas of Manipur Central district with 88.73 per cent and the lowest proportion in the rural area of Manipur East with 3.33 per cent.

Therefore it is clear that Hinduism is the predominant religion in the state and the concentration of the Hindu population is found in the plain area of the state, that is in the Manipur Central district. In the remaining districts Christian population dominates though it comprises 26.03 per cent of the total population of the state. The Muslims representing a distant third major religion in the state are found mostly in the Manipur Central district. Other religions like Sikhism, Jainism and Buddhism do not have a large number of followers in Manipur. They are generally found in the urban areas.

Tribes of Manipur

Like the castes, India is the home of many tribal communities, many of whom remained considerably backward because of geographical isolation, pursuit of primitive mode of living and alienation from the social mainstream.

The proportion of scheduled tribes to the total population is 31.18 per cent which is several times higher than the corresponding percentage of 6.94 for the country as a whole.

	Percentage of scheduled tribe to total population		
India	1961	1971	1981
	6.87	6.94	7.3
Manipur	31.93	31.18	21.4

The highest distribution of scheduled tribes is found in Manipur West district followed by Manipur East district. The third highest position goes to Manipur South district. In absolute number, Manipur South district has the highest number of scheduled tribes population followed by Manipur North, Manipur East, Manipur Central and Manipur West respectively. Among the district Manipur West contains the lowest scheduled tribes population.

Distribution : The concentration of urban areas of Manipur is found in Manipur Central district which is predominantly a plain area. In Manipur South district there is only one town viz. Churachandpur. In the remaining three districts which are predominantly hilly and the ancestral home of the scheduled tribes, there is no urban areas. It is therefore natural that the majority of the scheduled tribes live in the rural areas of Manipur.

Literacy : It has been noticed that the performance of scheduled tribes is a little better than the scheduled castes, in so far as literacy is concerned.

The percentage of literate to total scheduled tribe population in districts of Manipur are as follows ;—

	Total Literates	*Percentage*
Manipur	96,020	28.71
Manipur North	17,949	21.70
Manipur West	9,026	20.52
Manipur South	31,827	34.60
Manipur Central & Tengnoupal	17,439	31.22
Manipur East	19,779	33.01

There are in all 29 scheduled tribes in Manipur according to 1981 census. They are :—

1. Aimol
2. Anal
3. Angami
4. Chiru
5. Chothe
6. Gangte
7. Hmar
8. Kabui
9. Kacha Naga
10. Koirao
11. Koireng
12. Kom
13. Lamgang
14. Any Mizo
15. Maram
16. Maring
17. Mao
18. Mansang
19. Moyon
20. Paite
21. Purum
22. Ralte
23. Sema
24. Simte
25. Tangkhul
26. Thadou

27. Vaiphei
28. Sahte
29. Zou.

Activity: Everyone of us is doing something which is economically active or otherwise. We know the difference between a village and a town. In the villages, cultivation is generally the main occupation of the villagers while in the towns, the people do varieties of works like working in the office, factories or selling goods in shops etc. Therefore, the types of occupation in the rural and urban areas generally differ. In the rural areas many cut short at their studies due to many reasons and mostly boys become actively engaged in the agricultural occupation of their parents. It is therefore natural for a less industrialized state like Manipur to have higher proportion of workers in rural areas than in urban areas.

In Manipur nearly 67 per cent of the workers are cultivators. In all districts, the proportion of workers under this main category is the highest. Among the districts the highest proportion of workers under this category is found in Manipur West district with 89.91 per cent followed by Manipur North district with 89.28 per cent. In Manipur East and Manipur South districts the proportions are 85.41 and 85.30 per cent respectively. The lowest proportion is found in Manipur Central and Tengnoupal district with 54.40 and 53.20 per cent respectively.

Except in cultivation, the percentage of persons engaged in other activities such as livestock, forestry, Fishing, Hunting, orchards, mining and quarrying are very low. According to 1981 census only 3000 persons were found engaged in these industries.

But so far as manufacturing, processing, servicing and repairs of household activities are concerned, 9.34 per cent of the total population were engaged in these activities. The bulk of the population under this category is found in Manipur Central district and their proportion to the total workers in the district is 14.69 per cent. In other districts the working population under this category is too small and the proportion is less than 2 per cent. Next to Manipur Central, the second position goes to Manipur South district with 1.02 per cent workers and the third position to Manipur North district with 0.68 per cent,

Other than activities mentioned above, only 1.65 per cent workers are engaged in general work.

So far as trade and commerce is concerned 3.55 per cent workers are engaged. Under this category Manipur Central is leading district. The proportion of workers under this activity in Manipur Central is 5.31 per cent followed by Manipur North with 0.91 per cent. The third position goes to Manipur South with 0.87 per cent and fourth and fifth go to Manipur East and West district with 0.36 and 0.20 per cent respectively.

Other activities : All types of economic activity not covered by cultivators, agricultural labour or household industry will come under this category. Under this category come factory workers, Government Servants, municipal workers, teachers etc. The total population under this category is nearly 57,492 persons. The distribution of workers under these activities is highest in Manipur Central.

The proportion of workers in the four hilly districts—Manipur North, Manipur West, Manipur South and Manipur East is greater than that found in Manipur Central and Tengnoupal. These four hilly districts are predominantly inhabited by the scheduled tribes. The proportions of workers from scheduled tribes are greater than the workers from other communities. Whereas the proportion of workers for the state as a whole is 34.57 per cent, that of the scheduled tribes stands at 43.29 per cent. The scheduled tribes have the lowest proportion of non-workers.

The working population among the scheduled tribes is predominantly agricultural. Almost 90 per cent of the tribes are agriculturists. Less than 9 per cent of the workers are engaged in "Other Service". Hence the distribution of the workers in the other categories of work is highly unsatisfactory.

Conclusion : Almost nine-tenths of the total area of the state are covered by the hilly regions where the transport and communication facilities are far from satisfactory. The development of the state is more or less prominent in the central valley of the state where the capital city Imphal is located.

In the light of the above situation, the growth of population gives more pressure upon the fertile valley of the state.

Manipur is among the few states having a fast growth rate of population. The growth rate of Manipur with 37.53 per cent is the second highest among the Indian states. But as regards density of population Manipur is among the lowest in the country with only 48 persons per sq. km.

Traditionally the hilly regions of Manipur are the home of the scheduled tribes and the central valley is inhabited predominantly by the Hindu population. This geographical isolation of two major groups of people, namely the Hill-people and the plains people vis-a-vis absence of satisfactory transport and communication facility has done more harm than good for the over all development of the state.

In the hills the major occupation is cultivation. In the valley also agriculture is still a major occupation. However, the growth of minor industrial projects and other non-agricultural occupations are found in the valley. The availability of non-agricultural occupations is a major factor for immigration of the people from the hills to the valley.

The scheduled tribes represent about 31 per cent of the total population of the state. The improvement of the scheduled tribes is the improvement of the hills of Manipur. The natural resources are mostly in the hills. It is the responsibility of the state to bring the living condition of the hill people at par at least with that of general population.

Nearly 66 per cent of population is engaged in agriculture. But nearly 92 per cent of the total land area is hilly and covered with forests. Reserve forest area covers 1377 sq. km. while the protected forests spread in 4171 sq. km.

Forest reserves are being developed for better species of timbers. Bamboo is found in large quantities. Main crop is paddy, while wheat and maize are also grown.

The state has no large scale industries. Handloom weaving is the largest single cottage industry. Other cottage industries are sericulture, bamboo and cane articles, carpentry, leather goods etc.

Irrigation is done mainly through minor irrigation canals. Loktak is the only major power project in the state.

ETHNIC GROUPS IN MANIPUR

From time immemorial Manipur had been the home of a number of ethnic groups broadly categorised in modern times under the appellations of Meitei, Naga, Kuku, etc. The

Meiteis who become a major community as a result of confederacy of a number of cognate groups like Angom, Khumal, Luwang, Moirang, etc. which became its exogamous units might have been one of the earliest settlers. The fact that the Meiteis were able to establish against many odds, a well settled and close society and also a kingdom with a written chronicle dating from the first century A.D. speaks not only of the antiquity of their settlement but also of the endeavour leading towards the growth of a distinct culture in this small kingdom.

Scholars are of a view that Manipur had been in the past one of the trade routes between the east and the west and naturally a meeting place of immigrants from the east as well as from the west. The eastern stream consisting of mostly the Burmese which got assimilated into the Meitei society was known as the "nongpok-ha-ram." Since the wake of Hinduism in the Meitei society the flow of western stream became more regular than before and the assimilation of the western stream or the "nongpok-ha-ram" underwent into three directions : first, the assimilation of the Brahmin immigrants within the Meitei Hindu society to form the Brahmin caste; second the assimilation of other non-Brahmin Hindu immigrants, and third, the assimilation of the Muslims by retaining their Islamic faith. The adoption of Meitei language, family names and dress, among others, were the major features of assimilation of the Muslims. The native Meiteis along with the assimilated non-Brahmin Hindus became the Kshatriya caste and within the Meitei Hindu society they have a close-knit dual caste organisation of the Brahmins and the Kshatriyas.

Though Hinduism had its roots in Manipur prior of 18th century ; it was only during the time of Garib Niwaz, an 18th century Meitei king, that mass proselytism of the natives took place into the fold of Rama cult. Ramaism while in its teething stage was overshadowed by Krishnaism under the Chaitanya school whose Bhakti cult, absence of caste rigidity and devotion through singing of Sankirtan found a firm foundation to become the state religion in the Meitei Hindu society. The reason for the popularity of Chaitanya Vaishnavism may be attributed to Sankirtan itself which, infused by the artistic genius of the Meiteis create and atmosphere where dance and music become the dominant element of their religion and life, providing an emotional outlets of the people.

As a result of a strong force of cultural identification of Manipur with the Hindu India coupled with the political situation prevailing during the past one or two hundred years, the flow of immigrants from the west on increasing ultimately in the growth of separate ethnic groups represented mostly by those coming from Assam, Bengal and Bihar. The late settle from the west who retained their communal identities form the minor ethnic groups. Mostly engaged in trade and commerce, their actual involvement in the social milieu or the mainstream of social life with the other major ethnic groups is found to have been very much ingrained.

One of the most interesting features regarding the growth of ethnic groups in Manipur is the spread of medley of tribes in its hills. The settlement of the major Naga groups like the Kabui, Mao and Tangkhul in Manipur may undoubtedly be said to be one of the oldest enjoying in the past autonomy within their territorial boundaries. The eastern hills of Manipur are the ancestral home of the Tangkhul while the northern and western hills remain the abode of the Mao and the Kabui respectively.

It will not be possible to have an exhaustive account of all the tribal communities and their distribution pattern in Manipur. It may however be mentioned here that the large number of separate ethnic groups is due to the influx of mostly the tribal groups liberally grouped under Kuki from the Burmese territory during early times. Naturally the south and south-eastern hilly areas of Manipur have been settled mostly by these tribal groups. The settlement of the Kuki in the areas between the plains of the Meiteis and Burma and also in the hill slopes close to the fringe of the plains suggests the policy of the early Meitei kings towards having buffer communities for saving the plains from the onslaught of external forces.

A large number of tribes received constitutional recognition as the scheduled tribes of Manipur as a result of the modification of the list of the scheduled tribes of Manipur in 1956. Accordingly the Naga and Kuki appelations have been dropped and individual tribal names, numbering 29, have been recognised as the scheduled tribes of Manipur. These 29 tribes are as follows : Aimol, Anal, Angami, Chiru, Chothe, Gangte, Hmar, Kabui, Kacha Naga, Koirao, Koireng, Kom, Lamgang, Mao, Maram, Maring, Mizo, Monsang, Moyon, Paite, Purum, Ralte, Sahte, Sema, Simte, Tangkhul, Thodou Vaiphei and Zou.

If we go back to a few decades it will be found that tribal population in Manipur in 1941 showed a declining rate of 1.3 per cent over that of 1931. However, in 1951 the growth rate hit 26.8 per cent. The only possible reason for this alarming growth of tribal population in Manipur from 1941 to 1951 may be attributed to the influx of tribal population from Burma for shelter in the hills of Manipur as a result of the last World War II. It will be pertinent to have a glimpse of the tribal population of Manipur in the last two censuses of 1961 and 1971 and the decadal growth rate.

Tribe	*1961*	*1971*	*Growth Rate*
Aimol	108	836	674.0
Anal	4868	6670	37.0
Angami	632	70	— 802.8
Chiru	1809	2785	53.9
Chothe	1035	1905	84.1
Gangte	4856	6307	29.9
Hmar	15365	23312	51.7
Kabui	29218	40257	37.8
Kacha Naga	9734	13026	33.8
Koirao	406	1620	299.0
Koireng	531	458	— 15.9
Kom	5477	6550	19.5
Lamgang	1866	2622	40.5
Mao	28810	33379	15.8
Maram	4928	4539	— 8.6
Maring	7745	9825	26.8
Mizo	2746	7483	172.5
Monsang	1342	930	— 44.3
Moyon	647	1360	110.2
Paite	17029	24758	45.4
Purum	82	—	—
Ralte	80	154	92.5

Sema	4	3	— 33.3
Simte	2818	4177	42.8
Sahte	—	3	—
Tangkhul	43943	57851	31.6
Thadou	47994	59955	24.9
Vaiphei	8215	12347	50.3
Zou	6761	10060	48.8

It will be seen that between 1961 and 1971 there has been a very irregular trend of growth of the tribal population of Manipur. Higher decadal increase or fall of population is often found among the less populous tribal communities than among the more populous ones. This phenomenon is indicative of the irratic changes in ethnic identification of the less populous tribes on the one hand and the affiliation of a few unscheduled tribes to this or that scheduled tribe on the other. A probe into the factors or the circumstances leading to the steep rise or fall in population among some tribal groups from 1961 to 1971 will be a very significant socio-demographic study.

The inter ethnic relationship between the different groups of people particularly between the people of the plains and the tribes of the hills was largely determined in the past by two factors : (a) geographic distance and (b) religion. The physical distance between the plains and the hills of Manipur was aggrevated by unsatisfactory communication facilities or the absence of roads, and situation though very much improved today leaves much to be desired when it comes to wider coverage of interior tribal villages. A strong force of social distance began to operate between the plains people and the hill people as a result of the conversion of the plains people particularly the Meiteis into the fold of Hinduism some three hundred years ago. Hinduism with its concept of "Purity" and "impurity" created a social distance between the Hindus and the non-Hindus in the past though it has been considerably minimized today as a result of expanding growth of urban population increasing rate of literacy and introduction of democratic institution. Besides, the increasing growth of trade and commerce having a contageous effect upon the inferior rural areas including the remote hilly areas helped narrow down social distance of the past to a considerable extent thereby creating a climate for the growth of healthy relationship between the various ethnic groups.

While the Meiteis have accepted Hinduism as their religion, the tribes of Manipur began to accept Christianity under different denominations to such an extent that the followers of traditional religions among them have become the minority group. The acceptance of a major world religion like Christianity was a major factor of social change in the tribal belt of Manipur. Apart from enthusing the fervour of a new religion, it is responsible for the adoption of the Roman script by the tribes and for an uninhibited pull of tribal culture towards westernisation.

The third major group which is more cultural than ethnic is that of the Muslims whose contributions, like that of the tribes, towards the development of the state is considerable. The early Muslim settlers, most of them being contemporaneous with the Brahmin immigrants, got themselves assimilated within the larger Manipuri society by adopting local family names, Meitei language and other facets of culture. Among the local family names of the Muslims, mention may be made of Aribam, Khullakpam, Yumkhaibam, Ippam, Phisabam, Wangmayum, Meraimayum, Khulaibam, Baseimayum, Phundreimayum, Pukhrimayim, etc. It may be of interest of note that some of the family names like Aribam, Khullakpam and Yumkhaibam are common for both the Muslims and the Hindu Meiteis. Besides, the Muslims are found to settle as close neighbours to the Hindu Meiteis. These are indicative of the receptive attitude of the early Meitei kings in their relation with the Muslims.

Since the early days there had been inter-dependence between the Meiteis, the Muslims and the tribals in one aspect or the other whether econo-political or socio-cultural. In spite of ethnic diversities, there had been a bond of unity among these three groups and they undoubtedly form the tribe in the cultural history of Manipur.

LIFE STYLE—THE KABUIS (MANIPUR)

The word Kabui is still a mystery to the Kabuis themselves. It is an alien word of which no definite origin is known to the Kabuis. The Kabuis of Manipur nowadays call themselves 'Rongmei' also. It is a combination of two words 'rong' and 'mei' meaning 'South' and 'people' respectively. Thus Rongmei stands for the 'Southerners.'

The ancestral home of the Kabuis lies in the mountain ranges in the Tamenglong sub-division of Manipur and adjacent mountainous areas of Nagaland and Assam. The Kabui settlement area within the territory of Manipur happens to be the southern portion of the vast tract of Kabui country and hence those who are settling in the southern part of their habitat within Manipur call themselves the Rongmei—the Southerners.

In present day literature, the word Kabui has been widely used within and outside Manipur and the name Rongmei is less known to other communities.

History : The original home of Kabuis of Manipur lies in Tamenglong area which is a vast tract of hilly region situated along the western borders of Manipur. It is reported that many early settlers into the valley of Manipur came from Tamenglong area. It is also reported that the earliest settlement of the Kabuis in Imphal is about a century old.

The Kabuis are one of the major tribes of Manipur. The major settlement areas of the Kabuis are located in the Imphal west sub-division. The Kabuis are also found in neighbouring areas like Assam, Nagaland, Tripura and Arunachal Pradesh.

The Kabuis possess Mongoloid features. The colour of the skin varies from extremely fair to dark-brown.

Family and clan : The Kabui family is patrilineal and patrilocal. To trace down descent through the male line is the customary principle. As regards residence patrilocality, that is a man staying at his father's place, is the general practice, yet there are also exception where a man stays either at his wife's father's house after his marriage or at his mother's father's house. In either case, the circumstances may differ from person to person. When a person stays at his wife's place after his marriage, the type of residence is known as *Naomungmei* among the Kabui.

By tradition it is usually the youngest son who remains with his parents ever after his marriage, but the other sons also continue to have their sense of responsibility for the old parents, even after they set up separate household after marriage.

The Kabui population has been divided into a number of exogamous clans. The following four clans are found among the Kabuis of Imphal :—

1. Gangmei
2. Golmei
3. Kamei
4. Longmei

It is interesting to note that all these clans or exogamous units have been identified with the exogamous units, i.e. the *salais* of the Manipuris which are as follows—

	Manipuri
Gangmei	Angom
Golmei	Khermal
Kamei	Ningthouja
Longmei	Luwang

Among the Kabuis of Imphal, clan hierarchy is not found. All the clans are considered to possess equal social status in day-to day activities. The clan is not a factor or a condition at all so far as residential concentration is concerned.

In the past, the general tradition among the Kabuis was to have a headman from the Kamei clan only. Though the same tradition continues till now, much emphasis is given on personal qualities, like competence and ability to lead and a sound knowledge of customary practices. If such a person cannot be found from among the Kamei clan, head-manship will go to a person from any other clan.

Dwellings: The patterns of settlement in all the Kabuis village are more or less similar. The residential houses are built on both sides of the commonpath which cuts through the central portion of the residential areas.

All the settlement areas have rectangular or near-rectangular shape, and the houses are built facing the common path.

Houses built in traditional Kabui style are decreasing in number for the reason that traditional house type is no longer preferred and the people have constructed their houses similar to those of the neighbouring Meiteis in appearance. Nowadays, both thatched and pucca houses are found. The thatched house. have earthen floor and wooden and bamboo skeleton. The walls are plastered with a mixture of mud, cowdung and pieces of straw. Thatching is done with a local grass called 'ee'.

Dress : Nowadays menfolk have adopted western dress. Neckties are considered as things of educated persons. Genearally a local handloom cloth called *Khudei* is worn more or less in *Dhoti* style by men while in home. The womenfolk wear a wide sheet of cloth known as *pheisoi* to cover mainly the lower part of the body. This cloth is worn in two modes— one around the waist and another over the breasts. If the *pheiosi* is worn over the breasts wearing of a blouse is not always necessary. Girls and young women are usually seen wearing the *pheisoi* around the waist and a blouse and a piece of cloth as wrapper for the upper part of the body. These clothes are woven by themselves at the loin-loom and black, red, white and yellow colours are predominantly used.

Ornaments : Generally they wear necklace of glass and cheap stone beads of different colours, brass bangles and armlets. Those who cannot afford gold ornaments purchase gilded ornaments which is easily available in the market.

Hair Style : Men cut their hairs but women do not cut their hair. Long and black hair is prized most and considered an object of beauty. The indigenous method of taking care of the hair is by washing it regularly with a milky liquid obtained by washing uncooked rice in it.

Food and Drink : The Kabuis are non-vegetarians. They take meat and fish in addition to vegetables and pulses. Their staple food is rice.

Rice beer is indispensable on all ceremonies and drinking of ricebeer called 'Zou' in Kabui is not prohibited. Smoking of cigarettes and Bidis is very popular. They also smoke in a *hukkah* but generally by old-folks tea is a popular drink.

The Kabuis are neat and clean. Their language is Kabui. G.E. Grierson put Kabui under the Naga group which is a branch of the Tibeto-Burman sub-family. But they have adopted the Meiteis and Bengali scripts.

Life Cycle: In order to have handsome baby, pregnant women, during the fifth month of pregnancy, offer prayer to god by engaging a priest known as *muh* who sacrifices a cock in honour of the god and also prays on behalf of the pregnant woman.

There is little restriction in respect of the pregnant woman. Rounding of paddy at the mortar with a pestle is considered a good exercise of the pregnant woman. As regards restriction on diet, bananas and eggs are normally avoided by the pregnant woman. It is considered desirable for a pregnant woman not to attend on sick and ailing members of the household though there is no customary restriction on her for looking after the sick members of the household.

The delivery of the child takes place on a mat near the fire-place inside the house. As soon as the child is born, the navel cord is cut preferably with a sharpened piece of bamboo. Each wrist of the newly born baby is loosely tied with a black thread which is considered as a sign of human being. The after-birth is buried near the mother's bed and close to the wall. Before the burial, the after-birth is pricked with a pointed knife by way of destroying it.

After the delivery, the mother will remain inside the house for five days. The child is fed on mother's breasts for quite a long time and weaning of the child is gradually alone when the child attains its second or third year of age. When the child is three months old and develops some biting habit, the food-taking ceremony known as *Nasammei* is performed on any auspicious day. On this day, choice-food, say a beautiful bird is cooked and the child is fed with it.

There is no name-giving ceremony. There is no definite period or time when a child is given a personal name by his parents or grand-parents or any other member of the family.

Ear-piercing Ceremony: The Kabuis call this ceremony *Nanu*, which is performed for one day in the Manipuri month of Lamda (March-April) in every Kabui village. The main purpose of this ceremony is to pierce the ear lobes of every child born during that year. The piercing of the ear is done by an elderly person with a needle and thread. Some old women go to a nearby pond or river in the early hour of the morning to fetch water. For filling up water, *tumbas* (dry rind of gourd) are taken. In addition to the *tumbas*, a *dao* and a lance are also taken, when they return they stop in front of the house of every child whose ears are to be pierced on that day. Two old women from the group will enter the house and give some water for washing the face of the child. If the child happens to be a boy, one of the women will carry a lance with her while entering into the house. If the child is a girl a *dao* is taken inside the house. After this the families of the children for whom the ceremony is performed, will bring cooked food of various preparations and indigenous salt-cakes and rice-beer to the place where the old women assemble. The preparations are consumed by the village elders. The headman of the village will bless the children and pray for their welfare. After this prayer, an elderly person performs the ear-piercing of the child. In order to distract the attention of the child, old boys and girls make shouts and noises. The day of *Nanu* is a day of rejoycing and old men and women sing and dance in front of the house of those children for whom the day is a special one.

Sex life and Marriage : Premarital and extra-marital sex relation is reported to be considered a social anathema.

Child marriage is generally not practised by the Kabuis. A girl is seldom married before her attaining the age of 15 years. Similarly the minimum marriageable age of boys is 20 years.

It has been stated earlier that the Kabuis are divided into a number of clans namely Kamei, Golmei, Gangmei and Longmei. Each clan is an exogamous unit and a man cannot marry a woman if she belongs to the same clan. A man cannot marry his father's brother's daughter or mother's sister's daughter, because parallel cousins are regarded of brothers and sisters, and marriage with any one of them is unthinkable. However, marriage with mother's brother's daughter is allowed and preferred. When the parents of a boy are in search of a bride for their son, boy's mother will first ask for the hands of her brother's daughter, if any to become her son's wife before looking for other girls. It is also customarily obligatory on the part of a man to offer his daughter in marriage to the son of his sister. Marriage with father's sister's daughter is not permissible.

Widow remarriage is permissible by custom but in actual practice, it is a matter of personal inclination and the circumstances leading to widow remarriage may differ from person to person. As regards types of marriage, monogamy is the general practice, though a few instances of polygamy take place. There is no tradition among the Kabuis that polyandry was ever practised by them in the past.

Selection : Now a days much importance is given to family background and the moral character of the girl or the boy. Economic condition, educational qualificaiton, physical beauty etc. are also play a vital role while selecting a boy or a girl.

Acquiring Mates : There are two modes of acquiring mates—These are by negotiation and by elopement. As regards marriage by negotiation, the initiative is taken by the parents of the boy and very rarely by the parents of the girl. If the boy and the girl to be engaged belong to the same locality, some of the preliminary formalities associated with the negotiation may be conveniently relaxed. But generally some elderly women from the boys side will go to the girls' house taking with them an iron hoe which is a symbol of proposal. The women will talk to the parents of the girl on behalf of the boy's family. Until the marriage proposals have been finalized, two males who act as go-between will go to the house of the girl more than once. Such a person is known as *naothanpao*. The two *naothanpaos* from the boy's place will first contract two naothanpaos from the girl's place and the four will meet the parents or guardians of the girl and talk with them, when the parents of the girl give their consent, further discussions follow regarding *Mankat* or bride-price.

According to the Kabuis rule and custom, the *mankat* for a girl will consist of a pair of iron hoes, a cloth for the girl's father, two daos, two spears, two dishes, a necklace, a pair of buffaloes, four *tadiu* (bangle) and four *munthang* (armlet).

Marriage Ceremony: The marriage ceremony is held at the house of the boy, when the bride's party arrives at the boy's place the bride is lightly embraced by the mother of the boy and she is taken inside the house, while entering the house, the bride is asked to step over the threshold of the door with her right leg. Inside the house, the bride and the groom are seated on the edge of a bed or on some high seat while their feet are on the floor. The marriage ceremony is performed by a priest known as *Muh* The solemnising part of the ceremony is called *meirakmei*, which involves chanting of the marriage hymn and sacrifice of a cock after reciting the hymn. While sacrificing the cock, a plantain leaf is spread near the feet of the bride and the groom and upon the leaf are placed one iron hoe and a piece of ginger. No Kabui marriage is complete without performing *meirakmei* ceremony.

On the fifth day after the marriage, the parents of the bride bring cooked food for their daughter. This function is called *Pukpaoba.*

Bridal Gifts : There is no limit to bridal gifts from the parents. These presents generally consist of clothes, utensils, ornaments, weaving loom and other necessary for daily use at home.

Elopement : Elopement is also another mode acquiring a mate; when a girl elopes with a boy, the ceremony of *venkhong-tamba* must also be performed so that the boy and the girl be recognised as husband and wife. Payment of *mankat* is not strictly enforced, but it is always considered fair on the part of the boy to give the *mankat* by way of honouring the customary practice.

Religion : The Kabuis believe in their ancient religion which some educated persons among them call as Kabuism.

The Kabui pantheon is a very elaborate one. Under a broad classification, the deities of the Kabuis who are closely associated with the cultural life of the people may be grouped into three categories—the Supreme deity, the village deity and the household deity. The Supreme deity of the Kabuis is called Lagang (Ragang). He is considered the most powerful god having the power to create or destroy both the animate and inanimate objects. The village deities are known as *Bambus* who are propitiated in order to bring peace and prosperity within the village areas. The household or ancestral deity of the Kabuis is called *Kairao*. But most of the household are found to have acknowledged *Sanamahi*—the household deity of the Meiteis of Manipur, as also their household deity and as the Meiteis do, a rear corner of the house is usually reserved as the seat of this deity by many Kabui household. The acceptance of the Meitei deity *Sanamahi* by the Kabuis living in the urban areas of Imphal as their own is very significant. They have very close cultural relation with the Meiteis of Imphal.

Inter-Community Relationship : The Kabuis are one of the Scheduled Tribes of Manipur who have a distinct social entity of their own and they do not fall within the fold of caste hierarchy of the Hindus. One of the most significant events concerning inter-community relationship took place sometimes by the end of 1969 in Majorkhul when the newly appointed traditional Headman offered a feast in which many Hindu guests joined and dined with the Kabuis.

Social Control : Every Kabui village is found to respect the traditional norms and mores concerning communal life. The elders have considerable influence upon the day-to-day social activities of the inhabitants within each village.

In order to look after the propagation of customary practices and ancient traditions, every Kabui village has a headman who acts as the titular head without receiving any remuneration but respect. He is assisted by other elders from the Kabui clan and only in the absence of a suitable man possessing the requisite quality and rich knowledge of ancient traditions and customs, the headmanship may go to a person from other clans. Similarly *Luplakpa* and *Khunbu* normally belong to the Golmei clan.

Taboo : Kabui custom is full of *neimei*, i.e. taboos. When a woman died at child birth, *neimei* was observed for 3 months and the house wherein the delivery took place had to be destroyed. Similarly, when a kite or a dog sat on the roof of a house, *neimei* is observed. Previously when a death took place or a major festival like *Gan-Nagi* was observed, *Langthingmei* (which means closure of the entrances of the village area, thereby allowing none to cross the gate from within or from outside) lasted for at least one full day, but now it lasts for about an hour or so.

Dormitory System : One of the imperatives of dormitory system is that young boys and girls are compelled to sleep in the dormitory at night. But now-a-days, Kabuis living in urban areas have discarded this system due modern influence and proper place in the cities.

Till the first quarter of the present century, the strict and regimented nature of customary practices of the Kabuis remained more or less unchanged. But now the modern influence has penetrated the Kabui villages and brought the changes considerably.

LIFE STYLE—THE GANGTE

Culture had been used and defined to convey various meanings. The famous critic and poet, Mathew Arnold, defined culture as "sweetness and light". Philosophers like Cassirer and Sociologists like Sorokin and MacIver defined culture as "moral, spiritual and intellectual attainments of man". Tylor is the first Anthropologist, to use the term saying that "culture or civilization is that complex whole which includes knowledge, belief, art, morals, law, customs and any other capabilities and habits acquired by man as a member of society." In short, by culture he means "social heritage".

Functionalists like Malinawski and Radcliffe-Brown take the holistic view of culture and defined heritage as to "consist of a material part and a non-material, intengible, imponderable part". Lowie defines culture as "the whole of social tradition", while a more recent view of Linton is that culture is "social heredity" or inheritance. The latest view on culture is that of Kroeber who says, "Culture is what we learn from other man, from our elders or the past, plus what we add to it." This is the same with what Tylor means by "capabilities and habits acquired by man" and Lowie by "the whole of social tradition", which in fact conveys much the same meaning as Linton's "social heredity" or inheritance:

It is, therefore, clear that by culture it means, "what is socially transmitted, what is received from tradition and what is acquired by man as a member of society."

In much the same way, the terms Tribe and Clan have been indiscriminately used without any clear definition.

In the Notes and Queries on Anthropology (1929) edited by a Committee of Section H of the British Association for the Advancement of Science, "clan" has been defined as "An exogamous, unilateral group of persons all the members of which (clansmen) are held to be related to one another and bound together by a common tie of clanship. This tie may be a belief in common descent from some ancestor, real or mythical, it may be the common possession of a totem (sic), p. 76, or the common habitation of a village or district. Sib, sept, gens, totemkin have been used synonymously with Clan." The Notes and Queries on Anthropology (1929), basing on Prof. Wissler's definition of Tribe in his "An Introduction of Social Anthropology", selected the following as the outstanding characteristic of a tribe :

(1) Designation by a specific name ;
(2) Possessing unity in speech or a dialect peculiar to a group ;
(3) Claiming possession of a definite range or habitat ;
(4) Constituting an inbreeding or intermarrying group.

Based on the above definitions, Tarakchandra Das in his THE PURUMS (an old Kuki tribe of Manipur) does not agree with persons such as Col. J. Shakespeare, earlier writer on the Kukis, who called the Aimol, Anal, Chothe, Kom, Lamdang, Chiru, Purum, Tikhup, Gangte, Paite, Khotlhang, Vaiphei, Lusei, etc. as clans and claims that they are definitely tribes and not clans. His main contentions are that exogamous and unilineal principles being the two most important characteristics of the clan, the Purums and other groups cannot be called clans. They are by and large endogamous groups with "lapses on rare occasions" and as such should be treated as Tribes. In support of his arguments he made references of Prof. T.C. Hondson, who, in his writing on the "Naga Tribes of Manipur, 1911", called the Chirus as a tribe and not a clan and to Prof. Lowie, who, in his "Primitive Society", gave emphasis on the exogamous nature of the clan when he said, "We find as one the most common traits of the sib, the law of exogamy" and "that exogamy is one the most common characteristics of the sib." He further quoted Prof. J.H. Hutton, who, in his introductions to the Lakkers by Mr. N.E. Parry and the Notes of the Thadon Kuki Clan by Mr. W. Shaw treated them as tribes in spite of the fact that the people are being given clan treatments by the writers.

It is no doubt true that the Purums, so also the Gangtes and others, are not exogamous group. But basing on one rigid definition of the clan to come to the conclusion that because the Purums or the Gangtes are not exogamous groups, they cannot be called clans presupposes subjective approach. There are a number of clan systems and as such a definition applicable to a particular clan system may not be applicable to other systems. Keeping this in view, therefore, Radcliffe-Brown said that in a society where a clan was divided into sub-clans, lineages and sub-lineages the rule of exogamy was application only to a smaller group of persons on limited degree and commended to the excellent description made by Prof. Evens-Pritchard on such segmentary clan system of the NUER and by Prof. Fortes on the TALLENSI. This is true in the case of the Gangtes, the Thadous, the Vaipheis, etc. They are segmented into sub-clans, lineages and sub-lineages and the rule of exogamy is applied only within three generations, details of which will be dealt with a later stage. Radcliffe-Brown further said that "a clan system, however, also provides a division of the tribe into a number of distinct separate groups, each having its own identity", and added that "the unilineal principle of reckoning relationship in one line (male or female) is utilised in a great variety of ways in different kinship systems" and that "one important way in which the unilineal principle may be used is in the formation of recognised lineage groups as part of the social structure." The unilineal principle is prevalent among the Gangtes and so also the various ways of utilisation of the principle which will also be described in detail. Added to this, the characteristic of clanship in regard to belief in common descent from an ancestor, real or mythical, is also found among the Gangtes and will be discussed in detail.

Gangte is a generic name originally used to denote the children of Tukgke, who had three sons namely, Thanglun, the eldest, Hilkheng, the second, popularly known as Teklah and

Thangjom, the youngest. They all once lived in a valley called GANG which was believed to have been located somewhere in Burma. GANG stands for the valley of Gang and TE stands for the people. Therefore, literally, Gangte means the people of Gang.

The children of Thanglun are not numerically large. Almost all of them live today in Pangen village, while the children of Hilkheng, alias Teklah, are slightly bigger in number than the children of Thanglun and are concentrated in two villages called SEMPAT and LUONGPI. The children of Thangjom numerically preponderant over the children of the two brothers. The children of these three brothers form separate sub-clans in order of seniority. The children of Thanglun are the senior most sub-clan of the Gangte (Tukgek) clan, then comes the children of Hilkheng (Teklah) while the children of Thangjom are the junior most in relation to the elder two sub-clans. The children of these three brothers still claim to belong to one and the same ancestor called TUKGEK (alias Gangte). These sub-clans are further segmented into sub-lineages. In the case of the Thanglun and Hilkheng sub-clans their number are not large and as such I will not be dealing on them in detail. I will mainly be dealing with the Thangjom sub-clan.

The Gangtes are a patrilineal society and their descent being based on the unilineal principle is reckoned from father to the eldest son. The Thangjom sub-clan can be divided broadly into eleven lineages, which are shown below in a heirarchical order of seniority.

1. Suktung
2. Saknung
3. Helthang
4. Chontou
5. Jathuom
6. Phalchung
7. Sitsuong (alias selpho)
8. Kaihmang
9. Tuipite
10. Munthang (alias Saichangte)
11. Tuokim (alias Bailong)

These lineages are further segmented into sub-lineages and so on. In fact, the segmentation of the Gangtes into a number of sub-clans, lineages, sub-lineages, etc. etc., is determined by the number of male members born in a society and that the names of these sub-clans, lineages, sub-lineages, etc. are personal (male) names. The sub-clan which bears the name of the eldest person is the senior most sub-clan. Seniority and juniority of the persons in the family, in other words, seniority of the sub-clan is based on the direct lines of the genealogical trees. The same procedure is followed when the sub-clan is divided into lineages and sub-lineages.

The senior sub-clan or lineage or sub-lineage is known as UPA in relation to the junior sub-clan or lineage or sub-lineage who is known as NAOPA. Consistent with the unilineal principle followed by the Gangtes the right of inheritance is vested to the eldest son of a man who is known as UPA, who is associated with a number of prerogatives. These prerogatives are institutionalised in the villages organisation called HAOSA (chieftainship) and its council of Ministers, collectively known as SEHMANGUPA. Thus the institution of HAOSA is the centrifugal force where the Gangte culture and tradition, law and custom, etc., stem from.

The question of Upa and Naopa is entirely the outcome or the product of marriage and as such the institution of marriage should have consistency with the right of inheritance based on the unilineal principle. As has been rightly described by Prof. Redcliffe-Brown in his introduction on African Systems of Kinship and Marriage, "Marriage is a social arrangement by which a child is given a legitimate position in the society, determined by parenthood in the social sense." Marriage among the Gangtes is purely governed by social values accorded to it.

Normally, a Gangte family is of monogamy, but there is no restriction to the practice of Polygamous form of marriage as well. Polygamous marriage is mainly practised by the chiefs and outstanding persons and is considered as an expression of their social status. However, there arises complication in regard to giving what Radcliffe-Brown has termed as "a legitimate position in society" in the case of polygamous form of marriage.

But in so far as the Gangtes are concerned this does not give much complication. In a Gangte family of polygamous marriage, the eldest son of the first wife known as KHUNPI CHA has the legitimate position irrespective of his age compared to the sons of other wives. For instance, A marries B, but unfortunately no heir was born out of this wedlock. Several years after the marriage, A, with the full consent of his wife B and also his parents and his council of Ministers, marries C, the second wife, who has been blessed with a son. It so happened that after the birth of the son out of the second marriage with C, B, the first wife, has also been blessed with a son. Now the son of C, the second wife, is elder by age to the son of B, the first wife. But the rule of inheritance is that it goes from father to the eldest son. Therefore, the question arises as to who should be the heir. Since it is said that the right of inheritance goes from father to eldest son, it is quite natural that the son of C, the second wife, should be the heir. But it is not so among the Gangtes. Marriage being a social arrangement by which a child is given legitimate position in society determined by parenthood in social sense, although younger by age, the son of B, the first wife, is the rightful heir of A. This is true in the case Phalchung and Sitsuong lineages of the Thangjom subclan. Phalchung was the son of the first wife and Sitsuong was the son of the second wife. But although senior to Phalchung by age, Sitsuong being the son of the second wife he was not given the right of inheritance.

The Gangtes prefer Mother's Brother's daughter ; known as NEIHNU marriage. If a man has no Neihnu or does not marry the Neihnu it is still preferred that he should marry a girl from his mother's side who can still be regarded as representing the Neihnu. Father's sister's daughter, known as TUNU, marriage is strictly prohibited. Any girl from father's side is taboo for a man and cohabitation with such girl is incestuous. They belong to a man's exogamous group. But in exceptional cases a man can marry a girl from his father's side if the distance of their relationship is three generations above. Any marriage lower than this is not allowed for they still form an exogamous group. When father's father's father's brother's son's son's daughter marriage takes place the children of such marriage will call their mother's brother as HEPU who would have otherwise been called paternal uncle, HEPA NGAK. But such marriage is not encouraged because it disturbs the social structure as evidenced from the relationship between a man and his mother's brother.

Marriage price among the Gangtes varies from lineage to lineage ranging from three to seven Mithuns. Bride price is taken on the consideration that the parents of the bride suffer economic disadvantage as a result of their daughter being taken away from them. This is coupled with sentiment and prestige of the bride's family.

In a man's social life among the Gangtes there are three sets of indispensable relatives without whom a Gangte appears unable to exist. Life is a vacuum to him without such relatives ; and such relatives are the outcome of marriage. Kinship terminologies of such relatives are, namely, TUCHA, sister's son or fathers's sister's son, or in other words, receiving relatives and SONG-GAO, mother's brother, or mother's brother's son, or in other words, giving relative. These two sets or relatives are reciprocal relatives. If a man is a Tucha relative to another man, the latter is Song-gao relative to the former, and vice versa. The third set of relative is called BEHCHA. Two persons who stand in a Behcha relationship call each other BEHCHA. They are in self reciprocal relationship.

In case a Gengte lives among the people with whom he has no close relatives, he will in some way establish these three sets of relatives by extension of classificatory terminologies of Tucha, Behcha and Song-gao. He will find out someone as his Tucha relative whose relatives have married from his own lineage or sub-clan. In the same way he will establish the Song-gao relative with some body to whose lineage or sub-clan he or his father or distant relatives have married. Song-gao relative is, in fact, inactive and therefore is not very essential as is a Tucha. But this relative in turn gives him a chance to be a Tucha relative to his SONG-GAO relative. But in the case of Behcha relative, one need not go to the extent of establishing such relationship. If such Becha relatives are not available, any person with whom a man has a very good friendship can be a Becha relative.

Although there are instances of love marriage, arranged marriage is the practice of the Gangtes, and that the parents of the boy and the girl take the initiative in such case. When the parents of the boy think that time has come for their son's marriage they will first of all approach the parents of the girl called, the NEIHNU of their son, accompanied by their Tucha and Becha relatives, who will officiate everything on their behalf.

The parents of the boy together with their Tucha and Becha relatives will take one Jar of Ju (rice bear) called Jubel with them, and over the Jubel negotiation will commence. If the parents of the girl resent to the proposal, they will give them one Jubel in return signifying their disapproval to the proposed marriage. In case the proposal is acceptable to the girl's parents, the boy's parents will go again for the second time to finalise the negotiation. At this stage, certain categories of persons, such as, a widow or widower, or a person having any defect on the part of the body or a person who has more than one wife cannot take part in the negotiation. On this day, the marriage price, the date of marriage and any other matter relating to marriage are discussed and finalised.

On the approaching day of the date fixed for the marriage, the boy's party will leave for the girl's home. In that party the boy will not be included. Either of the parents or both the parents of the boy together with their Tucha and Becha and the young boys and girls of the village will go to fetch the bride. Full payment of the bride price may not necessarily be made on this day, but certain token bride price in the form of cloths called PHAWIPI AND PUONDUM should be paid.

On their arrival to the girl's village they will be intercepted by the young boys of the bride's village and there ensues wrestling between the boy's party and the bride's party. This wrestling is called BUONTUOLKHAW. Strong and expert wrestlers from both sides will be selected and there will be competition among them. But conventionally the boy's side allow the girl's side to take the upper hand in spite of their stronger strength and dexterity in the art of wrestling. It is considered that the boy's side had already won the competition by winning the hands of the girl and therefore, they should be equalised in wrestling as a consolation.

The parents of the bride will give a feast to mark the departure of their daughter. One half of the animal killed for the purpose is given to the boy's party to be taken along with them. The neck portion together with some portions of the spleen and the heart will be specially prepared and will be eaten by the boy's father or who ever represents him together with his Tucha and Becha on the one hand and the bride's parent's Tucha and Becha on the other hand, as witness meat for the payment of the bride price or for the witness of the balance due to be paid.

The next morning, when all the necessary formalities are over, the girl will be sent off and most compulsorily taken away from the village before sun rise.

The marriage rite takes place at the boy's residence being officiated by the village priest.

Within one year after the marriage, the boy's party together with the bride will go back to the bride's parents and is called MOUSULLEH. On their arrival at her natal home, the village priest will perform a cleansing rite for the bride so that she can thereafter take the liberty of taking food in her parent's house.

When a child is born in a Gangte family, a boy or a girl will be sent to the residence of the maternal uncle of the child to herald the birth of the child, who will give one Cock and one Pot of rice bear Ju (Ju um Khat). This is called NAO AKLA. This Naoakla takes place within five days after the birth of a female child.

A nyme is given as soon as a child is born and is called NAO MIN CHU (fighting for the name of the child). This is so because of the superstition that if a child's name is not immediately given after the birth, the THITHA (evil spirit) give their own name to the child, resulting thereby to the ill-health and short-life of the child. However, after some days the name of the child is given formally. If the child is a boy and is the first issue of the parents he is named after the last syllable of the name of his paternal grand-father which in turn becomes his first syllable of his name. If the child is a girl and is the first issue of the parents she is named after the last syllable of her paternal grand-mother which in turn becomes the first syllable of her name. The second boy and the second girl will be named after the choice of the parents, but preferably they go to the parents of the mother of the children, i.e. maternal grand-parents.

When a male child is about five years old formal christening of the child called NAOMINSAK is done. One pig will be killed on this day. Ju will be taken (sipped) by turn in the manner described below : The father of the child will sip first. He will then request the chief of the village to sip next. After the chief, will come the seniormost Sehman of the village, and then the Thiempu, then the other Sehmangs in order of seniority. Lastly, the KHAWSAM of the village council's turn comes. This turn of sipping the Ju is called JULEP CHEP. This will be preceded by JUPHI performed by the priest. He fixes the sipping pipe from which all will have to sip the Ju. He then sips the Ju himself and then spit it out in scattered drops which is called JUPHI. The significance of this Juphi is an act of propitiation for the good health of the family who performs the Naominsak.

Sipping of the Ju for the second phase continues. But here the Julepchep is not done. This phase of sipping Ju is begun by the Becha of the family and then followed by the Tucha of the family after whom comes by turn all the villagers present on the occasion.

The Tucha of the family will arrange for the sipping of the Ju which is called LENGSIK. This is the standard with which the turn will rotate. Becha of the family will commence this turn of sipping and then the Tucha will come. Every Becha and Tucha will call each of the family members after their turn. This is called KITOK. In between the Kitok young boys and girls will be called for sipping.

In the evening a feast will be served. Here also the social structure as expressed in the sipping of Ju is indicated. The head of the animal called SAPANG will be taken only by the chief and his councillors. Before eating the feast the THIEMPU (village priest) will perform SAKAO PAIH (offering of a token piece of meat). The manner of performance of this rite is that the priest will throw a piece of meat together with a piece of bamboo. This rite is performed with an act of prayer for the good-health of the participants of the feast.

In the daily life of the Gangtes the social actions and behaviours are in expression of the social structure. In much the same way in their drinking, in food also an expression of their social relationship could be observed. As has been described by Prof. Fortes among the Kachins of the Burma in respect of distribution of meat, so also among the Gangtes social structure is observed in their distribution of meat on the occasion of Naominsak.

Tuchas and Bechas have their own portions of share to the animal killed on the occasion. For Tuchas fore-legs, for Becha the hind-legs. The seniormost Tucha is given the right fore-leg. In the same way for the seniormost Becha, the right hind-leg, is given while for the second Becha, the left hind-leg is given. Usually there are four Bechas who share the hind-legs. So the two hind-legs are cut into four parts and distributed amongst the four Bechas. The seniormost Becha will be given the uppermost part of the hind-leg of the right side. The second Becha will be given the same portion as given to the seniormost Becha of the left hind-leg. The lower portions of the right and left hind-leg will be given to the third and the forth Bechas respectively. The same is true with the Tuchas. These shares of meat are called Tucha and Becha sa.

Before killing of the animal for the purpose the Thiempu will perform a rite for the appeasement of the soul of the animal to be killed which is known as GANTHA TAIH. Then the animal will be pinched with a sharpened or pointed bamboo or wooden bar just at its front right leg pit.

When it is killed the Tuchas will clear its belly and be busy with the intesting work. It is called SAGIL SAK. The Bechas will burn the animal and then they will cut into pieces preparing for cooking. When it is cooked the Bechas will prepare for serving the meal. While male Bechas are engaged in distribution of the meat, the female Bechas are engaged in distributing the rice.

Female Bechas (becha nupi) will cook rice while female-Tuchas (tucha nupi) will draw water. When the feast is over, all the cleaning of the utensils and posts are done by the Tucha Nupis.

The following day is Sa-Aa-JELNI. Becha-nupis will twist thread and make SA-AW for the baby and the mother.

The Thiempu will put the twisted thread (saw) on their necks. A portion of the animal killed the day before (on the Naominsah day) the Sa-aw-jelni was set aside. This is known as Sa-aw-jel-sa. This portion will be cooked on the day of Sa-aw-jelni, performed on the following day of Naominsak ni. This portion is taken from the part of the top of animal killed. This is called AHUOI. Angong-vel (the skin of the neck) is also included in the Saw-aw-jel-sa. On this day Sa-aw-Ju is taken.

When Naominsak is done portion of the animal killed is kept aside for the Upa. This portion contains the head, intestine, splean, heart, the flesh and skin portion of the stomach. These portions are taken only in parts excepting that of the head from which the jaw and the lower portion of the head are taken out. The portions mentioned above will be sent to the Upa along with Ju. This is called SALU THAK. The meat will be carried by a small girl, chosen from amongst the villagers whom the performer of the ceremony likes best. Along with the girl will go the performer's family, their Tucha and Becha. This must be in the evening, most preferably at dusk.

From what has been discussed it is clear that the characteristics of a clan, such as the unilineal principle, the belief in a common ancestor, segmentation of clan into sub-clans, lineages and sub-lineages, etc., providing a number of distinct separate groups, each having its own identity are prevalent amongst the Gangtes and as such I am tempted to call the Gangtes as clan rather than a tribe. Moreover, it is clear that Gangte is not a clan name in as much the same way as the Paites, the Hmars, the Simtes, the Zos, the Vaipheis, etc. are not clan names.

Das has taken one definition applicable to a simple society and come to the conclusion without going deep into the social structure of that particular society. The society and the nature of social structure should not be studied in isolation of one another. A society should be studied in the context of its social structure and function.

LIFE STYLE—THE TARAO

Tarao is a small tribe. They are found in three villages like Laimanai and Leishokehing of Tengnoupal district and Sanakeithel village in the midst of Tangkhuls in East district. The total population of the tribe is 472 according to a census made in 1981. This population of 472 is distributed in 75 households. The largest number of households of the tribe is found in Sanakeithel. It consists of 27 households in this village. There are three families living outside the three villages mentioned above. Tarao is not a recognised tribe by the Government of India. However, it is a very important and distinctive tribe of Manipur from cultural point of view.

Origin

In common with the Chin-Kuki-Mizo tribes, the Tarao believed that they emerged out of a hole or cave called "Tukleikhur" in the earth. The cave was supposed to be situated at the foot of Enthlouna Hill or Haobi hill on the bank of the Burmese Chindwine River. They lived in a subterranean world before they sprang out of a cave. They did not like to live in the underground world. They liked to leave the place. A man named Katrimsha explored how to come out of the cave into the surface of the earth. He found an outlet leading to the upper world. But a fierce tiger was guarding the mouth of the cave. The tiger killed Katrimsha and ate him up. There was none to inform his whereabouts and the people did not know what to do. The second man, Chana made his attempt to lead the people out of the cave. But he was also killed and eaten by the tiger. The third man named Khurpuin made his attempt to come out of the cave and lead out the people on to the world. He was the master of the cave of Takleikhur. He dressed himself in war costume. He also met a tiger at the mouth of the cave. He took a branched tree resembling horns of an animal. He challenged the tiger. He said that he would fight the tiger with a branched tree and the tiger would attack with its sharp teeth and that they would see who could get the upper hand over the other. Then Khurpuin charged the tiger with the horn-shaped branch of tree. The tiger was frightened and ran away. He asked the people to come out. He led the people out of the cave and settled on the surface of the earth.

Affinities

The tarao people have more affinities with the Chin-Kuki-Mizo tribes than any other ethnic groups. Linguistically they are very akin to the tribes of Chin-Kuki-Mizo group at least in respect of sharing a common belief in the cave theory and linguistic affinity. Sarabjit of Calcutta University made a study on the Tarao Tribes in 1932. By that time he could meet informants who could assert a tradition that the Tarao were from the Pawis of Falam in the present Chin State of Burma. The Pawis of Falam are the central Chins belonging to different tribes locally known as Laizo (Zahau), Matu etc. The same author stated that the Marings formed one of their coletoral branches originating from one of their ancestral brothers. Assuming that the Tarao and the Maring were of Chin origin, the tribes in Falam area in Chin State are the R-group of tribes in their speech as in the case of the Tarao and the Maring. The Chin-Kuki-Mizo tribes can broadly be divided into two divisions as the R-group and the non-R-group basing on linguistic factors within the Chin-Kuki sub-group of the Tibeto-Burman linguistic family. The Laiza (Zanau) and Matu of Burma and Lushai and Hmar of India belong to the R-group of languages and they have other distinctive dipthong sounds formed by TL, HM, HL etc. which the non-R-group of people do not have in their speech. The non-R-group includes the Paite, Tedim, Chin, Thadon, Vaiphei etc. So the Tarao and Maring of Tengnoupal district of Manipur belong to the R-group besides having dipthong sounds of TL, HM, HL as other R-group of people have in their speech. Interestingly the tribes of Falam and Hake of Chin State have a style of keeping the hair in a knot over the occiput of the head in a way a man among Maring does. There are other points which suggest the affinity of the Tarao and Maring tribes with the Chin-Kuki-Mizo tribes particularly the central Chin tribes.

Population

The population of the Tarao was at the verge of extinction at different points of time in the past. Lieutenant Col. Dun recorded that there were 25 persons in 1891 having only six persons that could fight. After 29 years in 1910 the total number of the Tarao came to only one hundred. After 22 years in 1932 there was a marked decrease of the population to only 18 adults with 4 to 6 old men distributing in 20 households. As stated earlier the population of Tarao now rose to 472 distributing in 75 households in three villages after 49 years in 1981. There has been a high rate of mortality among the Tarao. There were 63 cases of death during 1950, 70 and 50 cases of death during 1970-81 among the Tarao. The percentage of mortality is worked out at 35 per cent for a period between 1930-70.

The Tarao believed that they were the chosen people of God called Rapu or Sangku. The name of the present oldest village is Laimanai meaning, servant of God in Meitei language. The Meitei king in the days passed believed that the Tarao were the chosen people of God and that they were the servant of God to do the works of God. On that ground the king exempted the Tarao from forced labour for the State.

The relationship of the Tarao with the Meitei king and the God seemed not always favourable. Their spiritual relationship to the Meitei king fluctuated. The Tarao people used to water betel vines of the king. They felt tired of the work assigned to them. So they poured hot water to the vines and they withered. The king got angry and cursed the Tarao people. He cursed them that the Tarao would never exceed 20 households in any single village. They believed that they would not exceed 20 households till recently when their household exceeded this limit in the Tarao villages mentioned above.

In 1967 one hundred and ten persons migrated from Laimanai to Sanakeithel out of some discord in the parental village. Out of the 110 persons, 25 persons died of dysentary within a year.

Tarao is a patrilineal society. The traditional way of marriage is by service for three years by a boy. The boy was to serve for three years for his father-in-law and stayed there till the completion of the term. The tribe is divided into three exogamous clans. The exogamous clans are (i) Khulpuin, (ii) Chana and (iii) Katrimsha. Each of these clans is further sub-divided into a number of lineages.

(i) Khulpuin

This clan is the most important from the time of their mythological emergence out of the cave to the present day for their spiritual well being. The original form of Khurpuin changed into Khulpuin when the descendants of the original person adopted it as their group identity. However, the meanings of the two forms and same. (Khurcave in the R-group of the Chin-Kuki tribes are Khul also means cave or hole in the non-R-group.) Hence Khurpuin or Khulpuin means master of the cave. Khurpuin became the leader of the people after he led them out of the cave. The legend states that he became the first chief in Houbiding village. He had a daughter named Thapcha who had given a virgin birth to Sangku, the goddess. She eventually saved the world of the Tarao from a deluge at the sacrifice of her own life.

(*ii*) *Katrimsha*

This clan is divided into four segments. They are Toleksanai, Tuilamthangna, Salaisanai and Longlan. The Longlan social unit has been extinct. There is no living member representing this unit now.

(*iii*) *Chana*

Chana is also divided into two social units. They are Tlaitlap and Thanonin. So there is only Tlaitlap social unit now under Chana as Thanonin became exinct.

Economic aspect of the Tarao

The Economic life of the Tarao is very deplorable. They partly depend on shifting cultivation for their livelihood. They cannot make both ends meet by shifting cultivation. Life in the three villages, though equally immersed in poverty, illiteracy, ill-health, has different dimensions. The villagers of Laimanai have sufficient forest land for jhuming cultivation. So also the Tarao in Sanakeithel are permitted by the village authority of Sanakeithel to practise jhuming cultivation. But the product of jhuming cultivation is not sufficient for them. Out of 180 persons in Laimanai village, 94 persons are jhumers and 71 persons take up basketary works as their secondary occupation. Male, female and children do basketary work in order to supplement their jhum products. Annual scarcity of food is the usual phenomenon for a Tarao village. 20.55 per cent of the total population practise basketary work. Non-tribal middlemen collect the baskets at a low rate and sell them at a good profit to the nearby markets. In Leishokching village there is no land either for wet cultivation or forest area for jhuming cultivation. Most of them live on odd jobs and basketary works etc. There are three L P. School teachers, two J.B. School teachers, two drivers, and two in military services among the whole tribe of Tarao. None of a Tarao holds a degree. The students form 38 per cent of the population. After J.B. School level they find it difficult to continue their studies. Out of 16 matriculates there are 11 college students. There are as many as 282 individuals who can neither read nor write among the total population of 472.

LIFE STYLE—THE MOYON-MONSANG

The Moyon-Monsang people live in Tengnoupal District of Manipur. They are living side by side with their fellow tribes like the Anal, Chiru and Chothe. The Moyon and the Monsang are grouped separately according to 1971 census report of Manipur. Their names were also recognised as two separate and distinct tribes of Manipur. However, the two groups are very much alike in maximum respects. Numerically the two tribes are very small. According to the census report of Manipur (1971), the Moyon numbered only 1360 while the population of Monsong was only 930.

In common with the Chin-Kuki-Mizo tribes of Manipur, Mizoram and the Chin State of Burma, the Moyon-Monsang people claimed to have emerged out of a cave or hole called Khur according to their oral tradition. Linguistically they are akin to the Chin-Kuki-Mizo tribes. As such they are a group of people classed as old Kuki in anthropological literature just to allude to the earlier arrival of the Chin-Kuki tribes in Manipur. At one time in about 1948 the Moyon-Monsang people joined a political organisation of the tribes of Manipur called Khul Union. The Secretary of the Khul union was a man from Monsang.

Both Monsang and Moyon are divided into two moieties as in the case of the Anal. Monsang is divided into (1) Simputi and (2) Rinhe moieties. Similarly Moyon is also divided into two moieties known as (1) Simputi and Jangveni. The name of the first moieties in both the cases of Moyon and Monsang is similar and it is known as Simputi. So the Simputi moieti in Monsang is further sub-divided into (1) Nagarati, (2) Karati and (3) Thumli unilineal social segments. The Rinhe moieti of Monsang is also divided into (1) Rohin (2) Wanglar (3) Thesong (4) Hiengam (5) Songsir and (6) Khartu lineages.

The Simputi moieti of the Moyon is divided into (1) Nguru (2) Langlom (3) Serbum (4) Chara. Similarly, the second moieti called Jangveni is further sub-divided into (1) Roel (2) Wanglar (3) Chinir and (4) Nungchim.

The Moyon-Monsang and Anal tribes have peculiarity in having moieti system in which the tribe is divided into two halves. Because of the moieti system the tribes have distinctiveness from the rest of the tribes of Manipur. The wife-taking or wife-giving system is very much distinctive resembling the marriage circle of the Kachin of Upper Burma.

THE ORIGIN OF THE MOYON-MONSANG

The word Moyon-Monsang is a term given by the Meitei to refer to the Moyon-Monsang people. Moyon-Monsang call themselves sirtibujur (meaning-man of the cave). But this term is not used to identify themselves in reference to other groups now. The term sirtibujur came from sirti and bujur which were originally derived from siir (meaning-cave) and Jur (meaning man) respectively.

According to a legendary story the Moyon-Monsang people emerged out of a cave in the dim vista of the past. The cave was believed to be located somewhere in central China.

Men lived for many generations in the underground world. People sprang out of the cave. But at the gate of the cave or hole there was a tiger watching the gate. The tiger used to kill and eat people who came out of the cave. He made them his prey easily. People liked to come out of the cave and live a better life on the overground world. An intrepid man named Mirang made arrows and a bow for killing the tiger. He delegated a cock to see whether the tiger was at the gate of the cave or not. He further advised the cock to crow whenever the tiger was not at the gate of the cave but not to crow when the tiger was watching the gate. Mirang said that he would kill the man eater. The cock came back without crowing on seeing the tiger at the gate at first. The cock went again to the gate of the cave. The tiger was not there in the gate and the cock crowed. Mirang came with his bow and arrows to kill the tiger. He asked for help from all the birds with a promise that the birds would be entitled to eat the crops of men in their fields. The birds surrounded the tiger and overpowered it. In the meantime Mirang shot his arrow from his big bow and killed the tiger at once. Mirang sang his song of victory thus :—

Hia ye, khurna kahang suhpeh
Men bo, samang pa ning o
Kimang chung ning achii
Samangpa ning-o, kiman chung
Ning o atsa ae,
Mirang Sapao Kim an chang
Sing nge,

Free translation :—On coming out of the cave. A giant tiger said, 'He is tall and strong' But, I, Mirang killed the tiger, So I am strong and tall.

The head of the slain tiger was cut off. Mirang sprayed the blood of the tiger to the birds to mark the agreement between man and birds that the birds will freely eat the grains in the jhum fields of human beings. It is said that the wild sparrow (bariih) is bearing the blood stain of the tiger till today. The birds are feeding freely on the grains cultivated by human beings uptil now as result of the agreement made between Mirang as representative of human beings on the one hand and the birds on the other hand. As part of the result of the said agreement the horn bill is allowed to live peacefully and happily in the woods. The horn bill agreed that his quill and tail feathers should be used on ritual and festive occasions by human beings for decoration as headgear. The cave door was closed forever. The detached head of the tiger was hanged over the cave door.

The hanging of the head of a sacrificial animal at the gate of a house in tribal villages in Manipur indicates that the house and the inmates are under ritual taboo. No stranger coming from other village is allowed to enter the house under ritual restriction. Similarly chopped head of an animal hanging at the village gate signified that the whole village is under taboo. No outsider can enter the village. No villager also can go out during the period of ritual taboo. Any one violating the rules of restriction is fined as the magical efficacy is supposed to be neutralised. A fresh rite is to be performed and the whole process repeated.*

The tiger killed many persons. But no one knew how many of them were killed. A man named Thompungpa devised a means to count the number of persons killed by the tiger at the time the people were coming out of the cave. He instructed the people that every household should bring as many stone slabs as the members of their family killed by the tiger. Each household brought stone slabs corresponding to the member of the dead in their family. Thompungpa counted the number of stone slabs brought by the people and he could determine the number of the dead. So many people were found lost and eaten by the tiger. The tradition of erecting stone at the village gate is said to be originated from the practice in this story.

The people left the cave and followed along the phertsa river. At last they reached a place called Tengpherjur quite suitable for settlement. Hence they sang song like this :

Tsajur no bongnge aii
Phertsa Kahienote ye ;
Tungpherjur to kahein phaya,
Buno tiska pa ye.

Free translation :—

On coming out of the cave
we followed the phertsa river,
We arrived at Tungpherjur,
And found the place suitable
For throwing feast of merit.

---

* It is said that the practice of hanging head of sacrificial animal over or at the gate of a village or a house owed its origin from the hanging of the head of the slain tiger by Mirang.

CHAPTER VI

MEGHALAYA : LIFE STYLE—THE KHASIS, GAROS AND JAINTIAS

THE KHASIS today live in the Khasi and Jaintia Hills of Meghalaya. The remarkable plateau of the Garo-Khasi is joined at its eastern extremity by the Patkoi Range to the Himalayan system and by the hills of Manipur to the Arakan Yoma of Burma. The highest points of the table land are the Shillong Peak, 6450 feet, the Suer, 6390, the Rablong, 6283 and the Diengici, 6077. The whole of the plateau is inhabited and cultivated.

On the Southern slopes, the hills rise abruptly from the plains and present a succession of precipitious faces into which the rivers and streams fed by the enormous rainfall of this region (400-600 inches a year), have cut deep gorges as they issue upon the plains of North Sylhet (now in Bangladesh). The lower portions of these hills are forest-clad but in the upper and central plateau the landscape is on of undulating hills, with occasional pine and oak groves.

LIFE STYLE—THE KHASIS

Origins

Gait mentions four language formations that have dominated the culture of India. They are following : The Dravidian, the Munda, the Indo-Chinese and the languages of the Aryan group. He further divides the Indo-Chinese into the Mon-Khmer, the Tibeto-Burman and the Siamese-Chinese. Following the findings of the great linguist Sir George Grierson, Gait says that the Khasis belong to the Mon-Khmer group and are in fact the only people remaining today in India that speak this language.

In 1896 Peal drew attention to 'singular shoulder-headed celts' found in the Malay Peninsula in 1875, when they were also found in Chhota Nagpur—the land of the Ho-Mundas. Two tribal groups have been found that still use the iron version of these 'celts'; a certain Naga tribe and the Khasis. Further more the Naga tribe calls their celts *mo-gyu*, the Khasis call their *moh-khiw* or *mp-khu*. It has also been found that the burial system of the Ho-Mundas and Khasis are very similar. Both cremate the dead and then gather uncalcined bones and put them in stone cairns or what the Khasis call *mawshieng* (bone-stone). It is possible to deduce from this that the Khasis are connected with people who inhabited the Chhota Nagpur at the time of the stone age. It may be that both groups received there culture-elements from a common source, even if they were not related to one another.

Agriculture : Among the Khasis the system of agriculture is comparatively elaborate and carefully adjusted to the productive power of the soil. In the flattish valleys, with which the central plateau abounds, rice is grown in terraced and well irrigated fields and such fields are found also on the northern margin of the region wherever the conformation of the surface admits of them. With this exception, however the rest of their crops like unirrigated rice, potatoes, millets, chillies etc. are grown on hill-sides by Jhuming method.

Mines : The Khasi and Jaintia Hills abound with coal. The largest of these fields are in Cherapoonji and Lakadong. Iron is another mineral that exists in the Khasi and Jaintia Hills.

Next in importance stand the vast stores of limestone which exist on the southern part of Khasi region.

Administration : The greater part of the Khasi Hills consisted of the territory of the native chiefs. The people governed themselves through their elected rulers, who were responsible to their respective *durbars* or councils. All petty crimes committed by their subjects were dealt with by them and their *durbars*, only heinous offences or those cases in which subjects of different states were concerned being tried by the court. Now this power is vested in the Deputy Commissioner and his court.

Land tenure : Among the Khasis the land ultimately belongs to the people. The chief may have some land and property of his own as on individual but he has no extra privileges over the land by virtue of being a chief.

The land is the peoples', whether they be lands that are owned by the families and clans or state lands that are owned by the people of a state as a whole. The chief owns no land as such and can levy no taxes on the people for the use of the land.

Punishments : The Khasis had a high sense of morality and of law and order. The severity of some of the laws would shock our conscience today but Khasis were severe with the law breakers because they did not want any repetition of the crime.

Murder was punishable by beating the culprit to death. Adultery was punished by life imprisonment or a fine and one pig. A husband finding his wife and a man in *flagrante delicto* could, as under the law of the ancients, kill both of them without being himself punished for murder. Rape brought an imprisonment for life in case of a married woman and a heavy fine and a pig in case of an unmarried woman. The breaking of the incest taboo brought the dreaded punishment of ex-communication and an eventual exile from the village. Arson was either punished by life imprisonment or deportation beyond the bounds of the Khasi Country. Punishment for robbery or theft was the stocks or the culprit was compelled to sit on a bamboo platform under which hot chillies were burnt.

Religion and Myths : The Khasis have a very strong belief in *U Ble Nongthaw* (God, the creater). They believe that there was a time when the world was young and good or without sin, and men communicated with their Maker freely ; animals talked like men, and god, man and the animals lived in perfect harmony. They also believe however that their religion is a god-gived one—a way to show man how to restore that broken relationship. To the Khasis, therefore, their religion is a 'way' or a 'practice' or as they call it "*ka nuam khein ka niam bishar*" (the religion of figuring out, the religion of judging or reasoning). Thus, to the Khasis, all that they do-divination, sacrifice, prayer, naming of a child, cremation of the dead etc. is just an attempt to find that way back to God. All these ideas have been handed down from generation to generation in the following myth :

Long, long ago, on the very first day, God created heaven and mother earth. Mother earth had five children, the moon (male), the sun (female), the water, the air and the fire. The moon and the sun in turn gave birth to all the heavenly constellations and from the other three children were born all the things that are on the surface of the earth. When all these things came into being, the world was clothed in beauty. The mother earth requested God to give a ruler that would rule over all these things. God agreed to do so and called a council of the sixteen tribes that dwelt with him. After sometime it was decided that seven of the sixteen would descend to the earth to live there. It is for this reason that the Khasis call themselves 'the people of the seven huts and the seven nests.'

Under the region of the seven tribes the earth prospered and God and his whole creation communicated with each other freely. God even made a covenant with the seven, promising to communicate with them as long as they lived a good life. The symbol of this covenant was a great tree called *ka diengiei* planted by God on a mountain mount Diengiei, which was used as a ladder to go up and down as they wished.

Not long after this, however, a being arose from the sea, who, seeing that mankind was happy and prosperous, became jealous of him and of God and began to plot for man's downfall. With this in mind he befriended two brothers, Sormoh and Sorphin. In course of time he said to his two friends : "now look here, this Diengier is a big tree and if you do not watch out it will some day grow so big that it will blot out the sun and the moon and the stars, thus enveloping the whole earth in a terrible darkness, and we shall die of suffocation." This advise seemed very sound to the two brothers and they decided to pass the news to the others and get their opinion on it, while the tempter seeing that he had accomplished his aim, returned to his home under the sea.

When this matter was brought before the others they all agreed that it was a good idea to cut the tree down and so they asked the smith to make them a good strong *wait* (a kind of knife) and an axe. Having secured these two, they want to work on the tree and worked it all the day but in the evening they returned home with the idea of working at it next day also. But in the middle of the night when all was quiet, the tiger went and licked at the wounds of the tree and the tree was whole again. So next day they were astonished to find that there was no marks of any cuts on the tree. However they worked at it again. But tiger did the same thing again.

Next day they called a council of the people to solve this mystery. Just at the meeting, a *phreit* (a little bird) appeared and addressed mankind thus, "I chanced to hear uncle tiger the strong, the strong saying that soon he would roam the world in peace as it was going to be dark because of the Diengiei. He said he would keep on licking the Diengiei to heal it of its wounds." When the council heard this, terror struck and they were all puzzled. The *phreit* spoke again ; "O ye men, do not be afraid. Tomorrow after you have worked for the day instead of taking your instruments away, tie them to the tree with the sharp edge jutting out and when the tiger comes to lick it again his tongue will be hurt and that will stop him from repeating the performance". The next day they did as they had been told by the *phreit.* The tongue of the tiger had been sliced, fled away in terror. The manking was able to fell the tree. It was felt all over the world and wherever the sap of that tree mixed with the sand, it turned into coal. The result was that to this day there is no more Diengiei any where on the earth.

After the fall of the Diengiei men saw that he had cut his very life-line, no more could he communicate with his Maker, nor with the holy ones in heaven. But God who is merciful, seeing plight of man, took pity on him and came down to him for the last time to teach him how to get back to his home. So he came and showed man how to till the soil and to sow the seeds in their proper season and gave him the rites and the ceremonies that he had to keep in order to be able to find his way back to God. No more would God talk to man face to face but only through signs and symbols. And then God retired. But man realised that he was falling more and more away from the presence of his Maker. He realized that now he was under the domination of *ka-tyrut*—the queen of the spirit.

So man requested some animal to volunteer to go and plead for him before God. The cock volunteered to do the impossible. He went and bowed before the lord and to him that he had come to be *u ksiang* (mediator) between man and God. God asked him if he was prepared to take the consequences of man's sin and taboo. The cock said that he would do just. So God accepted the cock as mediator and as a symbol of his acceptance God gave the cock the ability to crow which was the means of telling man the hour of the day from the rising of the sun. God also promised that whenever man sought him he would make his will know through the entrails of the cock and all the shells of a hen's egg.

THE MYTH OF U THLEN—THE SERPENT

Like most of the primitive groups the Khasis too have a strong belief in a serpent deity which they call *U Thlen.* But no body seems to knowwhat this *thlen* really looks like. It is thought of able to take the shape of various animals like a mouse, a cat, a bech, a fish and sometimes even as an inanimate object such as a great big black kettle. However the word *thlen* is the word that is used to denote a kind of python that is found in these hills. It is considered to be as *Leishillong* (spirit or God of the Shillong Peak).

The Khasis suspect that there are people having *thlen* at their house. Thus to this day we find the belief among the Khasis that there are people who are suspected of having the *thlen* and who go out in the dead of right to get people and to bring their blood, finger nails and hair as a sacrifice to the *thlen.* If they cannot get to kill a person, it is said that they sometimes just cut a piece of the victim's clothing or hair. The *thlen* moreover will not accept the blood of a person that was in any way imperfect or handicapped, like that of a deaf and dumb person or a lame person. Furthermore the *thlen* will accept only the blood of a Khasi for according to a story it was only Khasi that had not eaten all his meat, while others have eaten up all their share. The account is as follows—

Long, long ago the little village of Rangjyrteh was a great commercial centre and people from all over the country came to this market with their produce. It so happened that if the villagers came to the market in odd numbers, the one forming the odd number would just disappear very mysteriously. So people began to be very afraid to go to the market at Rangjyrteh. Hence they prayed to *U-Blei* or *Ka Blei* for help, and *U-Blei* (*God*) who was merciful ordered *Leishillong* (spirit or God of the shillong peak) to look into the matter. Leishillong took chief syrmoh or chief kyrsan along with him to see *U Thlen*. He found that it was a spirit that lived in a nearly cave. He ordered chief syrmoh to kill the monster. He took a red hot piece of iron and said to *thlen* that he had brought him some pork to eat. On hearing this, the *thlen* opened his mouth and syrmoh thrust the red-hot iron into his throat. Then syrmoh told the people that they were supposed to eat meat of the monster. It was a very long reptile and whose death caused a land slide forming what is now called the *Mawiew Gorge*. The body was cut to pieces and served.

Everybody did as he was told—save one—an old woman who wanted to take a small portion home to her grand-daughter. But she kept forgetting to give it to the child. One day while she was all alone she heard a voice saying ; "shall I live or shall I die." And an answer from a mysterious voice came saying : "live, for a man had disobeyed my command." This terrified the woman and when she peeped into the little earthen ware in which she had put this piece of *thlen* meat, saw that it had come alive again and was now a little spirit. This spirit asked the woman to keep and take care of it. The spirit said that if the woman did so, in turn would bring wealth and prosperity.

Religion : For a Khasi, his religion is a 'practice' or a 'way of life' ; it is something that he does. There are certain rules that have been set down for him to follow and do, with respect to *U-Blei* or *Ka Blei* (God), the ancestors, the spirit and with respect to those that are living, his parents, uncles and aunts, brothers and sisters, friends and relatives. But his everyday life is hemmed in with rituals and ceremonies. From the moment he gets up in the morning and starts the fire for the day to the time that he creeps into bed at night his life is one long series of ritual. For instance, whom he gets up in the morning he 'greets' the *maw byrsiew* (the three stones in the fireplace on which the family kettle is placed). He does that by hitting it gently with a pair of tongs. Or again, he never kicks the fire place instruments, like the tongs, the bellows, and all the utensils that he uses for cooking, for that is *sang* (taboo). No one is served from a pot of boiling meal on the fire, but if it has to be done the house wife will first utter a formula : *tyrsaw tyrsiang* before serving it. For it is believed that to eat from a pot of meal that has not been allowed a cool off a little after cooking is bad luck in that it might cause the eater to meet with an accident.

When a person is about to partake of a meal he takes a grain of cooked rice from his plate and puts it out as a libation to the gods uttering some words of thanks giving-very much like the Christian practice of saying grace before a meal. Drinking water is usually taken out of a bronze pot with a cup formed from the half of a coconut shell. It is *sang* to make too much noise when taking out water in this way for it portends emptiness which might mean emptiness in the whole family life-emptiness of the family treasury or the family womb.

In matter of social calls, a caller is never supposed to walk right through a house. If he enters through the front door he is supposed to come back through it, for if he otherwise should walk out through the back door he is carrying away with him the *leiing* or the house hold deity.

An important form of hospitality is to offer the caller some betel-nut which is eaten with the pan leaf. When a visitor leaves, the host should not throw any rubbish immediately after his departure for that would be like 'shooting' the devils after him.

Good Natured People

The Khasis are light hearted and cheerful in disposition and appreciate a joke. The women are specially very cheerful and pass the time of the day bandying jokes with passer by with quite an absence of reserve. They are an industrious people, generally good tempered. They are courteous.

They are a very musical people. They love to sing and dance. They are a people that can adopt and adapt to new ways and modes with case.

Hunting, fishing and archery are their main forms of recreation : The bow and the arrow are their weapon *par excellence.*

They are inveterate chewers of Supari (betel nut) with the pan leaf. Men, women and children indulge in this. They are also hard drinkers and consume large quantities of spirits distilled from rice or millets.

To day the Khasis are playing a very vital and constructive part in the life of the Meghalaya, as college teachers, doctors, nurses, magistrate and judges. They are also merchants and businessmen. Several of the young men and women have had the opportunity to study abroad either in America or Britain.

LIFE STYLE—THE GAROS (MEGHALAYA)

The Garos inhabit the Garo Hills district on the western extremity of Assam in Meghalaya state. Besides, there are large groups of Garo in the contiguous plains areas of the District of Goalpara and Kamrup in Assam. A sizeable population also lives in the Mymensingh District of Bangladesh.

Thousands of these Mymensingh plains Garos—mostly christians—migrated to Assam in the beginning of 1964 due to trouble in East Pakistan, now Bangladesh. Some thousands of these unfortunate people, deprived suddenly of their hearth and home, have been rehabilitated in the Garo Hills of Meghalaya. The population of Garos is just, according to 1981 census.

The Garos call themselves achik-mande (achik=hill; mande=man) just as the Lushais (another hill tribe of Mizoram) call themselves Mizos (Mi=man; Zo=hill). The original home of the Garos is not known. They themselves believe that their original home land was in Tibet.

Linguistic Resemblance

A legend to this effect has persisted amongst the Garos, for generations. In his monograph on the Garos, Major Play fair points out certain linguistic resemblances between the Tibetan and Garo tongues and also refers to the reverence which the Garos, like the Tibetans have for long and the value they attach to the Yak's tail, although the animal never inhabited these hills. But such scrappy pieces of evidence are not sufficient for establishing a historical connection of the Garos with Tibet. It is mere probable that like most of the plains tribals of Assam, the Garos moved into their present habitat through the north-eastern routes from China and upper Burma. This movement was a part of a great Mongolian influx into this part of India in prehistoric times. It is not only possible but very probable.

The Garos belong to the linguistic stock called by ethnologist the Tibeto-Burman. They have close linguistic affinity with tribal races inhabitating the plains of Assam, the North Cachar Hills and parts of Tripura. Grierson in his Linguistic Survey of India, encadres the languages of all these tribes under a single group called the Bodo. Among all these tribes, the Garos bear the strongest resemblances linguistically as well as physically to the Kacharis. In fact the resemblances are so strong that they have led Major Play fair to believe that these two tribes originally constituted one, subsequently separating themselves into two, the Kacharis spreading over the North and the Garos over the south bank of the Brahmaputra. Certain features common to the Nagas and Garos in the performance of their funeral ceremonies (the practice of tethering a bull to a Y-shaped post before it is sacrificed) and other customs, especially the practice of head-hunting, point towards a link between Nagas and the Garos. Head hunting was never in vogue amongst any other tribe in this region except amongst these two.

The description of physical features would apply with equal aptness to most of the tribals inhabitating the plains of Assam, particularly the Kacharis. All these tribes, as a result of living in the plains under the suzerainty of Assamese King and coming under the influence of Hinduism, have become completely assimilated with the Assamese. Although the older folk are still to some extent bilingual, complete disappearance of their tribal languages is only a matter of time like the disappearance of the languages of the once powerful King. Ahoms and the Chutiyas and numerous other races which had been inundating from time immemorial the fertile and alluring valleys of the Brahmaputra and its tributaries.

This process of assimilation did not extend to the hill-tribes mainly because of the inaccessibility of their habitat.

History : As regards the history of the Garos, practically nothing is known. They are no doubt still very primitive. Till recently, they were regarded as nothing more than cruel. This notoriety having been gained by them as a result of frequent and numerous raids carried out by them on the people of the neighbouring plains districts. On the occasion of each such raids a number of people were killed and their heads carried off as trophies, head hunting having been with them as with the Nagas, their most favourite pastime. Apart from this killing for sheer fun, human victims were required for sacrificial purposes also. The sacrifices were made to propitiate the gods after a fateful event such as the death of NOKMA (the head of a village or a clan). Similar human sacrifices were performed by the Jaintias of Meghalaya. The stone on which the victim were decapitated can still be seen on the bank of the Kopili river near Garampani in the Jaintia Hills. Head hunting was effectively stopped in the Garo Hills as late as 1876 only. Now the villagers themselves managed their affairs with the help of the village elders. A group of villages elect a LASKAR for life and he functions as a magistrate for the purpose of petty cases (serious crimes are rare). Read power is however, exercised not by the Laskar but by the heads of clans called NOKMAS who elect the Laskars. This system worked democratically and efficiently ; but with the establishment of the district councils, authority is gradually shifting from the villages to the centralised headquarters at Tura. It is doubtful if this is proving beneficial for the common man.

Domestic Life

Dress : The Garo dress is simple. The man's attire consists of a loin cloth, six or seven feet long and about six inches wide. A blouse is sometimes worn to cover the upper part of the body but more commonly it is left bare except in winter when it is covered with a wrapper of blue cotton cloth. A turban which is generally worn, goes round leaving the top of the head bare.

The woman's attire is similar—a cloth about a foot and half long and about a foot wide round the waist, sometimes a blouse or a wrapper and a turban, but except during the cold weather the upper part of the body is not encumbered by any covering. Such exposure, especially on the part of buxom young females, gives to outsiders (particularly young people) at first sight a funny sensation. The loin cloths are sometimes ornamented with beads or cowries. Both men and women are very fond of ear-rings, the women wearing up to fifty of them, the weight of which distend the ear-lobes, sometimes splitting them in two. On festive occasions and when dancing, both men and women ornament their head dress with rows of beads and stick to them feathers of the bhimraj (horn bill). Brass or silver bangles are popular with men as well as women. Important persons like Nokmas (headmen of the village) wear a heavy ring of iron above the elbow, which is called Jaksil. A belt covered with beads completes the attire. The men are often seen carrying weapons—spears or swords.

Cultivation : The Garo is essentially a cultivator. "cultivating soil," says Major Play fair, "with him is the beginning and the end of his life's work, and the occupation to which he devotes all the energy he possesses." Like the other hill-tribes of Assam they follow the destructive Jhumming method of cultivation. An extensive area covered by valuable trees is chosen each year for an entire village, the trees are felled and after allowing sometimes for the timber to dry the entire area is destroyed by fire. After manuring the land in this fashion, seeds are broadcast. Similar treatment is given to another area, the following year. As land in the possession of a particular village is limited in area the villagers have to go back to the same land after some years (The Jhumming cycle) and destroy once again the trees which in the meantime have grown. Because of growth of population the Jhumming cycle is gradually becoming shorter and shorter, from ten or twelve years to five or even three years. The soil erosion caused by this method of cultivation is enormous. Unless this devastation of virgin forests can be stopped by replacing the present methods of cultivation by permanent ones, such as terracing as practised by the Angami Nagas, most of these hill areas will turn in the not distant future into the deserts unfit for human habitation.

Crops : The principal crop is rice which is also the staple food. Millets, maize, vegetables, ginger and indigo are grown extensively. Cashewnuts and tapioca have been recently introduced. But the most important crop next to rice is cotton, abundant cultivation of which gives the Garos as economic advantage over the other hill tribes of Assam. By far the largest part of the wealth of the Garos comes from this product. Lac is also cultivated in several parts of the state.

Food and Drink : Rice is the main food and it is eaten three times a day. So far as animal food is concerned the Garos eat almost everything—Goats, pigs, fowls, ducks, dogs, cats, snakes, lizards, bats and even flying white-ants. Elephants' flesh is highly prized. The only line drawn is at the tiger's flesh. Dried fish called Nakam is a daily dish.

As with the other hill-tribes, drink is an indispensable part of life.

The liquor is not distilled but is always brewed out of rice, Maize or millet. Apart from its daily use, drinking in profuse quantities is a must in religious ceremonies and at feasts. The prestige of a nokma or any other person of importance being dependent on the quality and quantity of drinks served on such occasions in addition to the abundance of solids.

Dance : Along with drinking, dancing to the accompaniment of music is also an integral part of all religious ceremonies and social functions. The men dance with sword and shield in hand, interspersing the bodily movements with shouts of Kai. Kai. Men and women dance together in some dances and separatively in others. The only musical instruments used are those mentioned above, namely drums, wind instruments made of horn or bamboo, brass gongs and other form a communal amusements of skill or dexterity.

Hunting and fishing : Hunting and fishing are popular but hunting is hardly ever done with weapons. The usual method is to set traps which are often dangerous to human beings. In catching fish which is their favourite item of food, the Garo use similar methods of trapping by building weirs across streams and rivers, but in the Someswari river one comes across the sight of Garos killing fish in running water with spears made of bamboo. The Garos of this area are experts in this form of fishing.

Activities : The Garo is essentially an agriculturist. Except for weaving of cloth by the women folk and making of some bamboo and cane mats, dugouts and boats and rudimentary implements of metal, they have hardly any cottage industries.

But the district is very rich so far as mineral wealth is concerned. High grade coal is found in Hills of Meghalaya. A thermal power station has been set up at Nangalbibra near the Khasi Hills border. Extraction of coal on a commercial scale has already been undertaken,

CUSTOMS AND BELIFES

There are large communities of Garos living outside the Garo Hills in the plains of Assam and Bangladesh. The Garos are divided into various sub-tribes with varying customs and manners. But the main septs or clans into which the race is divided are three, the *Maraks,* the *Momins* and the *Sangmas.* Each sept is exogamous, marriage within the clans being strictly taboo. Some sub-clans like the *Abengs, Arengs* and *Siras* are beginning to branch away from the original clans and are developing into independent exogamous clans.

Like the Khasis the Garos are a matrilineal people. The unit or group on which society is based is the *machong* which has been translated by colonel Dalton as, 'motherhood,' which is not the same thing as a family. All members of a *machong* claim descent from a common ancestress or mother, descent always being through the female or the mother. The father, both amongst the Khasis and the Garos, is more or less an outsider and his family is hardly recognised by the children *Machongs* are generally named after animals, rivers, caves ; e.g. The *Rangsan machong* or the children of the bear, the dove machong, *wasra machong* (after the wasra stream) etc.

Marriage : Marriage is strictly exogamous. The husband and wife must belong to separate clans—a sangma cannot marry a sangma or a Momin. The children take the mother's clan. If the mother is a Momin and the father a sangma the children all become Momin, not sangmas.

The proposal for marriage always comes from the woman's side and it is the girl who normally chooses her husband. But an only daughter or the youngest daughter is generally given in marriage to the son of her father's sister or in the absence of such a first cousin to another person of her father's motherhood.

After marriage the son-in-law comes to live in his wife's parents' house and becomes the father-in-law's *nokrom,* that is to say, a kind of representative of the father's clan in the mother's family. After the death of the father-in-law the *nokrom* marries the widowed mother-in-law, thus becoming the husband of both mother and daughter. This custom, which is beginning to be discarded amongst enlightened sections of Garos. is rather extraordinary. Mere marriage with the widow is not sufficient. In order that the female children may be entitled to inherit the mother's property there must be nuptial consummation between the young husband and in his old wife.

When there is no *nokrom* for a widow to marry, she is not allowed to remarry without the permission of the family of the deceased husband. This custom is called the law of *akim*. The custom is still honoured in practice.

A man can marry as many wives as he wishes but if he marries two sisters he is required to marry the elder one first. Before a man marries a second wife he has to obtain the permission of the first, failing which he is liable to pay compensation (*dai*) to her. The first wife is called *Jik-mamung* or principal wife and the other wives are called *Jik-gites*, that is concubines, but this does not mean social inferiority of the *Jik-gites*. When a man marries his uncle's widow she always becomes *Jik-mamung* irrespective of whether she married earlier or later than the other wives. A widow who refuses to marry her husband's nephew is required to pay *dai* to the nephew.

There is no custom among the Garos of paying any marriage price which exists amongst the Mizos.

Divorce is common and easily obtained on grounds of adultery etc. A man or a woman is entitled to a divorce even without a cause in which case the party seeking the divorce has to pay the customary *dai* of rupees sixty only.

Inheritance : the law of inheritance is based on the principle of descent through the mother and not the father and is strictly restricted to female line. No male is entitled to inherit property. A daugher inherits and her daughter after her ; when a woman has no female issue, the property goes to another woman of the same *machong* or motherhood.

Land Tenure : Unlike some other hill-tribes of Assam amongst whom all land belongs to the village community and not to any individual, amongst the Garos it is the *nokma* or the village headman who is regarded as the guardian of all the land of a village. But this is in theory only. In actual practice a person is free to cultivate any plot he chooses within the village.

Land can be sold by a *nokma* only with the permission of her wife's *machong*.

Disputes : Disputes between parties are generally of a petty nature in which *dai* is claimed by one party from another. Since the introduction of British administration, a class of village officials called *Laskars* was created, who serve as rural police and also as honorary magistrates. The *Laskar* decides all disputes, the entire village taking part in the trial and he gives his decision.

When a dispute cannot be decided on the oral evidence adduced, trial by oath and ordeal is resorted to. There are two kinds of ordeals. The first is the *sil-soa* or ordeal by hot iron. A piece of metal is made red-hot by the *Kamal* (priest) who then administers an oath to the witness and the metal is made to pass over the witness' palm covered with some cotton and leaves. He is supposed to escape unscathed if he is speaking the truth. In the second ordeal called *Chokela-Soa*, an egg is placed in a bowl of boiling water and the person speaking the truth is expected to extract the egg by dipping his hand in the water without receiving any injury. In the old days, a person's veracity was sometimes tested by tying him up to a tree in a jungle and leaving him there alone for the night. If he was not devoured by a tiger he was supposed to have told the truth. The practice is still observed but now-a-days a bullock or a pig represents the human being.

Religious Beliefs. The religion of the animistic Garos of whom over 30 per cent have already been converted to Christianity is not but Hinduism in its elementary or crude form. Their conception of the origin of the earth and man, however resembles more the biblical version.

In the beginning there was nothing in existence but a vast watery plain. There was no land and darkness reigned over everything. Then *Tatara-Rabunga*, the chief god or spirit in the Garo pantheon, corresponding to Brahma of Hindus mythology, created the earth out of this nebula, deputing one of his subordinates, a lasser spirit called *Nestu-Nopantu* for the purpose. Nestu-Nopantu sent a beetle down to bring up a handful of clay from under the water, with which eventually the earth was fashioned. Of the terrestrial animals the first to be created was the monkey and of the aquatics the frog. Man, the paragon of animals, was the last to come. The first man and woman were Sani and Muni, whose children Ganchong and Dujong were the parents of Noro and Mande (Noro sanskrit for man ; mande-Garo for man), and these last two were the progenitors of the Garo people.

Apart from this conception of the origin of man and the earth, the Garo's religious conceptions are a mixture of Hinduism and pantheism. The lowest form of incarnation is to be reborn as an insect or a plant. The next higher being birds and animals and the last in human form. The greatest reward for a virtuous life is to be reborn in the same *machong*.

The Garos have numerous deities or spirits such as *Choradubi*, the protector of crops, *Saljong*, the god of fertility, *Goera*, the god of strength, *Susime*, the goddess of riches. The sun. moon and stars are believed to be spirits placed in the heavens for ruling the seasons. Thunder, lightning rain, wind have corresponding spirits controlling them and they have to be propitiated with sacrifice of birds, animals, etc. When there is a drought, the rain god is worshipped by pouring water contained in gourds on the head of the priest to accompaniment of drum-beating. On the other hand when there is too much rain the Salaksoa (worshipping of the sun-god) ceremony is performed by lighting fires for bringing in warmth and sunshine. In both the ceremonies a goat or a fowl is offered.

In all religious ceremonies sacrifices are essential for the propitiation of the spirits. Besides the sacrifices performed in the case of individual illness.

As they entirely depend on agriculture, there are many ceremonies connected with crops. The most important is the *wangala* ceremony, which corresponds to the Assamese Bhogali Bihu, observed after the harvest has been gathered.

No doubt Garos were greatly influenced in their religious beliefs by the neighbouring Hunduised Tribals of the plains. The tantrik from Hinduism, contains many elements which contain tribal features.

LIFE STYLE—THE JAINTIAS (MEGHALAYA)

The Jaintias are also called Pnars.

The early history of the Jaintias or Pnars is obscure as that of other hill-tribes of North-eastern states.

It is believed that they came to their present abode from either the Far East or from China via Burma and established their kingdom in the hills now known as Jaintia Hills. Later they extended their domination to the adjoining plains' districts Sylhet (in Bangladesh) and Nowgong in Assam.

From some records as well as from the inscriptions on coins and copper plates it is conjectured that Parbat Ray was the first king who extended the sway of the Jaintia kings over the plains districts.

The kingdom : Prior to the advent of the British to Assam, the Jaintia kingdom consisted of a tract of plains country lying between the town of Sylhet and the Cachar border and also the territory stretching from the foot of the hills overlooking the Surma valley to the Kalang river in Nowgong district. This kingdom was governed by the Jaintia Rajas who were then very powerful and maintained diplomatic relations with the Ahom and the Kachari kings of Assam.

They ruled over the kingdom of Jaintiapur up to 15th March, 1835, when the last of the Jaintia Rajas, Rajendra Singh was dispossessed of his kingdom by the British.

The People : The Jaintias or Pnars inhabit the Jaintia Hills portion of the Meghalaya. Some Jaintias also inhabit the forest areas of the district of Cachar and also the adjoining Sylhet district of Bangladesh where they had migrated for cultivating pan leaves. The Jaintias or Pnars belong to the same race as the Khasis. They have many customs in common and are similar to each other in many respects. Indeed to an outsider they look identical. They alone know the dissimilarities they have.

Language : The principal language spoken in the Jaintia Hills is Pnar which is closely akin to Khasi in form, content and pronunciation.

This language is said to belong to the Mon-Khmer family to which Mon-Palaung and Wa belong. Pnar language has no written literature.

Occupation : The Pnars are mostly agriculturists. Unlike the other hill tribes of Assam the majority of them are engaged in permanent and not shifting cultivation. Rice is the chief crop grown in the wet lands and a certain quantity of the crop is also grown as highland paddy. The Pnars are a hardworking people and are skilful in making wet paddy-fields. These fields are irrigated in beautiful terraces by indigenous systems of irrigation channels which involve much skill in survey and construction, bringing water from long distances to the fields. They also use the plough drawn by bullocks. Other crops like maize, potato, sweet potato, millet are grown in gardens and in the nearby villages as subsidiary food crops. The gardens are protected from damage by cattle with mounds of earth about 4 ft. to 5 ft. high over which some shrubs are planted. In the border areas adjoining Bangladesh various kinds of fruits, such as oranges, pineapples, lemons lichis are grown very successfully. Arecanut and pan leaves are also grown abundantly in these areas. Men and women work together side by side in the fields, in the gardens and in the forests. On the market days it is not uncommon to see women folk coming to the local markets carrying basketfuls of their produce for sale. They love life, they love their work. They sing, they joke, they laugh all the way, however hard and long it may be. They travel miles to attend their bazars. No work is considered to be below the dignity of any to undertake. There is no class distinction based on occupation.

Subsidiary occupation of the people are basket mat-making, and livestock nearing.

Customs and Beliefs : Like the Khasis the Pnars are a matriarchal people. The groups on which the kinship is based is the *Kur* which is subdivided into *Kpohs*. All members of the *Kur* claim descent from a common ancestress, descent always being through the mother.

Marriage is strictly exogamous. The husband and wife must belong to separate clans. A *Rymbai* cannot marry a *Rymbai* or a Blah. There are subsidiary *Kurs* also. A *Rymbai* cannot marry a *Najiar* and in other Kurs the kinship of which dates back to ancient times when daughters gave their names to a clan, or a mother of one Kur suckled the child of another, or when one Kur came to the rescue of another in need. The children take the mother's clan. If the mother is a-Rymbai and the father a Blah, all the children become Rymbais and not Blahs. The proposal for a marriage always come from the man's side and it is the young man who normally chooses a wife, not his parents. After marriage the son-in-law does not come to live in his wife's parent's house as a full member of that family. He comes after sunset to spend the night with his wife and early in the morning he leaves the house to have his food and do his work for the day in his mother's house and lands. His earning go to his mother and sister and not to his wife and children. He belongs to his mother's Kur in life, and in death he is owned by it. His dead body should not be cremated by the wife's relatives but by his own Kur who collects the bones and keep them in the family cairns. This custom is however disappearing slowly. Among the Christian converts it may be said to have been completely given up.

Among those who still follow the joint-family system under the mother, the brothers and uncles of the wife manage the property. Even among those who retain the old faith the custom is losing its hold. The educated now set up their own homes and man and wife together bring up and educate the children. The change has been necessitated by changed conditions. They set up new homes with their wives where they live and work together. The spread of education and easier means of communication have widened social contacts. It would be difficult to think of arranging marriage nowadays within the village or even within walking distance of the village. The man has either to stay with his wife and children or with his mother and sister and circumstances force him today to cast his lot with the former. This change has not, however, seriously affected the social structure. The children still take the mother's clan. The matrilineal system still rules.

The Pnars cremate their dead and their bones are gathered together to be placed alongside those of their ancestors under the clan ossuaries. They believe in life after death. This is evident from the religious ceremonies performed in sickness or in connection with the dead. When there is a sickness in the family prayers are offered to the ancestors to intercede to help drive away the evil.

Administration : During the time of Jaintia Raja the administration of the Jaintia hills was vested in the local chief called the *Dolois* and the *Sirdars* who belong to special clans and are elected.

Besides their function as administrative heads, the *Dolois* have also to perform certain religious rites. They are assisted by subordinate officers called the *Pators*, *Basans* and *Dans*. The *Pators* have jurisdiction over petty disputes in their respective areas, the Basans execute the orders of the Dolois as policemen-cum-peons ; and the *Dans* are assisted and assigned the duties of collecting tolls and taxes from the markets under each doloiship. There are other officials too under the employment of the Doloi, viz. the *Sangat*, the *Chutia*, the *Haramuid* and the *Duhalia*. The Sangot is an officer subordinate to the Pator and has powers similar to that of a daroga. The Chutia is the village crier and performs other menial duties such as making seating arrangements in the court and for *durbars*, the Haramuid is incharge of the musicians as a band-master with Duhalias under him whose duty is to play the flute, the *bhuri* and different kinds of drums used in religious ceremonies.

In some areas like Nartiang, Raliang, Jowai, Nongbah and Shangpung, the Dolois, the Pators and other officers are given paddy-lands to remunerate them for the services they render to the community.

When the Jaintia kingdom was annexed by the British in 1835, they adopted the same system of administration as was in vogue during the reign of Jaintia Rajas. The Dolois are empowered to hear all civil cases and all criminal complaints not of a serious nature.

The year 1947 ushered in a new era of autonomous administration for the hill regions of north-east India. Accordingly the hill regions and districts were given autonomous legislative and executive bodies called District Councils with powers to manage all affairs pertaining to their welfare.

Festivals : The Pnars by nature a cheerful people. They love sports, jokes, and merry making. Hunting, fishing, dancing and wrestling are favourite pastimes. Among their festivals the most important is *Behdeinkhlam* which is performed annually with great zest at the sub-divisional headquarters of Jowari and the neighbouring villages. It is usually celebrated in the month of July. It is a very popular and colourful festival. Men only, young and old, take part in the dancing to the tune of the drums and pipes. The festival lasts a week. The last day is the biggest. Towards moon that day chariots (raths or rots) are taken for immersion in the pool called Aitnar. The raths are tall, gorgeous structure made of bamboo and covered with coloured paper of different designs. Women and Children don their best clothes to watch the man-dancing and performing the concluding rites. When all the raths are brought to Aitnar, the men dance in wild joy, posturing, twisting, rolling and rocking. Water is splashed and mud is spattered all around. The festival strongly resembles the Rath-yatra festival and clearly shows the influence of Hinduism on the Jaintias.

The entire plateau of Jaintia Hills about 4000 ft. high, with its bracing climate and covered with pine forests and studded with golden orange groves is magnificent country, the like of which is not to be seen anywhere else in this part of the world.

CHAPTER VII

MIZORAM : LIFE STYLE—THE MIZOS PAWIS AND LAKHERS

THE MIZOS were, till recently, known to outsiders as the Lushais and they were little known outside greater Assam. They have come into prominence recently not only in India but also outside on account of disturbances in the Mizo Hills in 1966. The term 'Lushai' is derived from the word Lushei or Lusei, the name of one of the Mizo sub-tribes which was the principal ruling clan among the Mizos, when their land was annexed by the British in the latter part of the nineteenth century.

In a general sense, the term Mizo means a hill-man (Mi—man, Zo—hill or high altitude), but all hill people were not called Mizos by them. They used this term with reference to certain tribes living in the hills of Manipur, Tripura, Cachar and the Chin Hills of Burma, who were akin to them in language, customs and mode of living.

The Mizos inhabit what is now called the Mizoram which forms the southern extremity of Assam. It is bounded in the north by the Cachar district and Manipur, in the east and south by Burma and in the west by Bangladesh and Tripura. Its boundary with Burma extends over 300 miles and with Bangladesh over 200 miles. It is thus an area of strategic importance.

Mizoram runs lengthwise from north to south. The length being about twice the breadth and all the hills which are generally small and steep and separated from one another by small valleys, also range from north to south. The general height of the hills varies from 300 ft. to 5000 ft. above mean sea level, although there are peaks here and there which are above 6000 ft. The highest peak called the Blue Mountain and known to the local people by the name of Phawngpuii, is 7100 ft. The state as a whole enjoys a very pleasant climate throughout the year. In Summer, the temperature at Ajwal, the capital varies from 20.30° to 29.8°C and in winter from 11.8° to 21.3°C.

As the Mizos were known till recently by outsiders as the Lushais, the state predominantly inhabited by them was previously called the Lushai Hills. But now the state is known as Mizoram which means the land of the Mizos.

History : Although the history of the Mizos, who are racially Mongolian, relating to the period prior to their migration to their present habitat, is not known with certainty, it is widely held by various authorities that their ancestors were migrants from the Chin Hills of Burma. The migration of the Mizos was forced in them by the stronger clans of Burma. Dislodged from the Chin Hills they established themselves in the Mizo district (presently Mizoram state) in the latter part of the 18th century. These Mizos, under their overlords, in their turn, consolidated their hold in the region by driving out other kindred tribes like the Hrangkhols, Biates and Thadous to the north and occupied practically the whole of the present Mizoram excluding the Pawi-Lakher region.

There is a popular legend among the tribe that their ancestors emerged from *chhinlung*, a hole in the earth. According to the legend, once upon a time a great darkness descended on the earth followed by a catastrophe. In the midst of the darkness, all men were transformed into animals and beast of various kinds and human life on earth came to an end. Repeopling of the earth commenced once more when men began to emerge from chhinlung. When the process was still continuing and after all the clans had come out two persons of the Ralte clan came out together and began to chatter. This made god think that too many men had come out and so closed the hole with a slab of stone.

Mizo is a generic term which includes several sub-tribes. The more prominent among them are the Lusei, the Ralte, the Hmar and the Pawi (Poi). Each sub-tribe has a different diatect with close affinity to one another. There is another major tribe called the Lakhers (who call themselves Mara) inhabiting the southern most part of the Mizoram. There is dialect is altogether different from those of the other sub-tribes. The lingua franca of the Mizos which has become popularly known as the Mizo language or *Dulhian*, is the dialect of the Lusei clan. It has however, undergone much modifications by absorbing many words from the other dialects. There is good deal of similarity between the Mizo and the Manipuri language. The Mizo language is written in the Roman script introduced by the Christian missionaries in the latter part of the 19th century.

Religion : Before Christianity came to them, the Mizos, like other primitive people, were animists. They believed in spirits, good and evil, supposed to be living in the trees, mountains, rocks, streams and caves. The supreme spirit was called *Pathian* (God), the creator of everything and a benevolent being. But he had little to do with human affairs. For more important to the average man and woman were the *Huais* (the demons or the evil spirits) who caused harm to mankind. It was to appease these evil spirits that offerings and sacrifices were frequently made whenever someone fell ill or was visited by misfortune. The priest or the sorcerer was supposed to know which spirit was responsible for a particular illness and how to appease him. Offerings and sacrifices to be made were prescribed and also performed by the priest, the form varying according to the type of illness. In one case the sacrifice might be a pig, in another a hen or a cock or some other domestic animal. One very well known spirit is called *Khawhring*, which sometimes possessed certain persons, generally women. The belief was that the *Khawhring* lived in certain women and from there it went forth and took possession of other women. The woman possessed falls into a trance and speaks with the voice of the original hostess of the *Khawhring* making all sorts of demands or revealing some unpleasant secrets. Women who happen to be possessed by a *Khawhring* are shunned in society. No one wants to marry such persons and they often got killed too. One possessed by the *Khawhring* could be cured only by exorcism, accompanied by shouting, drum-beating and gun-firing.

The Mizos believed in the existence of other worlds wherein the spirit of the dead lived. One of them is called the *Pialral* (paradise) which was situated beyond the Pial river (Ral means beyond or the other side ; hence Pialral meaning 'beyond the Pial'). Those who are admitted into the *Pialral* are supposed to live in perpetual bliss and are freely fed with husked and cleaned rice. The other spirit world is known as the *Mitthi Khua* (dead men's village or the Hades). This is a much inferior world where life is more troublesome and difficult than in the world of the living.

Beliefs : According to Mizo belief, when a man dies his spirit leaves the body through the crown of his head and then proceeds towards the Rih Lake, a small lake in the Chin Hills of Burma, three miles from the boundary of Mizoram. The spirit however, soon returns and thereafter stays near his original home or village for about three months. It is, therefore customary, when the bereaved family sits for a meal, to keep one seat vacant or to set apart a little cooked rice and curry and put them near the main door of the house for the spirit of the departed one. On the expiry of three months the bereaved family performs the *Thitin* rite (i.e. sending of the dead) to bid farewell to the spirit of the deceased. Until this is done ? no member of the family would be invited to any function by their neighbours. After the *Thitin* rites has been performed the spirit acknowledging that he is no longer wanted by the bereaved family, would go his own way weeping towards *Mithikhua*. On the way there is *Hringlang Tlang*, that is a hill from which he could get a good view of the land of the living. As he looks back from there with a great longing his pace slows down. That is why he is made to wear behind his ears the *hawilo* (no looking back) flowers which make him unable to turn back, however much he might wish to do. Finally he reaches the *Lunglo* (heartless, feelingless) river, the water of which is clear and transparent. He drinks from it with great reluctance and much weeping in order to forget all about the world of living.

The journey, however, does not end there. He still has to face one more inescapable, dreadful experience. In the *Zingvawan* village there lives an immortal *Pawla* on the entrance of whose house all the paths to the world of the dead converge. There stands Pawla holding his big and powerful bow with pellets as big as eggs and he shoots at all the spirits that come that way. His bow is strong and the pellets so deadly that it causes painful tumours which take at least three years to cure. Those whom Pawla shoots at with his bow cannot enter

Pialral (the abode of bliss) but are destined to dwell in *Mithikhua*. A shot from the bow, however transforms the dead into real spirit and thereafter all human traces in them vanish.

There are certain persons on whom Pawla cannot shoot at. These are the spirits of the *Thangchhuah* and the *Hlamguihs*, who are entitled to enter *Pialral* straightaway. The Thangchhuahs are those honoured persons who have given five prescribed major feasts and also have killed in the chase certain animals such as an elephant, a bear, a sambher, a wild mithun, a wild bear, a barking deer, a flying fox, an eagle or a king Cobra. The *Hlamguihs* are those who die in infancy and generally buried under the house without any ceremony along with an egg, and it is the egg which rolling on, leads the spirit to *Pialral*.

About 90 percent of the Mizos have now embraced the Christian faith and the primitive beliefs described above have become more or less things of the past.

Dress : The typical dress of the Mizos in former days was very simple. Men's attire consisted of a single plain cloth about 7 ft. long and 5 ft. wide which was wrapped round the body with the upper edge running from one shoulder across the back and under the armpit of the other shoulder and then on to the first shoulder. In cold weather a second cloth was added. When the sun is strong he would use another cloth, if available, as a turban. While working in the Jhum amidst mosquitoes he would put on a white-sleeved cotton coat open at the front and fastened to the neck. The coats were usually ornamented on the sleeves. All the cotton garments worn by men as well as women were, till recent times, made by the womenfolk from cotton locally grown by them.

The women's dress consisted, in the main, of a cloth similar in size to the men's but of a finer texture wrapped round the body in the same fashion ; a petticoat which covered the parts from the waist to about the knees, kept in position by the cotton cord or a brass girdle worn round the waist and a blouse open at the front. Although the men were not particular about ornaments on their garments, the cloths and blouses of the girls were decorated with attractive designs of many colours. It may not be far from the truth to say that the Mizo's women excelled all other hill-tribes of greater Assam in weaving, despite their primitive methods and the out moded fashion of the looms to which they adhere till today. The typical Mizo cloth called *punachei* and the blouse called *kawrchei* are much sought after by outsiders.

As the man's coat has no pockets, a Mizo man would carry, wherever he went, a cotton bag, some with beautiful patterns in different colours, slung over the shoulder by means of a strap of the same material. Inside it, he kept his smoking tobacco in a metal container, his flint and steel in a neatly made box of wood or hide and also his pipe when it was not in his mouth. If he had to go out on a long journey or for work for the whole day, the bag became a receptacle for a bundle of cooked rice together with a small salt and a piece or two of roasted meat for his lunch and also a *dao* or a big knife with or without a sheath. He was also likely to carry a small gourd which contained nicotine water from the pipe of his wife or sweet heart. He would take a little of this in his mouth and having kept it there for a few minutes would spit it out. This was a substitute for smoking.

The Mizos use hats as a protection against sun and rain. The hats are made of finely split strips of bamboo with linings of smoked leaves and in shape they are a good imitation of solar hats. While working in the Jhum, they, specially the women, use as a rain proof a large shallow basket-work tray, shaped like an oyster-shell and made water proof by being lined with smoked leaves. The narrow end rests on the wearer's head while the broad end reaches down well below the waist, so that while bending down to work in the Jhum, the head and the body are not drenched. These rainproofs are also made of fine strips of bamboo or cane. They are, however, disappearing gradually.

Ornaments : With the exception of their ear-rings, Mizo men and women wear almost the same ornaments. Both the sexes had the lobes of their ears pierced, but a man would wear only a small wooden stud or a bead of amber suspended by a string drawn through the hole in the ear. Even, this, they would not continue to use till old age. A woman has her ears pierced while still a young child and small pieces of wooden plugs are inserted therein. These are later replaced with slightly bigger ones which, in their turn, give place to still bigger ones made of clay and so on till a ring of ivory disc about an inch or one and a half inch in diameter, with or without a hole in the centre, could be inserted. Women who had given up thoughts of remarriage after widowhood remove. Their ear-rings and slit the lobe of their ears into two. Bracelets are not much worn by women and if worn at all, they are of simple design. The most popular and valued ornaments are amber and cornelian necklaces. The amber beads came from Burma and used to be worn by men as well.

Tattooing of the body was not practised ; small circles were sometimes impressed on the forearm and the breast of men by piercing the skin with the spikes of certain plants and smeared over with soot.

Long hair in women are greatly admired and it was not an uncommon sight to see young women with hair reaching down in the knees. Pig's fat is used in lieu of oil in dressing the hair.

Smoking : Smoking is practised by men, women and children alike. A man's pipe consists of a bowl made out of a hard kind of bamboo for holding the tobacco and a long stalk of the same material is joined to the base to serve as the holder. The women's pipe consists of a clay bowl at the top where the tobacco is put and is joined to a water-container made of bamboo by a reed-like stem of bamboo. To this contraption is attached a small metal piece from which is hung a piece of pointed iron for use as a poker. A lid to cover the clay bowl with it is also provided. The whole contraption looks like a miniature *hookah*.

Social Life and Customs: The Mizos are divided into several sub-tribes, the more prominent among them being the Lusei, the Ralte and the Hmar. These are again sub-divided lineages and branches. Thus we find, for instance within the Lushai, the Rokhum, the Sailo, the Hauhnar clans and similarly within the Ralte, the Kawlni, the Lelhchhun, the Siakeng clans. Though, these sub-tribes might have, in the past, different customs and manners, having been ironed out as a result of the sub-tribes living together, mixing amongst themselves in the same village under the same rulers or chiefs. A stranger might live for a long time in a Mizo village without even knowing that such divisions ever existed amongst them.

The Mizos are a patriarchal people and descent in the male or the father's line. Thus, the children of a father who is a Ralte by clan become Raltes even though their mother belong to a different clan. There is no bar to a man marrying within his own clan nor is he restricted by custom to taking one wife only. If a Mizo takes more than one wife, generally, the first one becomes the principal wife and the others secondary wives. This is not, however, the case with the chief's who can take concubines even before they marry their real wife.

Divorce : Divorce is common and easily effected. A man can legally divorce his wife by saying, 'I divorce you'. Divorce often takes place at the instance of members of the husband's family, if they are not pleased with the bride. Although it may be initiated by either party, divorce usually takes place at the instance of the husband. The status enjoyed by men in this respect can be easily appreciated from the old saying that "A wife and a bad fencing can be changed at any time." Divorce can also be affected by the wife by refunding the marriage price. This is resorted to only when the wife finds her situation intolerable. If the wife leaves her husband in this manner, it lowers the prestige not only of the unwanted husband but also of the husband's family.

Before a divorce or separation is considered final, due allowance is made for the frailities of human nature and time is allowed for the husband to repent and call back his wife. Several broken marriages are mended in this manner. In some cases, the relatives of the wife make some demands of the husband who wishes to recall the wife as evidence of good faith and a guarantee of good behaviour in future.

Marriage : Marriages among Mizo young men and women are usually love-marriages. If after paying court to the girl of his choice, the young man wants to marry her, he conveys his desire to his parents through a friend. The parents then send their relatives or trusted friends as intermediaries to the parents of the girl to ask for her hands. If the girl indicates her willingness and the parents approve of the young-man, negotiations as to the amount to be paid as the marriage price ensue. The negotiations involve lengthy discussions and arguments, the suitor's side trying to beat down to as low as amount as possible and the girl's side taking the opposite posture. It is customary and considered to be of good omen not to come to an agreement quickly. Either of the parties would, therefore, raise new points for argument every now and then, such as whether the marriage price should be paid in full or in part, how much would be paid as the first instalment etc., thereby causing the intermediaries to visit the two families several times. After all the preliminaries are over and the wedding day fixed, the marriage is celebrated with feating, singing and drinking. On the night of the wedding day, the bride escorted by her friends, is taken to the bride-groom's house. On the way they are pelted by young folks with all sorts of dirt ; but on arrival she is received with an ovation by the crowd which pack the groom's house to capacity. Here the bride and the groom are made to sit together to enjoy the jokes and entertainment provided by friends.

The bride returns to her house after the welcome. She is taken again the following night to the groom's house and left there to live with him for good. The first visit to the groom's house is at present usually done at noon on the wedding day so that consummation of marriage may take place on the wedding night itself. The practice of throwing dirt at the bride and her party has practically disappeared.

It may be mentioned here that the marriage price given for the bride constitute the security or reciprocal price rather than a sale price. The price consists of the principal price and the subsidiary prices. The whole price is not appropriated by the father of the girl. The subsidiary prices are distributed according to customary practice among relatives and this consolidates the family ties and also makes the relatives concerned conscious of their obligation to help girl whenever necesscity arises.

The girl may or not remain in her husband's house after his death. It is customary to remain there for at least three months after which she is free to leave, after having performed a ceremony called the *Thlahual*. So long as the widow lives in her husband's house, whether it is within the three month period or thereafter, she is regarded and treated as the wife and is, therefore, expected to remain faithful. If she has sexual intercourse with any one during that period, she is considered as having committed adultery exactly in the same manner as if her husband were alive, and she is liable to the full penalty imposed on an unfaithful wife.

LAW OF INHERITANCE

As the Mizos are patriarchal their law of inheritance is based on descent through the father's clan. According to the customary law the youngest son inherits the property and a legitimate son has priority over the son of a secondary wife or of a concubine who is in his turn ranks above an illegitimate son. In the absence of a male issue, the nearest male relation of the deceased, such as his father or brother inherits but in no circumstances are females entitled to do so. In order to remove this disability the District councils enacted a law in 1956 permitting and recognizing the will of a deceased person. The logic of the youngest son inheriting the father's property is that he is considered to be the fittest person to look after his parents in their old age when his elder brothers would be fully grown up and able to stand on their own legs. This custom does not apply to chief (who is succeeded by the eldest son), the reason being that he is expected normally to be more mature and experienced than his younger brothers in matters concerning administration and also in his judgement.

In spite of the above mentioned law, a man during his life time may dispose of his property. He may even disinherit his son on valid grounds e.g. if the son unduly neglects to look after him or runs away from him.

Economic Life : As in the case of the other hill-tribes of north-eastern India, agriculture is the mainstay of the Mizos. They have practised from time immemorial the destructive system of shifting jhum cultivation by cutting down the forests on the hill-sides and burning them after drying them in the sun. As their land is extensive and is covered almost completely by forests and the population sparse, the Mizos till recent times, were self-sufficient in rice except when there was a famine (called *tam*). As a result of the yearly destruction of the virgin forests for Jhuming and the rapid increase of population and the fact that a comparatively smaller number of people take to rice-cultivation, the out-turn has decreased so much that they are no longer self-supporting in rice and have to import a large quantity from other states.

It is therefore necessary to replace this primitive method of shifting cultivation and their primitive tools with more permanent and productive methods as early as possible before these lands become unfit for human habitation.

So far as animal food is concerned, the Mizos prefer pig, fowl and the cow. They eat with relish smoked elephant's meat. Although many of them eat dogs, they do not eat cats, nokes and bets which are consumed with relish by some other hill-tribes. White-bellied rats are a delicacy. Neither their customs nor religion prohibit the eating of any kind of animal, wild or domestic. Fish which is searce, is caught with nets and also by poisoning.

The Mizos are expert in handicrafts although professional craftsmen are few. They manufacture for their personal use fine baskets, by painting finely split bamboo into various objects, each form being adapted to some particular use like carrying goods, keeping their valuables or storing grains. The women make different kinds of earthen pots, moulding them by hands, for cooking and also for brewing rice-beer. Iron wares are generally made by the village blacksmiths who also make tools for Jhum cultivation hunting and domestic purposes.

As regards drinks, their tastes are simple. With their meals they drink the water in which they boil the vegetables or meat. Intoxicating drinks are made from rice and is called *zu*. Before the advent of Christianity zu played an important role in Mizo's life, it being required for due observance of almost every ceremony and for entertainment of friends and visitors.

House : The Mizos are very particular about the location of their houses. They choose the hill tops for village sites after ensuring that a good supply of water would be available. Houses are built close to one another in an orderly manner, arranged in pairs of rows, the front of each pair facing each other. The two rows are separated by the village street. The steepness of the hill-side is hardly a problem as they seldom level the building site. That is why the floor of one house is frequently higher than the roof of the house next below it.

The houses are strongly built so as to withstand the seasonal cyclone storms which could create havoc even to stone buildings of the plains. The framework is of rough-hewn timber uprights which give adequate support to the strongly woven bamboo walls and the roof which is thatched with *sunn* grass or strong leaves. The floor is made of split bamboo strongly woven, resting on timber uprights. Of late, it has become a fashion to have dressed timber floors. Almost every house has a kitchen garden.

A typical Mizo house is very simple in design, always rectangular in shape with the floor raised high enough as to allow the domestic animals to live under it. Every house has a verandah where fowl in their bamboo coops, the stock of firewood, mortar and other implements are kept. There also would be seen the skulls of wild animals and other trophies of the hunt. The hearth is placed in the middle of the house. Between the hearth and the verandah is the children's bed and the parent's bed is placed on the other side of the hearth. There is no partition except for the verandah. Only those who have performed the *khuangchawl* ceremony, which is beyond the means of capacity of the common people, are entitled to have windows in their houses. Ill luck is supposed to befall transgressors of the rule. The fear of ill luck was, however, dispelled by Christianity and windows are now provided in almost every house.

The children's bed, the hearth and the parent's bed called *khumpui* (Big bed) are placed in the same line occupying about half the breadth of the house. The other vacant half usually serves as a place for chit-chat over the hearth are placed two shelves one above the other. The lower one is used for drying paddy to be husked for daily use and the upper one for keeping smoked edible herbs, smoking tobacco, well wrapped up, and other things which have to be preserved or cured.

Division of work : Although there is no clear cut division of work between men and women prescribed by the customary law, the more strenuous tasks are done by the men. Clearing of the forests for Jhuming, collection of heavy materials for construction of the house, building of the same and implements, Jhum-house, making of household furniture, tools and also of the village water holes are men's tasks. Collection of wood, drawing of water, making of garments, from ginning to weaving and sewing together, pounding and shifting of rice and cooking are the main functions of women. If a women has, of necessity, to engage the services of the village blacksmith. The latter is bound by custom to give priority to her. Likewise, a man is entitled to priority in the village water-holes even during the period of water scarcity when it takes hours to fill a bucket. Most other tasks such as, sowing, weeding and harvesting in the Jhum fields and also carrying the paddy to the house are done by men and women jointly.

Mautam : The term Mautam (Mau=bamboo, Tam=to die down) literally means the dying down of bamboo ; but it is not so much the withering of the bamboos that affects the life of the people as the dire famine that invariably follows. The Mautam is said to visit Mizoram at regular intervals of 50 years. The last one occurred in the year 1959 and the preceding one in 1911 and the next previous one in 1862. The next Mautam is, therefore anticipated about the year 2007.

In the year a Mautam occurs, two particular species of bamboo, namely the Mautak and the phulrua, flower and then bear fruit and die down shortly afterwards, throughout the state. This is invariably followed by a rapid increase of rodent population which devours the entire rice crop and thereby causes famine.

When a Mautam year approaches, the cultivators take every possible preventive measures in their own simple way by setting up traps around their Jhums and keeping watch at night. During such a famine the people have to depend for their sustenance and survival on wild roots, jungle fruit etc. Due to under-nourishment various epidemies break out causing heavy loss of life.

Administration : Previously Mizo district was one of the autonomous districts in the state of greater Assam. There are thus two tiers of administration in Mizoram, viz. the District Council with powers to make laws in matters relating to tribal customs and practices and the Government of Mizoram, which deals with the subjects which fall outside the purview of the District Council. Each village is now administered by a village council elected on the basis of adult franchise. These councils are responsible to the District council which regulates by legislation their functions and powers.

Prior to the formation of the District Council on whose recommendation the institution of chiefs was abolished, each village was practically a separate state, rules by a *Lal* or chief. Although chieftainship was hereditary, the Government of Mizoram acting through the Deputy Commissioner had the power to dismiss a chief. This power was, however, nearly exercised. The chiefs were drawn principally from amongst the members of the Sailo family of the Lusei clan. If there were more than one village under a chief, the village wherein the chief himself resided was called the *khawpui* or the principal village and the other villages were called *khawapers* or sub-villages. The sub-villages were generally placed by the chief under the charge of his sons. Sometimes, the chief gave away a village to a son for ruling over it as an independent chief without paying any tribute to him.

The chief was assisted by a council of village elders, called *Upas* who were appointed by him. This council discussed all matters affecting the village and also decided all disputes.

In addition to other privileges enjoyed, the Upas were entitled to priority in the choice of land for Jhum cultivation and were also exempted from impressment for labour to which the Mizos were liable during British regime.

Besides the Upas, the chief generally appointed the following village officials :—

(i) The Tlangau (the village crier) who announced the orders of the chief in a loud voice in the morning or in the evening when everybody was indoors. He received as his remuneration a basket (kho) of paddy from each house every year.

(ii) The Thirdeng (village blacksmith) whose duty was to make and repair tools such as hoes, daos, axes and sickles and he received three kerosene tinfuls of paddy from each household. Every household had to pay this fee whether the blacksmith was engaged or not.

(iii) The *puithiam* (the village priest) also received a basketful of paddy from each household for whom he performed the sacrifices. The chief had a separate personal priest known as *Sadawt*.

(iv) The *Ramhuals*, though not officials, were important people in a village who were allowed the first choice of Jhum land for a year on payment of a comparatively larger quantity of paddy as tribute to the chief than the quantity fixed by custom for the rest. In the past the chiefs appointed *Zalens* who were also entitled to the choice of Jhum land even in preference to the *Ramhuals*. The *Zalens* were usually near relatives of the chief and they were not required to pay any paddy to chief, but in times of need, the chief had free access to their granaries.

The village chief was by custom and tradition entitled to *buhchhun*, that is, a paddy contribution from each household, approximately 40 kilos, free construction of his house which was generally much bigger than the house of the commoners and the right fore-leg of every wild animal shot by any of his villagers which was called *Sachhiah*.

A chief could turn out from his village anyone who incurred his displeasure or whomsoever he considered undesirable. A villager also had the right to migrate to another village if the chief of the latter village agreed.

LIFE STYLE—THE PAWIS

The Lushai Hills of greater Assam is the home of several peoples with distinctive cultural heritage, most of them being Mongoloid and speak languages that belong to the Tibeto-Burman family.

The Pawis occupy the area of South-Lushai Hills sub-division of the Lushai Hills. The mighty Kolodyne river flowing from the east to west separates the Pawis from the Lushais. There are the Chin Hills to the south and east, and the Lakher-land to the west. Although most of the Pawi villages are within this area, there are villages predominantly inhabited by Pawis under Lushai or Fanai chiefs outside this area.

Although the Lushais and Pawis are neighbours, they speak two different tongues. Lushai, however is widely known and serves as the *lingua franca.* The women folk with their innate conservatism, call it *Mipatawng* or languages of the menfolk.

The Pawis and the Chins are the same people and in the stream of migrations that flowed through Burma the Pawis got deflected towards the Lushai Hills. The legends and folklore indicate that in the past the relationship between the Pawis and the Lushais was far from being cordial. The Lushais used to call the Pawi country *ral ram* or enemy country and the folklore speaks of Lushai damsels being carried off by the Pawis. The Fanais, who live between the Pawi and the Lushai country earned their reputation as diplomats, as they were often asked to negotiate settlements between the Pawis and the Lushais.

On the other hand, the Pawis and the Lakhers got on very well together and intermarriage, though not common, has been quite frequent. This was mainly because the Pawis and Lakhers used to join hands in their expeditions in the South Lushai Hills.

The first Lushai expedition was launched in 1869 and in 1871 the Lushai country was penetrated from Cachar and Chittagong. These expeditions did not touch the country beyond the Kolodyne. The Shendus continued their raids, particularly in Chittagong Hill Tracts, in the country side near Demagiri. Matters came to ahead in 1881 when Lieut. John Stewart, who was engaged in survey, was killed by Hausata who was Chin. This led to the Chin-Lushai expedition of 1888-89, as a result of which the Chin and the Lushai Hills came gradually under the sway of the British Raj.

In 1891, the Pawi chief, *Zakhupa*, made an attempt on the life of Mr. Murray, the political officer at Lungleh, and a punitive expedition was sent to deal with him. Gradually the Pawi and the Lakher country came within the orbit of British administration. To deal with the Pawis, the British established military outposts at Lungleh, the sub-divisional headquarters, Darzo and later at Tuipang.

Thereafter, acculturation proceeded and the main instruments in this process were the Lushai interpreters who brought in the Lushai language and even contributed to the adaptation of some of the Pawi customs on Lushai lines. Nevertheless, the Pawis continued to have social relationship with the Chins of Burma.

The pivot of the Pawis social organisation is the village. The chief with the elders has been maintaining law and order and dispensing justice according to custom.

The principal occupation is agriculture by shifting cultivation. As they prefer maize and millets, the Pawis do not grow much rice. For their wearing apparel, they still depend on their own type of handloom. On the festive occasions they wear silk, which is hand-woven from the yarn obtained from Burma. The loin cloth and wrapper are still commonly used by men and they still wear long hair in bun above the forehead. The Lushai call the Chin *Pawis* for this particular hair style. It is interesting to note that the Lushais call the Sikhs, with their long hair, *Vai-Pawis* or foreign Pawis.

The dress of the womenfolk is beautiful. Normally a woman wears two pieces of cloth, one around her like a skirt and the other on the top of it, which comes down up to the knees. Often they wear a choli type of blouse and in addition a chaddar which gets more elaborate and expensive according to social status. The womenfolk still wears a lot of bead-oranaments around their neck, arms, ears and ankles. A Pawi woman still wear a metal girdle on her hips, which produces a sound when the wearer walks. The length of hair pins often indicates the social status of a woman, and coiffure is more elaborate than that of the Lushais. They are still picturesque and living as they still do in their mountain fastness, they have avoided the Procrustean influence of the west. In short, they are not as sophisticated as their neighbours in the North.

Inheritance : Amongst the Pawis the eldest son inherits the paternal property, and this rule is applicable in the case of succession to chieftainship as well. Pawi young men were not subjected to the discipline of the young man's house, which was the rule amongst the Lushais. The standard of 'Good Form' imposed by the Lushai code of chivalry has been absent amongst the Pawis. The hold of the chief has been rather weak. The people had a tendency to be litigious and rake up old feuds.

The Pawis trace their origin to a mythical tiger. The dance associated with the head of a tiger is really picturesque and a lot of religious significance is attached to it. The Pawis are great dancers and unlike the Lushais both men and women take part in some dances, the most notable being *khelkhawn.*

The chiefs and their elders are free to govern the villages according to customs and tradition of their own.

Education had spread rather slowly amongst the Pawis, but there was a popular demand for association in the administration of the village. This has found fitting recognition in the Sixth Schedule of the Constitution. The Regional Council, a self-governing organisation which gives them a considerable amount of autonomy in the sphere of village administration in all its aspects, was inaugurated in 1953. This council is composed of twelve members from amongst the Pawis, Lakhers and a few other tribes and comprises of the areas inhabited by them in the South Lushai Hills.

Skirting round the blue mountains, with an elevation of about 7000 ft. which is the highest in the area, Pawi-land is salubrious in winter and inaccessible in the rains. Blue Mountain still nurtures wild goats and has the loveliest collection of wild orchids. Pawi-land is indeed a fine country for a fine people.

LIFE STYLE—THE LAKHERS

The Maras or the Lakhers, as the Lushais call them, inhabit the southern tip of the Lungleh sub-division of the Lushai Hills, now known as the Mizoram. Most of the Lakher villages are enclosed by the bend of the Kolodyne river which debouches from the hills near Haka in Chin Hills and flowing in a southerly direction, passes through the southern tip of the Lungleh sub-division and flows down to the Bay of Bengal near Akyab. The Lakhers are interspersed both in the Lungleh sub-division as well as in the Haka sub-division of Burma.

The Lakhers, says Dr. Hutton "must be classed, at any rate in so far as their language and material culture are concerned, with the Kuki tribes who migrated in historic times down the value of the Chindwin from its sources to the Bay of Bengal, continuously throwing off branches of their race westward into the hills, while the vanguard, having turned north again up the same range, are still involved in a slow drift back like their own fabled river, which runs down to a rock in the ocean and thence flows upwards to its source. The Lakhers include in their composition, more than their immediate neighbours, of the races that preceded them, of which the Indonesian race, everywhere submerged by the Mongolian flood, appears to have been one, while Bodo, Mon-khmer and Melanesian elements seem to be definitely traceable. He goes on to say, "There is much, however, to suggest that underneath has externally Kuki culture, the Lakher is something of a Naga at heart. His attachment to his village site and to the graves of his ancestors is essentially Naga, as distinct from the migratory habits of Kuki tribes. His want of discipline, as contrasted with the Lushai, is again Naga, as contrasted with Kuki. . . . Place-names, as by the Naga generally (the sema largely excepted) are taken by the Lakher from natural features, instead of from the traditional sites of former villages. The *Bongchhi*, the sacred ficus, is obviously closely associated with the external souls of the village and affords a close parallel to the Lotha *mingethung*...... The absence of any institution corresponding to the Lushei *tuai*-men who wear women's clothes and follow women's pursuits—also suggests that the Malay elements present in the Lushai may be weaker in the Lakher, while the use of conch-shell ornaments with patterns of circle and dots in black is clearly a link with the Angami and with other Nagas, Konyak in particular.

Hutton, however mentions certain features of Lakher culture which are neither Kuki nor Naga but are in contrast to both. First of all, the Lakher practice of reaping paddy by pulling up rice by the roots is peculiar. The Lakher also exclude women from taking part in sacrifices on account of the possibility of their menstrual uncleanliness.

In physical characteristics, the Lakher men are well-built and have good physique. The women are taller than the Lushai and Kuki women and rather slender. They have a light brown complexion and are darker than the Lushais. They have a broad nose, high cheek-bones and Mongoloid eyes. Like several other hill tribes, they age prematurely and women, particularly after marriage, become rather sloppy in their looks.

Unlike many other hill tribes of north-eastern India, men always wear *Pagri* (Turban). The Lakhers are very proud of their hair and most of them tie it up in a knot on the top of the head. A boy's hair is normally cut at the age of nine and afterwards it is not allowed to be cut at all. The *Pagri* are wrapped on the head more or less in the Sikh style and usually a hairpin is run through the hair-knot.

Women wear far more clothes than men. They cover their lower limbs with a dark blue petticoat, the lower part of which is embroidered with silk. On the top of this, they wear a skirt which is shorter than the petticoat and displays the embroidered end of the petticoat.

Women are fond of using *Cowries* as well as conch-shell ornaments. They also wear metal belts around the waist and over the buttocks. The quality of the belt indicates the wealth of the wearer. They also wear a sleeveless jacket and a silk top garment to cover the body. In fine, Lakher women are very fond of garments and use various kinds of beads to embellish their figure.

Administration : The unit of administration in Lakher society was a village. The village community consisted of the chief, the patricians and the commoners, the village elders and the village officials. In matters of marriage, birth, death and certain sacrifices of private nature, clan relationship took a predominant place. In Lakher society chieftain families and patricians had certain privileges which were not enjoyed by the common run of people.

The elders or the *Machas*, were selected by the chief to administer his village. Normally, they belonged to the clans of the nobles, but Plebeians of outstanding ability were also often chosen as elders. The elders received a share of money paid by a loser in a case and a share of any animal killed (known as Sochhiah in Lushai). They were also exempted from doing certain duties which the common run of people in the village were obliged to do.

The chief had full control over his village and any disobedience was punished by expulsion from the village. The villagers were obliged to perform certain duties for the chief personally and the entire village generally. In Lakher Society, the unit of the village was the household and not the individual. The normal obligation to the chief were the repair of his house, carrying his load while going on a journey and a share of the crop harvested by each family. He was also entitled to get meat-dues and other dues which were enjoined by custom.

The chief dispensed justice with the help of his court of elders. His decision was final. There were very few cases where the decisions of the chiefs and his elders was not obeyed implicity.

The Lakhers used to live mainly by agriculture. The only implements they use for the purpose are a dao and an axe. All crops are grown in Jhum. Their agricultural year previously used to begin in December when the chief and the elder decided which particulars sites would be selected for the purpose of Jhum. Thereafter, the lots were divided amongst the people who cultivated the plots according to the distribution made by the chief. The main crops are rice, millets, maize, tobacco, ginger, beans and arum (Kochu). The Lakher method of harvesting paddy is rather peculiar. The paddy is pulled up by the roots and not cut by a sickle and the plants are tied up in bundles and left for a few days to dry. Thereafter the usual process of beating follows. The paddy is stored in a granary and remains there to be collected according to need from time to time.

The Lakhers used to get their fish from the Kolodyne river and rivulets flowing into the Kolodyne. They trapped animals for meat. Being quite a self-sufficient community, they devote a lot of time to making baskets with bamboo-cane and in this art they have acquired considerable proficieney. Surprisingly enough, wicker-work was taken up by men rather than women. On the other hand, weaving and dyeing are done entirely by women. They consume a lot of tobacco, practically all Lakhers, both men and women, being heavy smokers.

Customs : Lakher women enjoy absolute freedom and have equality of status with men. It is indeed a tribute to Lakher Society that prostitution have never existed amongst them. There were occasional aberrations but the Lakher, in his own subtle way, had a answer to this problem. Unlike the Lushais, the Lakhers did not have any ***Zawlbuk*** or the bachelor's house, where the young men of marriageable age used to sleep. A teenager did not sleep in his parent's house but in the house of the girl whom he happened to be courting at the moment, pre-marital relationship between young boys and girls not being discouraged.

The following Lakher song expresses the attitude of a Lakher teenager to his exploits :

> "On each side of me you two lovely
> sisters are sitting,
> I love you both, but if I tell you
> not to get married, but
> to wait,
> I shall be laughed at."

Marriage

Marriage price amongst the Lakhers is quite high and this works as a deterrent to easy divorce and fortifies the position of the wife. Marriages used to be arranged by choice or by arrangement between two families. Bride-price was shared by a long-line of relations and even aunts. Sharing of bride-price is so complicated that litigations regarding such claims continue more or less endlessly and are never finally settled. Adultery is rare and so are bastards.

Inheritance : Inheritance amongst the Lakhers is patrilineal. The eldest son takes all the property and also takes the responsibility for his father's debts and death ceremony. Women cannot inherit and if a man dies without a son, his brother inherits his property. Remarriage of widows is quite common if the women is young. After remarriage a widow lives with the husband but the children have a choice to live either with her or with their paternal uncle.

Amongst the Lakhers there was a custom of child-marriage which was entirely unknown amongst the Lushais. There were cases where the parents of two children married them at an early age before they attained puberty. There were also cases where a young man of marriageable age married a girl child or a girl who had attained puberty married a boy much younger than herself and who had not attained puberty. There had not been cases where a child after attainment of puberty, had taken dislike to his or her spouse and in such cases separation was allowed on return of the bride price.

Although after the establishment of Lakher Mission at Serkawr, many Lakhers were converted to Christianity, the impact of new religion on the Lakher Society is not great. Even as far back as 1947, most of the Lakhers followed their old religion. The recognised *khazangpa* as the creator of the world and protector and preserver of the Lakhers. They also believed in the spirits of the mountains and the hills and the woods. The method of the propitiation of *khazangpa* and these spirits was through sacrifices. The most important sacrifice was the propitiation of *khazangpa* who according to them, possessed human attributes inasmuch as he had a wife, a child and partook of food and beer like human beings. The belief was that *khazangpa* dealt with an individual according to the work he had done and the manner in which he had behaved with his other fellow beings.

The Lakhers also believe in a soul who, according to them, is invisible but resembled his body and size. Illness and bad luck are explained as wrought by *khazangpa* or the spirit and sacrifices are prescribed as remedies. Religious and social behaviour is modelled by *ana*, i.e. 'what is forbidden'. This was the key word on the life and behaviour of the Lakhers and as Parry has mentioned, "The *anas* are really the Lakher equivalent to the Ten Commandments and though to the western minds many of the prohibitions may appear absurd, some of them are of undoubted social value and are no more illogical than most of our superstitions. Thus it is *ana* to shift the boundary of another man's field, it is *ana* to throw weeds into another's field, it is *ana* to steel eggs, it is *ana* for a women to give birth to a child in another person's house and all these prohibitions and many others a sound, as they prevent people from causing inconvenience to others." There is a belief in the existence of a paradise, but according to them, a soul has to stay in a no-man's land called *Athiki* for a long time before he goes to paradise. There is also a belief in another land and they call it *Sawvawkhi*. There is a strong belief amongst the Lakhers that the spirits of the children are reborn to the same parents.

The Lakhers had thus a national system of religion and social organisations to suit their needs. After 1947, District Councils were established for the Lushai Hills. Chieftainship has been abolished and education on modern lines is being imparted in the schools. Gradually the Lakhers are coming into the main stream of Indian nationhood.

CHAPTER VIII

A PORTRAIT OF NAGALAND

Population : Nagaland is one of the smallest States of the Union of India, occupying the 21st position in regard to population. The total population of Nagaland, according to 1981 census was 7,74,930.

The district is the main administrative unit throughout India. During the 1981 census there were seven districts.

According to 1981, population in the seven districts were as follows :—

No.	*District*	*Area (sq. km.)*	*Population*
1.	Kohima	4041	2,50,105
2.	Mokokchung	1615	1,04,193
3.	Mon	1786	78,938
4.	Phek	2026	70,618
5.	Tuensang	4228	1,52,332
6.	Wokha	1628	57,583
7.	Zunheboto	1255	61,161

If the geographical location of a place is more favourable, then the potentiality to sustain a heavy population increases.

There are two natural processes which go on unassumingly over the years, so that population changes continuously—Birth and death. There is one more factor which affects population, it is migration. A population decreases by the number which migrates outside and increases to the extent of persons migrating into it. The density of population per square kilometre is only 47 persons.

Housing : The housing facility in Nagaland is comparatively very poor. In villages people use thatch and palm leaf (takopat) roofs and most of the structures are of bamboo and wood only. While constructing a house ropes of creepers, climbers, bamboo, split, bark etc. are used. Walls are generally of bamboo mat. Majority of houses have only one room, having one fire place for cooking purposes and a few cots inside the same room to sleep. In these houses only the wife and the husband with their minor children sleep at night because all the grown up children sleep at night dormitories. In all the villages there are male and female youth dormitories where boys and girls sleep at night until they reach the marriageable age. The moment a boy attains marriageable age, he constructs a new house for his family in the village. Thus every year, the number of houses in a village goes on increasing.

In most of the villages, the church building are very prominent. By and large, the church building is also the largest building in the village. Dimapur is the only town in the state capable of having pucca buildings in view of easy communications and availability of building material.

As discussed earlier, most of the Naga houses in a village are one-roomed. They are self contained, having an average length of 20 ft. and a breadth of 15 ft.

Social norms : In Naga Society, the village is the main pivot on which the activities of each individual revolve according to social norms and tradition of his village. All aspects pertaining to security, climate, water supply fertility of soil, availability of cultivable land and woodland were taken into account before selecting a village site.

Village founders had to perform rituals sacrificing animals and observing genna to establish the village, giving it a suitable and acceptable name. Hence a Naga has great sentimental attachment for his village even if he is settled in an urban area. It is the place where all his kinsmen, clan folk are closely knit in ascending order. It is here where human values are realised through the success or failure of individual. Nearly 90 per cent of Nagaland population live in the villages.

Naga Village : A Naga village is usually well defined and demarcated by natural features based on customs and traditions. A village boundary with its neighbouring village, is marked either by natural ridges or rivers. The village would contain village reserved land, wood land and sufficient jhum land as the village practise shifting cultivation.

Establishment of new village is to be done through permission of some of the old villages so that the new village shall be able to acquire rights over the land surrounding the new villages.

Owing to growth of population in the villages, the jhum land at the disposal of the people could not accommodate the excess population and therefore, the surplus population moves to a new place where jhum land is available. Of late, new villages are situated at lower altitudes. In the past they were situated on top of hillocks.

Education : The history of education of Nagaland is hardly a century old. Prior to independence there were only two private high schools, two government middle english schools and about a hundred primary schools. Christian missionaries were often the pioneers in setting up schools in different parts of Nagaland. The state has made tremendous progress in education in the past independence years, specially after Nagaland had been made a full-fledged state. Now there are 52 high schools, 7 colleges, 193 middle schools, 973 primary schools and a polytechnic. Besides there are basic training school and adult literacy centres. The Mokokchung is considered to be the most literate district followed by Kohima and Tuensang.

Language : India has a variety of languages of which quite a few still remain to be properly studied and classified.

According to the 1981 census, there are 16 tribes in Nagaland and each is having a local language or mother tongue of its own. None of these is being used as a state language. There is speech form known as 'Nagamese', composed mainly of broken Assamese, Bengali, Hindi and Nepali. This peculiar speech is used as a common language next to English. Naga local language use Roman script. The Angami and the Ao local language have now been developed to an extent that students appearing for the High School Leaving Certificate examination can also offer these two languages as vernacular subjects.

Speakers of tribal language form smaller proportions in urban areas than in rural areas.

Religion : Prior to 1872 Nagaland was a land of animism. Even now a number of Nagas are following this religion. They perform sacrifice by killing animals like the pigs, fowls and dogs to propitiate spirits, offer their prayers to the moon and sun and the spirits of the village. Their aim is to receive blessings from deities and spirits for a bumper harvest, for health and happiness in this world and beyond.

The 1981 census showed that Nagaland was the only state in the country where the Christian population was more than 50 per cent.

One feature in Nagaland is that the followers of tribal religions come next to the Christians.

Tribal Population : The total tribal population of Nagaland according to 1981 census was 650885. There are no Scheduled Castes in Nagaland. Almost the bulk of the tribal population live in rural areas.

If we study the general characteristics of the tribal in India, we find that they prefer to live in rural areas. But if we study the percentage distribution of scheduled tribes in rural and urban areas in Nagaland, we will find that the tribal occupy a noticeable position in urban areas also, indicating an accelerated modernization.

The table shows the distribution of rural and urban population in three districts of Nagaland (according to 1971 census).

Percentage

	Total	*Rural*	*Urban*
1. Kohima	80.00	91.44	37.72
2. Mokokchung	91.30	96.30	32.45
3. Tuensang	94.70	94.70	47.98

Promoting Education : There are a number of difficulties in way of promoting education among these classes. One major factor for their not sending grown up boys and girls to a school is essentially economic. It entails dislocation of the traditional pattern of division of labour in the family. That is why in almost all the tribes in India, their percentage of literacy is found lagging behind.

As Nagaland is more or less a tribal state, the gap between the percentages of literacy of the state's population and that of its tribal population is not so wide. The literacy rate of the state stands at 27.40 per cent to our country's rate at 29.45 per cent. The percentage of literacy among the Scheduled Tribes in Nagaland is 24.01 as against 6.94 for all India. It may, therefore, be concluded that unlike other states in our country the growing literacy rate among tribals of Nagaland is an encouraging sign.

Prior to the formation of a separate state, Nagaland was a district in Assam known as Naga Hills and the present Tuensang district was a part of the then NEFA (Arunachal Pradesh).

In the 1971 Census, the Scheduled Tribes as listed in the Constitution (Nagaland) Scheduled Tribes order, 1970, have been adopted which are as follows :—

(1) Naga
(2) Kuki
(3) Kachari
(4) Mikir
(5) Garo

In the major head Naga covers the sixteen tribes as the Naga Scheduled Tribes. They are :—

(1) Angami
(2) Ao
(3) Chakhesang
(4) Chang
(5) Chirr
(6) Konyak
(7) Kheimnungan
(8) Lotha
(9) Makware
(10) Phom
(11) Rengma
(12) Sangtam
(13) Sema
(14) Tikhir

(15) Yimchungre
(16) Zeliang

Economic Activities : In Nagaland, males and females occupy the same status in society without any discrimination and there is no reason to keep the women folk hidden in huts.

The demographic situation is one of the most important factors on which the economic activity of the people depends.

Among the Indian States, Nagaland has the highest percentage of workers to the state's total population having 50.75 per cent. But we cannot say that we are economically advance. The rise in the percentage of workers depends on the way of living of the people and the social customs of the tribal people. Hence rate of participation in work depends on many factors. Like natural resources of the state, kinds of occupations available, whether labour intensive or not and the degree of unemployment and under-employment prevailing in the state.

Nagaland being a tribal state and the mainstay of the people being cultivation, both the sexes work equally in their respective Khet (field). Besides that there is no division of labour as the question of specialization in a particular trade does not arise due to absence of industries, mining and quarrying or caste or tribal system affecting it.

A tribal economy cannot support a large number of dependents. Therefore the participation rate in the working force is very high in tribal societies. Unlike other states in India, in Nagaland ownership of land for cultivation lies with the people and the government does not settle land for such purposes. All the cultivators are concentrated in rural areas where both males and females work together equally. However, in urban areas population is concentrated for other services such as office employees, teachers and colleges, employees in shops, skilled labourers etc. works. Therefore, the housewives in the towns cannot participate in cultivation work as in the case in rural areas.

Nagaland being a tribal state, cultivators constitute 77.58 per cent of the total working population. Rearing of domesticated animal, forestry, fishing, hunting, plantation and orchards are some of the allied activities.

Mining and quarrying are little known to the Nagas. It reflects the relative scarcity of known deposits of profitable minerals as well as the insufficiency of organised enterprise. Borjan is the only coal mine in Nagaland, in Tuensang district.

Unfortunately Nagaland has very little flat land where permanent terrace and wet rice cultivation is possible. The bulk of cultivators has to depend on shifting cultivation in which so much waste of labour starting from clearing and cutting jungle or woodland till harvest is involved. No double cropping is possible and such cleared Jhum land has to be abandoned after two years' cultivation. From this fact, it is clear that the lot of cultivators are not available.

Conclusion : Nagaland is situated on the north-eastern corner of our country, India. Owing to its centuries old isolation from the mainstream of civilization coupled with inaccessibility on account of hilly terrain, the tribal people lived for generations together, fighting among themselves for the sole objective of survival on solidly founded villages. Even now Nagaland is a state of villages. Every village is a democratic republic where custom and tradition reign supreme. The entire state is rugged and rocky and agricultural potential is not high. The density of population is 47 persons per sq. km. Even then there is not sufficient land for cultivation because shifting cultivation is the chief means of livelihood for the people of the state. Unless cultivators take to permanent cultivation the state economy will not improve.

LIFE STYLE—THE NAGAS (NAGALAND)

The Nagas are the most singular race of Nagaland. They are of different classes, even though they have many characteristics in common. There are the Angami Nagas, the Ao Nagas, the Lhotas, the Regmas, Semas, the Nagas of the North-Eastern hills, and those of Cachar and Manipur, to mention only a few. The tribes are constantly forming new groups and associations, like the Chakhesangs, Zeliangs, Shamnyu-yungmangs and others. Thus the Nagas have quite a number of clans and affiliations.

The origin of the word 'Naga' is interpreted in different ways. One belief is that it is derived from the Sanskrit word 'naga' 'nagna' meaning 'naked', for the reason that the Nagas were comparatively ill-clad. It could also be from the vernacular 'nag' which means a mountain. Or it may be the corrupted form of 'log' meaning 'people'. In fact some Naga tribes use the word 'nok' for people, which closely resembles the Hindi word 'log'.

The Nagas are a kind of Indo-Mongoloids whose presence was noted as early as the 10th century before Christ, at the period of the Vedas. They were known as 'Kirata' or non-Aryans, and were described in ancient Sanskrit literature as subsisting on the flesh of the animals they hunted, roots and fruits of the forest, a warlike race, dressed in skins, and wielding formidable weapons. They are described as 'golden hued' in contrast to the dark complexioned people of the plains. It is also mentioned that they were rich, having exploited the plentiful minerals available in the hill regions and the forest produce of the mountain-sides. They were also expert weavers, a trait which exists amongst the race even now. It is mentioned in the Mahabharata that the great god Shiva took the form of a Kirata, with his consort Uma in the guise of a Kirata woman, and went in this form to meet the warrior Arjuna. Thus it is evident that the Nagas are not an alien race, but are a branch of the rich and varied tribes of India.

Nagaland is now a full fledge state. These are administered from Kohima. The southern base is Manipur, with Burma on the east, Arunachal Pradesh to the north, and the Assam valley on the west side. The Naga country is covered largely with hill ranges having many spurs and ridges, and occasional gentle slopes. The height varies from four thousand to about ten thousand feet above sea level. The population is concentrated on the higher hills. Rainfall varies from 70 to 100 inches in the year. Numerous rivers and streams flow through Nagaland, but there is a marked absence of lakes and tanks.

Much of the forest has been cut down to make way for cultivation, and most of the wild game has already been exploited. Thus there are few wild animals left, like elephants, tigers, leopards and so forth. The Indian hornbill bird is greatly prized by the Naga inhabitants. It is used for decoration, and magic is also associated with it. The Naga State has a population of 6.18 lakhs and an area of 16,527 sq. kms. according to the 1981 census.

The traditional belief is that the Naga tribes migrated from the south, except in the case of the Kacha Nagas whose ancestors are said to have come from the mountains known as Japvo. There exists an isolating tendency amongst the race. One can almost categorise the type of Naga by a mere study of facial characteristics. In some villages the men are of tall stature, while others are marked out by the beauty of their women. Some are even distinguished by peculiar traits of character. For example, the villages of Kidima and Nerharma abound in men who are fond of litigation, and Tofima has the distinction of possessing a large number of liars !

Various tales are told about the origin of the Nagas. The Angamis, Lhotas, and Semas are supposed to be descended from four brothers, and distinguished by the amount of clothing that they were authorised to wear. The eldest of these brothers was gentle and virtuous and so his parents gave him a picturesque dress to wear. The Angamis are his descendants. The second brother was troublesome and so he was given scantier clothing. He was the ancestor of the Aos. The third brother, from whom the Lhotas are said to have been descended, was much alike the, second in conduct, and so he was clothed in much the same manner. The youngest brother, the ancestor of the Semas, was markedly wicked. When his parents sent him to scare away the birds from the field, he neglected his task and plucked off all the pumpkins. Fed up with his naughtiness, his parents tied a piece of cloth round his waist, and leaving him just like that, turned him out.

It is also said that the Naga tribes were all descended from one father, but he was the son of a second wife. The children of the first wife were given proper clothes, but the child of the second wife could get only a small piece of cloth which was sufficient only to wrap around the waist, and so his descendants still wear the kilt.

Yet another story of the origin of the Naga tribes is as follows : In the village of Kezakenoma there lived an old couple who had three sons. The sons used to take loads of paddy to spread out to dry on a huge stone. The heaps of paddy would multiply when laid on the stone due to the influence of a spirit living in it. One day the sons quarrelled among them selves about their precedence in spreading loads of paddy on the stone, and fearing that there would be bloodshed, their parents broke some eggs on the stone, laid firewood on it, and set it afire. One being heated, the stone suddenly burst with a sound like thunder, and the spirit inhabiting it went up to heaven in a cloud of smoke. The three sons thereupon separated, and became the ancestors of the Angamis, Lhotas and Semas. It is said that the great stone, cracked when its spirit flew away, still exists opposite the house of the original founder of the village.

There are several legends concerning the origin of the Nagas of Manipur. According to the Tangkhul legend, one day a sow was tracked down a valley by the younger of two brothers. The sow littered by the banks of the Iril river, and the young man stayed behind to look after her. He found the country so fascinating that he decided to stay there. He would send the produce of the plain country, to his brother whom he had left behind in the hills, and get presents in turn from the latter. After some time the younger brother stopped sending gifts, which so enraged his elder brother, that he came down and forcefully obtained them. Subsequently, perhaps based on his legend, a curious custom came into existence according to which the Tangkhuls would swoop down on the day of the Naga sports and loot the women vendors, which made the Manipuris prohibit their women from frequenting the market.

Another legend concerns the Marring Nagas. It is said that they left the valley because of the heat and the mosquitoes taking fire with them. The fire was extinguished when they reached a ridge between Hundung and Ukrul, but to make up for it the deity taught them to get fire from stone. The sacred stone, maibung stands there till this day.

A legend concerning the Tangkhuls is given by themselves as follows : Some of the Tangkhuls were trapped in a cave, from which they emerged one by one. But a large tiger, who emerged. Thereupon they took recourse to a stratagem. They dressed up an effigy to make it appear as a live man, and left it outside to distract the tiger's attention. Having done so they rushed out together, and the tiger was so greatly baffled by seeing the crowd, that he fled. To mark the occasion they set up a large stone on the hill-top, which is there to this day.

A story which features the Nagas, the Kukis and the Manipuris, is about a jumping contest held between the representatives of the three tribes. The Kuki leapt from the top of one range to the crest of another. The Naga, too, jumped across, but his foot slipped and touched the water of the stream. The Manipuri tumbled right into the river. For this reason the Naga bathes only now and then, the Kuki scrupulously avoids it, and the Manipuri, because of his dropping headlong into the river, is rather fond of bathing.

A legend about the origin of the Marams is also interesting. A flood came and destroyed everyone except a couple of the name of Medungasi and Simoting. The couple wondered if they should get married, but since there was no one to advise them, they went out into the forest. Here a god appeared to the man and told him that they could marry but their descendants were forbidden to eat the flesh of the pig. Therefore to this day the Marams do not eat pork.

The origin of the Marring Nagas is also curious. It is said that fourteen of them, seven men and seven women, emerged from the earth. At that time the men and the women wore the same clothes (the dhoti). But in order to make a distinction, the men tied up their hair into a knot in front, and the women behind. The women lengthened their waist-cloth while the men shortened their. Not finding themselves comfortable in the plains they migrated into the hills, where they are living to this day. Another legend about the Marrings is that while they emerged from a cave, horrible beast would devour them. The beast, however was slain by a deity with two horns, and they could get out safely out of the cave.

A legend concerns the origin of the Vuites, another Naga clan. One day the head of the Thadous clan of the name of Asian Ningthon found two eggs in a basket. He ate one and found it bitter. The other he put aside, so that it may become mature and nice to eat. From this egg, however, there emerged a lad who became chief of the Vuite clan.

Though constantly at war among themselves, the Nagas have a certain unity also. They intermarry only among their own clan, and not among tribes other than the Naga community. Though differing in build and complexion, they have common characteristics like a coarse and savage face, and a dull timid disposition. In the use of weapons, too, they have a similarity, for they all use only javelins and spears.

The Angami Naga is a particularly lithe and agile person. He is capable of a great deal of hard work and endurance, marches long distances and carries heavy loads. He has a curious way of bathing. The water from some stream is carried in a hollow bamboo, and the soap is made by pounding into pulp the fibrous stalk of a creeper which gives a lather like ordinary soap. A practice which has a smack of modernity is the wearing of wigs. The wigs were not worn by women, however, but by old men whose hair had greyed ! They were made of bear's hair, with human hair hanging at the back.

The Angamis were very fond of wearing something as an ear-ornament. This was not necessarily a silver or gold ear-ring, but anything which took their fancy, like plugs of black wool, pieces of red paper or cloth, and even the cog-wheel of a watch !

The men also wore cowries in rows of three or four. Originally these signified exploits in war, but gradually they became emblems of love, and the fourth line of cowries was worn by a man who had an intrigue with a married woman or with two girls of the same name, with two daughters of one father, or with a mother and her daughter at one and the same time !

The Nagas eat mostly rice and meat, preferring beef and pork. Though they have now started taking tea, and milk which was tabooed sometime ago, their favourite drink is rice beer of which they consume large quantities.

A word must be said about head-hunting. According to the Nagas themselves they got into this practice by seeing an ant and a lizard fight over a berry which a bird had dropped. The ant cut off the lizard's head ! and thus provided the impetus to take heads. It is believed that the soul and its receptacle has its place in the head, so to bring home a head means capturing a great deal of spiritual power. Often it is the way to win the heart and hand of some lovely damsel in the tribe. Indeed at one time a Naga who had not won a head, could not get a decent girl in marriage. All these factors led to the Naga cult of head hunting. So much was the desire for heads that they were taken most cruelly and treacherously. A man would hide near a tank, and suddenly pounce upon and kill any woman or child who came to draw water. Or a group of Nagas would swoop down upon a village, particularly when the men were out in the field, and behead as many old persons, women, and children as they could, and be off before the men of the village returned. Davis records that when some men of Mozema went to Kohima, they killed one man, five women, and twenty young children, for their heads, and one of the on-lookers told him 'that he never saw such a fine sport, for it was just like killing fowls'. Fortunately all this is past history, and the last recorded case of head-hunting was in 1958.

Kutcha Nagas

The tribe we call Kutcha Nagas, very much resemble the Angamis, though of inferior physique. They are closely allied to the Nagas in Manipur, as well as to the Angamis and probably were pushed in front of the latter from the Northern North-East, as the Kukis were forced in by the pressure of the stronger tribes to their south. They have always been less warlike than their powerful neighbours, though they could be troublesome at times.

Angami Nagas

A strong built, hardy, active race, the men averaging 5 feet 8 inches to 6 feet in height, and the women tall in proportion. In colour they vary from a rich brown to a yellowish or light brown. They have a manly independent bearing, and are bred up to war from their earliest years. While the Kukis are monarchists, the Nagas are republicans, and their Peumahs, or chiefs are elected, and though they often have great influence, they are in theory, only primus inter pares, and are liable at any time to be displaced. Practically they often remain in office for years, and are greatly respected.

Their dress is a short kilt of black cotton cloth, ornamented, in the case of warriors, with rows of cowrie shells. They have handsome clothes of dark blue and yellow thrown over their shoulders in cold weather. Their arms are spears and heavy, short swords, called by Assamese name of *Dao* ; helmets and shields of wicker work and sometimes clothed with skins of tigers or bears. They also have tails of wood decorated with goats, hair dyed red. The war spears are plain ; the ornamental ones are covered with goats hair dyed red, and are sometimes used in battle. Their drill is of a most complicated style and requires much practice. An Angami in full war paint is a very formidable-looking person. They are divided into many clans. Several clans often inhabit one village, and if frequently happened that two clans thus situated were at deadly feud with each other.

No Angami could assume the "Toga virilis" until he had slain an enemy. To kill a baby in arms, or a woman, was accounted a greater feat than killing a man. Every Naga who was able to murder an enemy did so, and received great commendation for it by all his friends.

The Angamis when on friendly terms are an agreeable people to deal with, polite, courteous and hospitable.

Their houses are large substantial structures built of wood and bamboo thatched with grass, and the eaves come low down. Houses with any pretensions always have verandahs. Besides the house, there are granaries, often at a distance for fear of fine. The Angamis bury their dead in and about their villages, and strongly object to the graves being disturbed.

The Angamis have a vague indefinite belief in a supreme being, but look on him as too great and good to injure them. They believe themselves also to be subject to the influence of evil spirits, whom it is their constant endeavour to appease by sacrifices. Every misfortune is ascribed to evil spirits, and much money is spent on appeasing them by offering fowls.

The Naga women are not handsome but very pleasant looking, and many of the girls are pretty. They do not marry till they are nearly or quite grown up. Divorce can be easily obtained by equal division of goods.

The Nagas are skilful iron-workers and turn out very handsome spears. Their women weave substantial and pretty coloured clothes, and every man knows enough of rough carpentering to enable him to build his house and make pestles and mortars for husking rice. They make rough pottery, but without the potter's wheel.

According to Konyak custom, a person in hostile country carried a bit of egg-shell to ward off the dangerous emanations of enemies, and to throw eggs into a burning house to stop the fire from spreading.

The stones are used in building the "morungs" (bachelor's house), and the erect stones set up in front of one of them are painted in bands of reddish colour alternating with equal bands of grey stone. Red and black or black and white bands of equal breadth is a favourite pattern among Konyaks. The wooden 'drums' in kongan, for instance, are painted thus. Other morungs had unpainted stones, one or two, erect with flat ones round them to receive the heads of newly decapitated enemies, a custom apparently followed by the Dusun of Borneo likewise.

The trophies of Konyaks consisted of skulls decorated with horns. The horns are of buffalo with grass tassels at the end of them, above which beans from the huge pods of the sword-bean were strung. This sword-bean probably has a particular association with fertility. It is hung round the necks of their mithan by Semas and Lhotas and also used as a tally of loans. The Angamis and other Naga tribes as well, use the stem of this creeper as an intoxicant for catching fish. The grass tassels are attached to the skull to swing and rustle when the owner is dancing with it, and the same practice seems to obtain among the Dusun of Borneo again, a tribe which appears to have very much common with Nagas. Four were human skulls, on which bears jaws replaced the originals doubtless taken by some other sharer in the head. One skull was divided vertically and the left half replaced by a piece of hollowed wood with a hole for the orbit. Another was human with a wooden jaw. Three are monkey skulls, representing no doubt human originals, one being surmounted by a bit of cranium and with a wooden jaw; another combined with a human jaw and with several bits of crania, presumably the jaw of a young bear. One trophy consisted merely of two bits of crenia on a knotted string, and two more were basket balls of the kind familiar as the Ao Naga symbol of an enemy's head, one with a fragment of cranium attached and adorned with the horns of a serow, the other without horns but with a human jaw and fragment of bone attached to it.

The Konyak Naga dispose of their dead like *yacham* in trees, removing the head when ripe and burying it in a pot let into the ground among the roots of the corpse tree or a neighbouring tree and covered with a flat stone. The corpse tree is a *ficus*, for which there is some consistent veneration among Nagas. The Lhota Naga *mingethung*—head tree—is usually the same ; as also is that of the Wa in Burma ; while the Angamis say that a *ficus* is the priest of the trees. Similarly the *ficus religiosa* is worshipped in a tribe of the South India by women who desire offspring. Sir J.G. Frazer, in a note quotes Livingstone as saying of the *ficus*, "It is a sacred tree all over Africa and India." In a note on an Angami folk-tale, Folk-Lore, suggests that the Angami beliefs are borrowed from Hinduism, where veneration for the *ficus religiosa* is well known. It seems to me more likely that all these beliefs about and the veneration for, the wild fig, have their origin in some ancient negroid cult spread all round the Indian Ocean, which has grown up into Hinduism from below and traces of which one would expect to find in tribes which have obviously absorbed an appreciable strain of negroid blood. The Naga tribes appear to me to have not only never been seriously under the influence of Hinduism, but to be probably entirely untouched by it, except perhaps a few who live among Manipuri in the Manipur valley.

A huge comb in front of a Morung in Ukha, a Konyak village to the south-west of Yungya, being particularly noticeable. It kept the wild cats away (they wreak havoc with the chickens in these hills) and the Sema Naga say that it helps to make the eggs hatch, no doubt because it has already succeeded in hatching out a brood of wasps. The Thado Kukis, however state quite definitely that empty honey-combs are invaluable for warding off the onslaughts of evil spirits. One presumes that they are afraid of getting stung by the bees there might be in it, or as Mills suggests, that they cannot find the way through or perhaps that they have to stop and count the cells, while A.R. Brown, in *The Andaman Islanders*, gives this as an Andaman belief, the wax of the black bee—perhaps rock bee, as in the Naga Hills—being particularly efficacious in keeping off the spirits of the forest.

Hunting dogs are buried, like men, with houses over their graves, offering of meat, etc. If this be neglected the surviving and subsequent dogs do not hunt well. Similarly the Thado Kukis and Angami Nagas always bury their hunting dogs with four corner-posts (*Vakot*) to the grave like men. The Italians crowned them.

A rain hat in use made like an oval shield with a headpiece in the centre of the underside as in the case of a 'mortar-board'. One may find in this part of hills is the circular hat inside which the head fits. The oval shield type is used by the Angami further south, while with the tribes in between, rain hats of any type are much less popular and are rarely seen.

They believe that a great ant-hill with a buffalo's head carved in earth in the side of it will bring rich paddy.

A custom which is fashionable among the women of those Konyaks which the Changs call "Chagyik" of cutting their hair as short as possible all over the head and of plucking it out entirely along two broadish triangles one on each side of the centre of the head starting from the forehead as the base. Before plucking out the hair they rub in ashes, which apparently makes the hair come out quite easily. This practice is not confined to the unmarried girls, shaving the head is with the Angami and other Naga tribes, but is permanent; "a very evil custom and a parlous," as Marco Polo would have said. In a verminous country, however, it probably has its advantages.

The hair of boys is first cut short after they have 'touched meat' taken on a raid. Batches of boys whose hair is then cut together are thereafter treated as adults. For this ceremonial hair-cutting the cutting block used is made of seven sword-beans each stuck on a bamboo stalk, the opposite ends of which are bound together to make the handle. The hair must be cut with six taps of the beans on a dao. The Ao boys have their cut with a hammer made from a little bean.

Outside the morung they put forked wooden posts erected and tied to it with ropes, while a few longish sticks, forked or branched, were stuck into the whole group so formed.

They (Changs of Tuensang) executed a woman thief by throwing her repeatedly into a pit full of tree-nettles. This treatment should have a most discouraging effect on the Thievishly inclined.

Their village is a very stony one and with exceedingly strong defences—ladder wall, ditch wall, palisade, ladder again, wall and then solid wooden door. The curly-haired negroid type of head was very prevalent, and the carvings in the village more naturalistic than usual.

In the village there are stone sitting places, stone foundations to the morungs ; and I noticed one regular stone platform, like the Angami *Baze*, though rather rougher than a *Baze* would normally be. There were also the usual forked posts carved with the inevitable buffalo head. The human head seemed to be represented in carvings with peculiarly heavy eyebrows. One morung, at the edge of a cliff, had two posts to the outer verandah, carved with a man and a woman respectively.

The women have their Chins tattooed like Chang women, but in addition have a trellis pattern on their breasts and sometimes a circle with a dot in the centre of it on each cheek. The men occasionally have a face tattoo of two lines running away downwards from each corner of the mouth. The leg tattoo of the women is elaborate and elegant.

The great wooden dug-out 'drums' in use here had a curious cone left sticking up from what one must call the floor of the drum inside it, but not reaching to the slot edge, when the drum was hollowed out.

One can see here large numbers of skull trophies in which a cow's skull took the place between the buffalo horns usually occupied by a human skull. When a man wounds an enemy but fails to get his head, he hangs up a cow's skull in the place of the human skull which he ought to have got but didn't. The wounded enemy is probably regarded as dying in consequence of the *Genna* done with the substitute for his head. A monkey's or even a bear's skull, as used by Tacham and Yungya, would seem a decidedly nearer approach to human than a cow's. But the Naga is not a pastoral race and does not drink milk, nor has he been appreciably touched by Hinduism.

Cow is the only animal besides the dog to which the Angami gives an individual name, in some respects the cow is treated with respect. The Aos include a clan which tabu the flesh of the cow entirely. Both Aos and Changs believe that mithun of men is associated with the sky spirits, while the souls of men are conversely bound up with the mithun of the sky, so that when a mithun dies on earth a spirit dies in the sky, and when a man dies, it means that the sky spirits have sacrificed a mithun. It seems possible that one is in touch with some pre-Hindu belief that has been incorporated elsewhere into that so receptive system. There is an Angami custom which always suggests the primitive practice in which the Hindu use of caste marks on the fore-head arose. The seat of the Angami soul is in the forehead. To keep off evil spirits the young, who are more susceptible to such harm than the adult, lick and stick on to the centre of the forehead a bit of the leaf of some aromatic plant, usually wormwood, a spiritual disinfectant of great efficacy, which gives the exact effect of a caste mark.

There is a practice of penning up the village pigs in pens under the platform at the back of each *Morung* which is used as a latrine, the pigs serving for sewers. Individual householders hand over their pigs to be fattened thus by the young men of the *Morung*, and pay them for the services so rendered.

The villages have strong defences, a double rampart of earth and stone with perpendicular sides, a "panji" ditch in between crossed by two bamboos for a footway with a cane slung alongside as a handrail, then palisades, ladders and a wooden door. In addition to this the paths to the village were all blocked with branched stumps, sometimes with rows of them, which would entirely prevent anyone from running down the paths. It is an Angami practice.

In front of the houses rows of forked posts form a low wall to the porch front, and the gobles carry "house-horns". The forked posts were probably significant of the performance of some such ceremony as the *Lisu* of the Angamis.

The belts worn in these villages give a definite connection between the long strip of cane, which a Konyak so often coils round his waist, and the broad band of cloth, stiffened to a shining white solidity with filed and fitted cowrie shells, which the Chang affects.

They put a round water-worn stone hanging up in cane harness under the caves of the morung. The explanation given was that some Yungphong man chopped a man of Jakphong and took his head, and, in order that the blood-guiltiness might rest on Jakphong's own head instead of Yungphong's, a stone from Jakphong's land was brought away and hung in Yungphong. It is difficult to see what good that can do, unless the miserable ghost is deceived by the presence of a stone from his own land into thinking that the village is his own village and her enemies his enemies. They erect large white screens of split bamboo that signify the death of a great or rich man. White screens of one sort or another all over the Naga Hills have this significance. The Angami put up white and black clothes in a very conspicuous way, stretched on a scaffolding and looking like a sail when any proper man dies so that the dead-man might see them.

Woodthorpe's description of the white screens he saw in 1876 is as follows :

"It looks at a distance like a large silver chevron turned upside down. It is made of split pieces of wood with the white face turned outwards, placed close together vertically and fastened to huge curves of cane or bamboo, suspended between three trees ; the whole length varies from 40-50 feet, and the average width is about 6 feet, widening to 12 feet at the centre point."

Here, however, it struck me that these screens were merely another instance of the buffalo-horn symbol, and possibly a means of the soul's communicating its fertility "mana" to the village or the village land. But the form might be likened to the representation of a gigantic bird, and some further erections described by him gave him that impression. These were :

"large pieces of wood, cut, and the white face turned outwards, and joined, so as to resemble a bird with outstretched wings, and placed in the branches of several of the trees of the village, and have the appearance at the little distance of huge white birds beginning to take flight."

Whatever the intention of these erections put up by various tribes they all have the effect of catching the eye at a great distance, and letting one know that the village has lost some stout fellow by death.

All round these parts there is a general reluctance to part with any article of personal use or adornment for fear that the soul of the original owner will fall into the power of the purchaser, which looks as thought articles once worn became permeated with the owner's vital essence.

The Ukha men had the "ostrich-feather" Chang tattoo on the thigh, while the women had the same patterns as those of Pongu. Some of the men also had their throats tattooed with a vertical line pattern suggesting a stiff and high necklace with bone supports like those of some Konyaks. This pattern was seen at its best on the effigies of the dead. They are stated to be provided for the habitation of the soul of the deceased whom they represent. The body is disposed of in a wrapping of the "tonkopat" leaf (*Livistona Jenkin Siana*) and slung on four stakes about five feet above the ground outside the village. Seemingly the head is ultimately detached, for the skull is placed on the top of the effigy in order that the soul may pass thence into the wooden figure, after which the skull must be again removed. All the effigies at Ukha were made from a single piece of wood, but one which had the right arm bent at the elbow and pegged on to the body at the shoulder. The eyes were made of a shing round black seed, probably that of *Sapindus Detergens.* In some cases the dead were represented merely by a piece of conical basket-work resting on its base and being topped with a sort of deep basket work tray, the unfastened ends of the bamboo material curving over the top, to protect the skull.

The wooden figures put up as the memorials of the dead by the Angami seem to be likewise for the accommodation of the soul. Some villages leave them till they rot away ; others remove them after they have been up a year. Wooden effigies are used as abodes for the soul in the Pacific.

As among the Aos, the successful head-hunters in Angami hang up a circle of cane in front of his house.

The Konyak women all wear a very narrow petticoat some five inches in leagth and above it a belt, or a series of belts, each consisting of a number of separate threads made up into a bound loop at each end and fastened in front. The twisted threads are covered over with some sort of gum or wax, making them black and shiny like well-worn hide. The women all do their hair, or rather their head, for they leave little enough hair on it.

Most rich men seem to have their own drum-logs in Konyak made of buffalo-head. One wonders whether the metal gongs so beloved of Kukis and other tribes, and always a mark of wealth or importance, have merely replaced wooden and less portable ante-cessors.

The carvings on MORUNG ran to monstrosities like tigers with elephant-tusks, tigers with buffalo-horns, and in one case a two-headed tiger. The carvings on the houses were as at Yaktu, but often spotted with black on a sort of ochre-coloured ground. The MORUNGS contained large number of heads, mostly taken from Angfang across the valley, and the granaries had one of the most ingenious devices for defeating rats.

The village organization of Konyak in very Angami-like in its non-existence. There is no one who can give an order which has any serious chance of being obeyed, or who has any appreciable control over anyone else.

The Konyak women shave the whole of their heads, and this custom is found, in other Konyak villages further north. The explanation given in Longmies is that this clan is descended from slaves whose heads were kept shaven to make sure that their hairs should not fall into the Ang's food when they were preparing it.

The memorials of both men and women in Konyak carry rows of dancing chignons—decorated bamboo tubes with a tuft of human hair fastened on at the lower end. Mills wrote that the chignon is worn by attaching it to the extreme end of the wearer's back hair, which is bound on to the outside of the top end of the tube, the tube being covered with leaves and hairs so that the whole looks like continuous tresses. The women's memorial places had pot-making implements on them.

In villages there is a heap of stones, mostly oblong, in front of the Ang's house, to which a stone is added for every enemy head taken and exposed on the heap.

The houses of Kacha Nagas are frequently walled with planking, and sometimes roofed with the same huge wooden shingles as we noticed at Songpurr in the case of rich men's houses. No particular ceremonial status is necessary, however, as it is in the case of the Angami who wishes to have a shingle roof. The women have a curious way of doing their hair. An ordinary knot is made at the back with a rather long loop of hair sticking out straight behind, and then the knot is turned over and tucked in which brings the loop over so that it stays pointing forward over the left ear. The men had in some cases tattoo on their arms, while the women a very small lozenge pattern of the same shape as the Chang, on their foreheads.

LIFE STYLE—THE ZEMI-NAGAS (NAGALAND)

The Nagas have come a long way since the British first came in contact with them in the middle of the 19th century and took defensive measures to protect British subjects and the tea plantations from raids by hostile. The Nagas are now equal partners in the Union, with the formation of the Nagaland by joining the three hill districts of Kohima, Mokokchung and Tuensang in to India's seventeenth State.

Mountaneous Tract

An expanse of forests, mountains and streams, the State 6361 sq. miles in area with a population of about 4 lakhs, has more than 30 tribes with different customs dialects and religious practices. Many of them are converts to Christianity. Of mixed origin, slant eyes' straight hair and rather flat noses.

Head Hunter

How did the Nagas get their requatation for head hunting ? The custom springs from the belief in a soul force capable of bestowing vitality to an individual or community. Each community is said to possess a certain quantum of soul force which decreases with time, and has to be replenished if the tribes are to be healthy and prosperous and the harvests remain abundant. By keeping skulls in the house, the Nagas believe this soul force is augmented. Some anthropologists, however, state that this scalp-hunting is a form of vendetta.

Martial Race

A martial race, the Nagas built their house with defence possibilities in mind. The villages were sited on mountain spurs and surrounded by bamboo palisades or stone stockades. The eminence gave the Nagas a panoramic view of the countryside and kept them prepared for sudden attacks from other tribes.

Houses

The hearth is the centre of the Naga household and family and friends gather it to char or partake of food. It is here that decisions are made. The chores are divided among men and women, the latter fetching water and attending to domestic duties. The men work in the fields on the hill slopes, where their women folk occasionally help them. There is a fair amount of rainfall, about 80 inches, and rice and vegatables are cultivated. In the plains sugarcane, papaya, pineapple and oranges are grown.

Jhoom

Agriculture is the mainstay of the economy. The traditional form of farming is known as Jhoom, a shifting system of cultivation. Every year trees in a part of the forest are cut, the area cleared, sown with seed and a bumper crop harvested. This piece of land is allowed to lie fallow. It is cultivated again after a lapse of time. A fresh piece of forest land is farmed the following year.

The Nagas are now changing to other methods of agriculture. The Angamis of Kohima, for instance, have a terrace system of cultivation and make use of mountain rills to water their fields. Others have adopted modern farming tools and using high yielding seeds. Growing rice in built-up terraces has gained much publicity.

Usually a hut is constructed near the fields to store the produce. It also serves as a recreation centre. The tribals chat and sing at the end of the day's work. Their philosophy of living is a simple one to work for their daily bread and relax completely when the chores are over. Dances are reserved for festive occasions.

Women Weavers

While the men work as potters of silversmiths, or fish for a living, the village women are experts in weaving artistically patterned shawls and fabrics for their personal use or for sale to tourists. Their clothes are always colourful, and they were a profusion of ornaments made of silver or bone, and chains of coloured heads. Alcoholic drinks, made from rice, are popular both with the locals and visitors. Being mild drinks, women also partake of the brew especially during festivals which are frequently celebrated by the Nagas.

Festivals

One of the major festivals is the Sankarni Puja which coincides with Shivratri. Single boys and girls join in the Sankarni Puja which lasts over a week. Chanting songs, they smoke, eat and drink to their hearts content. Contribution in money and kind is welcome from the participant families as well as visitors.

Smoking and Drink

Smoking seems to be a universal habit and the Nagas take to it even from the tender age of three. Men and women chew tobacco, smoke biris, and welcome the offer of a cigarette. Milk as a food-even for nursing mothers and children is relatively unknown. Instead, rice gruel is taken frequently. Milch cattle are consequently few. The Nagas are fond of meat and are not averse to eating the flesh of any animal. They relish the flesh of snakes, field rats, pigs, cats, dogs and the mithun, a cross between a bull and the yak. Animals, brought by the Nagas from the plains of Assam, are herded into the villages for slaughter. They have a simple way of cooking, meat, dispensing with spices and fat. This renders the flesh particularly rich in protein. Fish, whenever available, is popular among Nagas and is also dried and stored for use during lean periods. The food is washed down with liberal quantities of spirits-zau and Dekrizau.

Dormitories

Special dormitories for boys and girls known as morungs, and under the supervision of trustworthy old couples, still exist in some villages. The dormitory serves a dual purpose. It is a sort of cultural centre for the preservation of music, dance, and artistic expression of the tribes, for the youths learn the rudiments of the arts there. It is also a kind of military camp. Since the single men are located at one place with ready access to arms they can in an emergency be called upon to defend the village at any time of the night. The young men have their gayer moments too. They visit other morungs as far as ten miles away to seek the company of the opposite sex and engage in amoral dalliance. Pre-marital taboos are few and the children born of such liaisons are not frowned upon but accepted in society and are looked after, generally by the mother.

Democratic Practices

The Nagas are well disposed towards newly married couples. The bride and bridegroom are helped by the villagers in setting up a home built on piece of land allotted to them and which incidentally, is owned by the village and not by individuals.

Indeed, the Nagas have certain democratic practices where the interest of the community is placed above that of the individual. The co-operative system functions at all levels and for practically every purpose, from building a house to harvesting crops. The whole village gives a helping hand when a major chore has to be done and in return the workers receive free food and drink. Occasionally, the rich provide a feast for the villagers and are then entitled to a sort of status symbol displaying a sign outside their houses.

Game trophies and heads of the mithun are also prominently hung in the porch. The Nagas have a crude but effective way of curing heads, burying them for a period of time so that the flesh falls off leaving the heads fairly decent looking. The whole village takes part in the hunt, either as beaters or hunters whenever the summons for a chase is given. Though eager to possess guns, the Nagas make the best of their primitive weapons and are capable of killing even big game with spears, dahs or bows and arrows.

Their main support being, hunting, they are adept in trapping animals, wild bears, elephants and even tigers. All game meat is equitable distributed among the poor and the better off. It is often smoked and set aside for future use. On festive occasions the killing of a fattened mithun which is tied to a post is almost a ritual—although a cruel one. Instead of shooting it outright the Nagas resort to disposing of it with a dah, one limb at a time, eventually severing the head.

Besides the tribes within state boundaries, there is an overflow to the neighbouring States of Manipur and the North Cachar Hills of Assam. They claim kinship with one another though their dialects differ. Predominant among the Naga tribes are the Angamis and the Rengma from Kohima, the Semas and the Aos from Mokokchung and the Phoms and the Changs of Tuensang.

All the tribes take pride in martial activities and tend to fight at the slightest provocation. Some of them have joined the Indian Army. Many members of the Ao tribe have taken to business. The Aos are generally more educated and advanced than other tribals. Ao girls wear modern, fashionable clothes and look smart.

There is much missionary activity among the Nagas. Christian priests of various denominations work there with American Baptists in a majority. There are also many Roman Catholic missionaries. Christianity has changed tribal marriage customs and the mode of life. Parents now prefer to keep their children at home rather than in the morungs, and send them to school.

The Sansaris, however, retain their customs and beliefs. The Phoms and the Changs in the interior of Tuensang dispense with clothes altogether. However, contact with the plains people obliges them to cover their nakedness but even so they wear the minimum number of clothes. The climate is pleasant so that there is no real necessity to wear clothes in summer ; even the winters are mild.

Dress

Tribal dress and accessories are eye-catching. The red blanket, a symbol of office of the headman (Gaon Burra) and a red jacket that of an interpreter (Do-Bhashi), are worn with pride though little or no monetary benefit accrues to the wearer, except possible signifying a position of authority and prestige.

In the interior, communications are still primitive though road building efforts are in full swing. Unlike other parts of India, the villagers can be entrusted with the responsibility of constructing and maintaining and if necessary, guarding the portions of road passing through their area.

But services only extend to the district headquarters. The Nagas still cover long distances on foot despite the heavy loads they bear. Of course, they like to ride in a bus and their pleasure in this quick and comfortable form of transport is evident.

Doctor

The old witch-doctor with his sacrifice of chickens and practice of other rites still holds away over the country-side. Medical aids are primitive. The cure for sores consists in covering them with leaves. The Nagas, being hardy, shrug off minor ailments and often manage without modern drugs. Treatment of the sick, the old, and injured persons poses a problem. Young men, however, volunteer to carry the patients for miles, and for days together to a hospital for treatment, provided they are convinced that the witch-doctor is helpless and the patient needs specialized medical care.

Scenic Beauty

The scenic beauty of the area strikes the visitor. He can never hope to see the place in one or two trips. It is a paradise for research scholars, anthropologists, botanists and tourists. It is worth a visit especially in the cold season when there is still a lot of greenery around.

History and origin

The Zemis are one of the sub-tribes of the so-called Kaccha Naga Tribe according to the Zemis of the North Cachar Hills. The word Kaccha Naga has been derived as follows. When the Britishers came to North Cachar Hills near about Dimapur they made Asalu as one of the headquarters of the British army. The people living in the Asalu village were the Zemis themselves. From the Asalu Head Quarters the District people started to move toward Kohing, but could not succeed due to thick forest. The people of the Asalu village stated that those who live there are all dacoits of Kahegami (meaning dacoits a head hunters in the Zemi language). So the Britishers did not proceed further, but came down to Dimapur side and entered a village of the Angamis near Kohima called Khonoma. When they entered Khonoma they called the people of Khonoma village as Angamis, (they derived this name from Kahegami, which they learnt from the people of the Asalu village. But the people of the Khonoma village (Angami) even today call themselves Thenemi). The British were enquired from the Angamis of the Khonoma village, as who are the people living to the western side of Kohima.

Kacchas

The Angamis said that nobody lives in that area but there are only Kacchas (Kacch is an Angami word meaning forest). That is in that area there are only jungles and no one lives there. But the Britishers moved and entered inside the western area, that is the Zeliang area at present, to their surprise they found some people living there. The Britishers mistook themselves at the Kacchas, (which they learned from the Angamis of the Khonoma village and named them as the Kaccha Nagas). According to the available information the people living in those thick forests were the Zemi Nagas themselves, whom the Britishers mistook as the Kaccha Nagas.

Western District of Kohima

Thus Kaccha Nagas are the Zemis living in the Western district of Kohima, while the Zemi themselves are living in the North Cachar Hills from an early time. According to the Zemis of the North Cachar Hills there are no marked difference in cultural and social activities of these two groups of Zemis.

The term Zemi

The term Zemi means 'Southern' or the plain regions in comparison to the Naga Hills. 'Nzieme' the name by which they call themselves. It is now an obsolete term previously used by the Zemi Nagas of Manipur to refer the Zemi Nagas of North Cachar Hills. The word is pronounced with a slight nasal aspirant.

The word has been derived from the root word Zemina meaning man.

First Inhabitants stated back to 13th Century

According to the Zemis of the North Cachar Hills of first inhabitants of the North Cachar Hills were the Siami and Zeme and their settlement may be dated back to the 13th century. The Siamis were Zemis in general, but since they know the art of making 'Teluiteu', (Naga Necklace) out of the soft stones (conches), so the Zemis gave the name as 'Siami' 'Siame' (mean artisans) to those families which knew the art of making necklaces. Their artistic works and stone pillers are still to be found in Melangpeu. Boloson, Asalu, Impoi, are other Zeme villages of the North Cachar Hills.

Kechingpethka

According to them, since the 13th century Zemis were living on the Borail Hills, before the Geographical division of India. This North Cachar Hill was called 'Kechingpethka' (Borail range). When the Ahoms and the Kacharis invaded this area, they asked the Zemes as to whom this land belongs. The Zemes answered that this land belonged to 'Kachingpeka' (that is Boro, or Bara that is elder). They actually meant that this is the home land which belonged to the eldest of the family of 8 sons. Since that time the name Borail (derived from Boro) came into use, which is still being used. During the 16th century there was another batch of Angami Naga migration into Barai Hills. The Zeme Nagas being the weaker groups went away and moved downward and westwards passing through the Borail range, and started colonizing beyond the hill areas.

Clanwise Migration

The Kaccha Naga as a tribe consists of three sub-tribes as follows, the Zemis, the Liangmes, and the Rongmes or the Kabuis. The first two groups speak the same language but little variation in accent and the last group, speaks a different one though there is a good number of word akin to the first two. According to the Zemi Nagas of North Cachar Hills all these groups belong to the same stock but later somewhat clanwise migration had to take place to different parts in search of fertile lands for cultivation. In olden times the Angamis carried on raids against the Zemes who thus had to migrate further and further away from their original place of settlement till they come down to, Borail range in North Cachar Hills. Thus scattered and separated by economical, political and social forces they had to live in different geographical units like North Cachar Hills, Manipur and Nagaland.

Same Social Customs

Inspite of the different geographical situations in which they are placed, the social customs and manners of these three sub-tribes are almost the same.

The Zemis are the Kaccha Nagas who had been for a long time the virtual subject of the Angami people of Khonoma (Hutton 1921, p. 352).

Different Dialect

They resemble the ruling people in manners of dress though they speak a different dialect. It is difficult to say that customs and measures are originally of Kaccha Naga and what have been borrowed from the Angamis of Khonoma.

Their Origin according to Sir Grierson

How and when from the Kaccha Nagas come before reaching the present abode is still in mystery. The tradition goes that their ancestors came from the direction of Japromo in Nagaland (J.H. Hutton, The Angami Nagas, 1921, pp. 352, 6) and spread towards the south. They have been connected with the head hunters of the Malay and the races of the Southern sea on the one hand and traced back to China on the other (J.H. Hutton, The Angami Nagas, 1921, pp. 352, 6).

It has been stated (communication made to the Royal Anthropological Institute, Quarterly from Man in India 1948, Vol. 48) that the Zemi Nagas apparently migrated to the present location from the neighbourhood of Mao and Kohima, by a route down the Borail range and reached North Cachar when the Kachari Kingdom at Maibong was established.

On the basis of language, their origin is assigned by Sir G. Grierson (1903) to the second wave of imigration that of the Tibeto-Burma, from the traditional cradle of the Indo-Chinese race in North Western China between the Upper water of the Yangtse-kiang and the Ho-ang-ho rivers.

The Kaccha Nagas of the North Cachar Hills came into contact with the Kacharis (Hutton, 1921, p. 13). The legends of the Kachari king Bhim are still current among the Kacharis. They believe that he is still sleeping in a cave among the hill immediately to the south of the Japro mountain when he will come out at sometime in the distant future to rule over all who eat form the wooden platter (Nagas in general).

The Zemi Nagas of North Cachar Hills though know about such a legend which is current among the Kacharis yet do not accept the possibility of a Kachari king ruling over them.

Ahom King

The Kaccha Nagas (E.A. Gait 1963, 1013) were also enlisred in the armies of the Ahom Kings who had relations inter-Manipur. During the thirties of the eighteenth century a Manipuri raid was made into the Angami country (Gait) 1963 as far as Kohima, which the Manipuris attacked and burnt and slaughtered large numbers of inhabitants. The Kaccha Nagas as neighbours and satellites of the Angamis suffered in the same way as the Angamis when the Manipuris raided into the Angami country as far as Kohima.

Angami Rule

The Kaccha Nagas were for a long time under the Angamis Suzerainty and even they had migrated to the area in the North Cachar Hills the fluctuating suzerainty of the Angamis over the Kaccha Nagas was still maintained until the establishment of the British rule. The Kaccha Nagas owe allegiance to the Angamis in that they had to pay a kind of tax during their subjugation which amounted to Rs. 2 per household per annum.

Over and above, they nad to assist them in their devastating raids on the plains. In some cases the Angamis made their settlements in the Kaccha Nagas country and where each settlements were made, the Kaccha Nagas as their subjects had to accept allegiance to the ruling Angamis. But the villages were so made that the Kaccha Nagas were free to pursue their own pattern in matters of village organizations and administration. As a result to such settlements it is but natural that the Angamis would dominate them and hence superimpose on them their own customs, ornaments etc. through the ages.

PEOPLE AND THEIR ECONOMIC PURSUITS

North Cachar Hills

The Zemi Nagas are found mostly in North Cachar Hills (J.H. Hutton 1921, pp. 252, 6) and also in Manipur and Nagaland. Those found in the North Cachar Hills sub-division have been living together along with the other tribes like the Dimasa Kacharis, the Kukis, the Hmars etc. According to the Zemis of the North Cachar Hills they come this sub-division from the north-east and migrated down the Borail range and still further to the west as far as the bank of the Kopilai river. Thus there is long continuous chain of villages, with few Kuki and Kumar villages at places from the bank of the Kopilai on the west to the eastern border of the North Cachar Hills.

Land

Land, the most important property, can be held by the individual or clan. The waste land of the village, where no structure has been erected by any person belongs to the whole community of a particular village. Each village has also a small patch of forest land and rigets to this land belongs to the whole community irrespective of clan. No individual person or clan or family can utilize such village a land for the purpose of cultivation or erecting a house. The only benefit enjoyed by them from such land is that any villager can utilize the building materials of constructing or repairing his house.

Clan Land

Clan land is allotted for cultivation by an agreement among the people of the clan. That is a person who wants to cultivate that land or a part of it will approach his clan's members who will sit together and give their consent. In case of disagreement, the person concerned will refer to the village council who would try their best to settle the dispute. Such cases generally end with the interference of the Kadeipeo and other members of the village council and it is seldom referred to the District Council for its final decision.

Kadeipeo

Though the lands within the officially demarcated areas belong to the villages as a whole there are some patches here and there within the boundary which are socially regarded as owned by the Kadeipeo at the time of the original settlement. These lands can be disposed of by the Kadeipeo in favour of any of his relatives or descendants. He may give a part or whole of the land to his daughter or daughters as a part of the dowry for their 'Chingrimiabam', meaning place for collection of fire wood ; when they go to their father-in-laws' house. The land thus given will then be in possession of their family and it will be subject to a traditional leavy or tax called 'Mpua' which every non-Kadeipeo must pay to Kadeipeo in recognition of the latters right over the land in case the land is cultivated (that too after consultation with him), 'Mpua' may be measured in terms of crops grown thereon, it may be a basket of cotton belts, chillies, rice etc.

Full Authority

The eldest member of a clan has full authority over the clan land. Allotment of land for cultivation may be made by himself as is the normal practice, after consultation with his immediate elders of the clan.

Livestock

Land and livestock are the only factor which play an important part of the economic life of these people. Since their economy is predominantly agricultural the entire social structure is dependent upon the ownership of land and cattle wealth like the buffalo or the mithun, is an important source of income as a consumption good especially during recemonious occasions. The price of the mithun usually varies from Rs. 20 to Rs. 25 according to the size and thus is a source of income for the owner. The Zemi households in the village make weaving and basketry for their own purposes. Though these traditional industries are not carried out in a large scale and do not find their way in the market but rather provide a utilitarian object to the producing household.

Blacksmithy

Blacksmithy as a profession among the Zemi Nagas is practised on a very small scale. It cannot be regarded even as part time industry in the village. There are no particular clan or clans who are attached to it. This is only when the cultivators want to improve their agricultural implements like spades, hoes, dao etc. that they resort to this work, and that too, in their own houses, with the help of indigenous assessories. There is no tradition connected with the industry and there exists no class distinction among those who practise it and those who do not. The services of other tribes like Kacharis are obtained and in fact the implements like daos, spears, etc. are manufactured by Kacharis of Maibang in the olden days were considered to be one of the best quality available in North Cachur Hills.

Shifting Cultivation

The principle basis of subsistence is shifting cultivation. As the Borail is extremely steep and cliffs and crags abound, the spurs lie close to each other and gorges and deep ravines are in between, the land fit for jhum exists only in scattered patches while the greater part is rocky and impossible for cultivation. Moreover the land can be put to cultivation only for two or three consecutive seasons. It is then left to lie fallow for at least ten years when the land has recovered enough for jhumming. During the period when jhum field is left fallow, the cultivators shift their activities to another plot of land and resume jhumming in the old plot when it is again fit for cultivation.

Changing Pattern

Since as is generally the case there is not enough land for shifting cultivation, it becomes necessary to change to permanent fields by which the same population could live as a fraction of the acreage needed for jhumming.

Wet Cultivation

Wet cultivation, even it is known to them, is impracticable for the simple reason that the land around the Borail Hills is unsuited for the purpose. Even lands fit for jhumming are few and far between, being found only in small scattered patches.

Clearing of Jhumming Land

Usually the land to be jhummed is cleared with daos (heke)

or axes (hrei) in the months of December-January and set on fire in March-April. The ashes are thoroughly mixed with the earth and holes are made with the help of the hoe (Kepen). The holes are to be made in such a way that the soil is to be upturned, will generally depend on the nature of the soil and the kind of crops (paddy) to be grown. In stormy or sandy hums the holes are usually made and in soft or laamy areas, the outer crest of the earth is upturned. There are certain kinds of paddy which are havested late in November-December and are of made sturdy growth and hence require deep roots for their proper growth. For these, holes are generally made even in soft soils otherwise the paddy plants will fall on the ground as they grow in cluster from the same one hole. But some kinds of paddy which are reaped early in September-October are broadcasted after the soil is upturned, for they are of stunted growth and do not usually need deep roots. At present broadcasting of seeds (after the soil is upturned) is the most popular practice perhaps because of poorer quality of soil and the need for early crops. The methods in practice seems to require less quantity of seeds also. This broadcasting method is possible only in plain or at least on very gentle slopes, whill on hilly steep sides, holes are generally made, for the seeds if broadcasted will be washed away down the hill sides by the rains. Sowing begins usually after the first rains, i.e. during the months of April-May. Paddy is the main crop and chillies pumpkins, millet, maize etc. are sown as side crops along with paddy, each in a separate hole. The harvesting of paddy begins in November and lasts until December whereas in the case of maize, chillies, etc. the harvesting period starts in August and that of millet, in October-November. Sickles (sapinen) are used to out the ears of paddy and the sheaves so collected are beaten against a stone until the ears are separated from the plant. Husking is done with the help of pestle (kemi) and mortar (gepa).

Cottage Industries

Though cottage industries like, weaving, basketry and black smithy are practised by the community yet it may not be wise to include them as subsidiary occupations though, of course they provide a source of income to the producting household.

This is due to the fact that the industries are not carried on a large scale but are practised only when occasion arise, as has been mentioned before these products do not find their way to the market but are rather meant for personal use. Of the industries practised by them weaving is the most important and the clothes are meant only for personal use. Of the clothes woven by them the most important are Menipai, Hemi', 'dimdia', used by men and armiang, 'peingum' used by women.

Ngkum and Hemui

A small wooden machine called 'ngkum' is used to extract the cotton seed. After extracting the seeds, cotton 'Hemui'. The spindle is made of a strong piece of bamboo or wood pointed at the bottom and above it has a round flat stone with a hole in the middle through which the wooden stem passes from its upper end. The thread is would round the wooden stem as the latter spins. The loom (dekrain) is a simple ten loom. The warp of moderate length and breadh is made and fastened at the end to a wall while the other end of the warp is tied to the waise, of the weaver with a cotton leather belt. No reed is used and the shed is operated by a half heald process which is also operated by the hand. The weft yarn is inserted in the hed by means of bamboo tube and a wooden string is used for beating up the weft. This kind of loom is common among them because of certain advantages it offers such as the compact taxture of clothes woven in a tension loom the ease with which the loom can be erected in any place or rolled up when it is not in use and the simplicity of the loom which enables its parts to be replaced easily and practically without any cost.

LANGUAGE AND RELIGION

Although the Zemis believe in spritual beings they cannot be rightly called animistic. They have well defined gods and goddesses who, they believe, take special interest in the life of the people. They believe, that there is a God known to them as 'Tingwang' who guides and controls the life of man and who is above all of the gods (hera) and spitits (herui). This supreme God is omniscient, omnipotent and omnipresent. He is to be worshipped and prayed and he is to be feared and respected. He is the supreme and dispenser of good and evil and it is who makes man rich or poor, great and small. Besides this Almighty there is a good number of gods whom they fear and revere. There are legends that eight of these gods are the children of a goddess called 'hezale' and two of them, 'chuprai' and 'munsenieu' are the most important and due propitiations to be given to them in times of sickness. The functions of the other goddesses are not known but they appear to be of less importance in their relations with the life of men. There are spirits good and evil, which manifest themselves in the jungles, the wood and trees, the valleys, the hills, the precipices, the rocks and rivers and the sky above. These spirits or herui are also to be propitiated and revered. The Zemis have no temple or shrine for the worship of gods and spirits, they are performed by 'ting-kupeu', the priest. The 'tingkupeu', directs all public ceremonies and fixes the day for them.

Tingkupeu

It may be noted that the office of the priest, or 'tingkupeu' is hereditary. The office while descending from generation remains however in the hands of the old man of the family, the second brother succeeding the elder or the son his father and so on. The priest also plays an important role in connection with the formation or shifting of a village to a new site. When a new village is to be built it is the duty of the 'tingkupeu' to go and select the site for the first house of the new villages and in this connection the 'tingkupeu' performs a ceremony, before the construction of the first house in the new site. The ceremony being attended by the elders of the village.

Selection of House Plots

On the spot where the house is to be built, a cock is tied from the leg by a rope to a post. Early in the following morning when the sun is high the cock is killed and its blood is offered to tingwang, praying at the same time that the place so selected for the new village will be free from any misfortune and calamities. The flesh of the cock is then cooked and eaten by those present on the occasion. It may be pointed out that the sitting place in front of 'tingkepeu's' house usually contains the graves of the decased 'tingkume' (plural of tingkupeu) and is regarded as a sacred place.

Sun and Moon

The sun (naimik) and the moon (hekeu) are not worshipped but are looked upon with reverence and respect. The hills, streams and rocks are believed to be the creations of Tingwang but solar eclipse (naimik'nra) and lunar eclipse (hekeu'nra) are the cause of the devil (nra) who swallows them up at certain seasons of the year resulting in failure of their crops and famine following its terrain. The thunder (hegikeube) is due to the quarrel between husband and wife living in heaven who turn all things upside down thus making the roar or noise in heaven. When sacrifices cannot be strictly followed as instructed by the 'tingkupeu', hail stones (gesak) will fall down from heaven to undo the works of man especially that of his fields. Earthquake (kaketaibe) is caused by some spirits who shake the earth which is usually followed by a poor, harves.

Life for Zemi

Life for Zemi is full of fears and horrors. The illness of a person is attributed to some wild spirits. In such case, therefore, the 'tingkupeu' the person who, they believe, has got spiritual insight and power is consulted. He is supposed to know the cause of the illness by the expedient of drawing lots and accordingly pronounces the cause which may be either due to the gods, goodesses or spirits inhabiting a particular precipice or rock etc. The 'tingkupeu' also declares the number of fowl or pigs to be sacrificed and offering to the gods is done according to his instruction.

When a person is suddenly attacked with unconsciousness and encounters fearful experiences or he meets with an unexpected death on the way or in the jungle, the cause of such misfortunes is attributed to the agency of wild spirits.

Herasiateuhe

In such cases an offering known as 'herasiateuhe' is performed and a dog, a pig or a fowl is sacrificed but their meat should not however, be eaten. Also when a person's health deteriorates, it is taken to be caused by the goddess 'chuprai' or 'munsenieu' as the priest attributes it and a fowl is to be sacrificed to the goddess in order that she may leave the ailing person in good health. The flesh of the bird killed should be eaten only by the ailing person while the blood is offered to the goddess.

Nvuikereura

Every year in its beginning there is a sacrifice called 'nvuikereura' or 'sacrified of ten hens'. This sacrifice is performed for the purpose of propitiating the Almighty God (Tingwang). The priest invokes the help of Tingwang to keep the people in good and sound health throughout the year. It may, however, be noted that there are two classes of sacrifice to the deities, viz., sacrifices to the family deities called 'kelakra' and sacrifices to the community deities called 'keluara'. If the ancestors of the past are not given adequate sacrificial articles at their death, their spirits may visit their descendants and trouble them. The number of animals to be offered depends upon the ability of the family or clan which performs the sacrifice. Sacrifice, to the community deities is done when the general condition of the community is not good, that is, due to epidemic diseases like cholera, small pox etc. On this occasion one or two white or black fowl are let loose and they are not to be caught by any body as these fowl are meant for the gods only. On this occasion no outsider or stranger is allowed to enter into the village and to prevent strangers from entering the village two bought of tree are put on each side of village gate.

Dreams and Vision and Dogams

A word may be added regarding the interpretation of their dreams and vision. It is believed that when a person has a bad dream at night like falling from a tree or into the river or stream or encountering fearful experience that person must not leave his house on the following day. He is believed to have been caught by the evil spirits which are to be a fowl. In this case the priest is consulted who after killing the fowl on some plaintain leaves, offers it to the spirits to free the person from their grip. When a person who goes on a journey sees a black cat crossing the path he is to turn back home otherwise he will meet with some misfortunes on the way, when he sees a snake crossing the road he must either kill it or return home. When a dog howls at midnight it is considered as an ill omen and some one living in the village may die. The howling of the dog is taken to be a sign of the presence of evil spirits which pass through the village.

Christian Zemis

The Christian Zemis belong to the presbyterian Church and follow the set pattern of the presbyterian church organization.

The believes and practice discussed earlier is mainly applicable to the non-christian Zemes. But these believes and practices still persist to a certain extent among the Christian Zemes, as illustrated by a case study.

Mr. John Jeme, who is Assistant Secretary, Executive Committee, N.C. Hills District Council, Haflong was staying at Bara Haflong. He told to his friend that one day his father was knocked off by a speeding jeep on the road. His father received injuries on the head and on the waist. Since the driver of the jeep knew him so he brought his father at home. At home his father remained unconscious for one night. Mr. John Jeme, though being a graduate of Gauhati University, and with a responsible post, did not think of taking his father to the hospital. His father was laying on a cot in a smoky room by the side of the fire made for keeping the room temperature high. The room was not well ventilated. The relatives and friends were sitting surrounding his father. He was given only some tea when he gained his conscious. The morning following the accident when he reached Mr. John Jeme's house, he learnt that they are waiting far a man who wants to pray to the God for the recovery of the patient. After some time the man came to his house. While he was praying all the persons sitting in that room lowered their head in regard to the prayer. That man (not the priest, but an elderly man) uttered few sentences in Zeme language, in a rhythmic tone for about 10-15 minutes. After the prayer was over the compounder of the hospital came at this house and saw the patient and asked them to take him to the hospital. They made a stretcher and he was taken to the hospital after about 3 hours. Later his friend learnt from the doctor of the hospital that since he was an old man he got a shock, and the injury was not serious. Thus this case fairly indicates that such believes and practices of the non-Christian Zemes still persists among the Christian Zeme to a certain extent.

Zemi Language

The Zemi Nagas of North Cachar Hills speak their own language which is known as the 'Zemi' language. The Liangmes who are the other sub-division of the Kaccha Nagas, speak the same language but with a little variation in accent or intonation and the Rongmes or Kabuis speaks a different one though there are quite a good number of words akin to the Zemis and the Liangmes. Sir George Grierson (Linguistic Survey of India, Vol. III, Part II), classed the Kaccha Naga language in the Naga Bodo group. In the 1961 (Part II. C) census there were 185 male and 189 female Zeme speakers in the Assam Hills division. The same holds true for the united Mikir and North Cachar district. They have no script of their own instead use the Roman script with few alterations in the alphabets. For example, A.I. (to be pronounced in high tone), 'm' (Pronounced, 'im') 'n' (pronounced 'in', 'ng (pronounced 'ing'), 'ng (Pronounced 'eng') are added to the alphabets while C. F. Q. V. X. Y. are omitted. The Zemis, except the Christian Zemis have no literature of their own. There are songs, folk stories, legends etc. which are never reduced to writing but are orally handed down from father to son through generations Past.

Zeliangruoing Committee

The Zemi christians have some written books, there is a Zeliangruoing literature committee which aims to bring about uniformity in text books, script, etc. This has evolved common script so as to facilitate production of common standardised text books, for schools, hymn books, bible extracts etc. The District Council has not yet taken any step to encourage their language. Though the District Council has provisions for the introduction of Zemi language in the primary stage and also for the preparation of text books in the Roman alphabet. The council has taken over all the Government Primary Schools but the medium of instruction still used is either English or

Bengali. The Zemis language has been introduced only in those Primary schools which are run by the Presbyterian Mission to which the Zeme Christians belong. The Zeme Primary text books which are prepared and published by the Mission are also in use.

Primary Schools

The villages which are nearer the town or have some access to the urban centres are having the primary school while the interior villages which are remote from the town are lacking even the primary schools. As a matter of fact, the idea of education is most readily appreciated by the Christian Zemis. In some villages the education is as old as the coming of Christianity.

Literate Person

According to 1961 Census the number of literate persons in the North Cachar Hills are 437 out of the total population of 8.338. This shows that the literate persons are very few among the Zemi Nagas and constitute only 5.2 per cent of the total population. Most of them have not yet realized the value of education or are rather not yet willing to part with their children for education.

FAMILY AND COMMUNITY RELATIONSHIP

Hekiria

Generally in the Zemi villages the type of the family is simple consists of husband, wife and the unmarried children. The term 'family' among Zemi means 'Hekiria', meaning 'Rows of houses' in broader sense thereby implying 'lineage' traced from the clan. In the narrower sense it may simply mean 'Kelak', i.e. House derived from the word 'Kelaktenbe' which means 'marriage'. When a man marries and sets up a house of his own, his house is called 'Kelak' or more correctly, 'Pekalak' meaning 'his home or his family', Being patriarchal society the Zemis trace their descendant through their fathers or forefathers. It is the social ideal that parents live together with their married children and only when the married brothers fail to live together due to various reasons then they live separately and establish a new house of their own after a year or more of their marriage.

Head of The Family

The father, being the head of the family, commands respect from all the memebrs which the latter consider as a part of their duty. In the absence of the father the eldest son or in his absence the elder or younger one takes charge of the family and that too if the members agree and if he can win their affection and respect. Otherwise, a disaccord may lead to the split up of the family. But no such case was however found during the field study. The mother also commands much respect in the family and keeps good care for the children when they are young and look after the needs and the requirements of the children.

In short, the family which is patriarchal in type is a well-knit unit and being patrilineal the members are descended from the oldest male resident in the house, within the family men and women enjoy equal status, except in the property inheritance which goes to the eldest son.

Beside doing household duties, woman render additional labour to man in their work in the fields.

Clans and Marriage

The Zemis have the following clans namely Mpame, Nkuame Henume, Nriame and Sogame, Ndaime, ane Hezanne. Of them Mpame and 'Nkuame' are considered as belonging to the same clan. Marriage within the clan is not the rule and all the clans mentioned above are equal in status. The clans are believed to be descended from a common ancestor by whose name the clan is known. As stated earlier, Mpame and Nkuame belonged to the same clan. They did not intermarry and were socially regarded as belonging to the same family. According to the Zemis, it is said that there was a man belonging to this (i.e. Mpa-Nkua clan) group and was nicknamed as 'Nkuampeu' one who rolls' and while competing in sports during festivals he uttered, as was his practice, a list of names of his grand fathers including his. Instead of uttering his own name he used his nickname (Nkuanepeu) to which the audience took exception. It is said that from that time onwards his descendants came to be known as 'Nkuames' i.e., the members belonging to this clan. At present the members of these two clans, i.e. Mpame and Nkuame though originally regarded as one clan can inter-marry but with a show of restraint or reservation Zemis believe that as the twice passes the relationship between them two clans become more and distant, and so they can inter-marry.

Low Exogamy

The clan is, however, sociologically of importance as the marriage unit and the law of exogamy obliges marriage outside the clan. It may be stated that there is no association of any clan with any occupation, as such the Zemi community is pre-dominently an agricultural community.

Patriarchal

Being patriarchal, the father is the head of the family and on his death the eldest son assumes charge of his responsibility thereby inheriting the larger part of the property. This was in vogue in earlier times. Only males can inherit the property. If a ma n leaves no male issue at his death, the property will be equally divided among the deceased's male cousins. The usual custom is for his father to divide the bulk of his property among his sons during his life time. When the sons marry, each son receives his portion of the acquired property from his father and on the death of the father, the eldest son, though he may already have been given his share, inherit rest of his father's property including the house which was in the father's possession at the time of his death. The property of any son who dies without leaving any male child during the father's life time reverts the latter but after the father's death it goes to the youngest son, while in the case after the youngest son himself dies without a male issue, his elder brothers share his property equally. If there is no father, a brother or son living, paternal uncle or, in the absence of such, any nearest male relative on the father's side would inherit the property. The personal of the mother including the cash and the ornaments etc. goes to her daughters. Failing daughter, her property goes to her father's heirs who take all the property including ornaments, even if she has a son. But presently it is found that though in the Zemi society only male members have the right to inherit yet it is not correct to say that the eldest son gets the largest share. When the grown up sons get married and established their own new homes, they leave their parents and live independently. It is customary on the part of the parent to ask the youngest son (even after his marriage) to remain with him. The idea is, that the parents now being old should be looked after and attended by one of his sons. In such cases the normal procedure is to leave the entire property at the hand of the youngest son at the time of his (parents) death and some amount of property also goes to other sons as willed by the dying father. The quantity of property to be shared among the sons may be less for one and more for others as warranted by their circumstances in which they are placed.

Property

If a man has only daughters and therefore leaves no male inheritor the property will go to the nearest and eldest relative of his family who in turn will be charged with the responsibility of looking after his (dead man's) widow and daughters, whether married or unmarried. And in case, the man dies living no issue, his property will go to his nearest and eldest relative who will take charge of the property as well as the widow thus left behind. The widow to be cared for and maintained must remain under the roof of that family, but if she prefers to leave the family and go to her own family, the responsibility of her husband's relatives ceases. But such action of the widow leaving the family of her husband is rare and is socially and morally denounced.

Relation among the Different Segments of the Community

The real unit of the society are the clans. In the past relation between the clans were not always in amity (J.H. Hutton 1921, p. 109) and this antagonism or rivalry coloured the Zemi life. The jealousy and suspicion of one clan for another had been a source of weakness. If there were disputes between two persons of different clans, then the clansmen on each side appear as partisans and foment the discord. However, only in cases of a breach of social code and religious observances the clans would unite.

Clan Enemity

At present there are no traditional clan enemity. The clans are strictly exogamous and on no account can a clan marry within the clan. The clan is also recognized as a unit for genna purposes (T.C. Hodson, 1911, p. 73) and what is genna to a clan, say for the death of one of their members, may not be genna for other clans. Except for the gennas for the religious and ceremonial purposes for the tribe as a whole. All these still hold true among the present day Zeme society. Each village possesses a wall defined area of territory not only of cultivated land but of waste and forest land as well. The village is a unit of socially organized community, acting as a whole and participating in the ritual associated with and intended to assist the cultivation of the community. Members of the same clan are found in different villages situated at long distances from one another. Since the villages are situated at long distances from one another and are not easily accessable so as the time passes, the kinship among the persons belonging to the same clan becomes remote, but sometime such relationships among persons belonging to the same clan of different villages are traceable as told by the Zemes themselves.

Women from other clans

In the exogamous community the male element is the permanent element of the society and the women are only brought in from some other clan while the unmarried girls are destined to leave their clan of origin on marriage. This is one factor which keeps the various elements of the community rigidly apart.

INTER-COMMUNITY RELATIONSHIPS

Homogeneity

The Zemi Nagas are distinguished from other Nagas tribes by its remarkable homogeneity and specially localized in the Borail hills (L.A. Waddel; 1900) and so are in contact with the Kukis, the Dimasa Kacharis and the Homars rather than with the Naga tribes. With the Dimasa Kacharis they have been in contact long after they came into this part of the Borail hills, the contact was rather peaceful. But they have not always been on good terms with the Kukis, boundary disputes and trespasses are the problems which can in no way be solved. The cause of the enemity has been inherent in the two communities, since British days (U. Grahn Baver, 1946, pp. 50-57). Both the two rival communities practised shifting cultivation and when the Zemis first came to these hills they claimed a large tract of land for cultivation. Since they follow cycle migration and come back after about 10 years to the former site only when it has fully recovered. The properties are buried on the old site to mark the place for reoccupation. In course of time the Kuki immigrants appeared and were in search of new lands to replace the one which was exhausted. The British Government in order to check onward a certain tract of land which certainly had been old Zeme sites and presumed to have been abandoned. Thus the Zemis were ultimately left with only that part of their land which was in cultivation when the boundaries were demarcated. As a matter of fact much of the good land was lost to the Kukis, which the Zemis could not forget easily. Excepting the Kukis, whom they look on with distrust and suspicion, their relation with other communities as Dimasa Kacharis and Homar has been peaceful. The fact of the dispute between the Zemis and the Kukis has been accepted by the Zemis, but the enquires regarding the dispute is yet to be made from the other end before the conclusions are made.

STRUCTURE OF SOCIAL CONTROL PRESTIGE AND LEADERSHIP

District Council

In spite of the present day political administration the ancient system of social organization of the Zemis is still in vogue. The District Council recognizes the functions and duties of their organizations as well as the members of office bearers. Each village has its own headman known as 'Kadeipeo' whose office is hereditary and who is assisted by a council known as 'Samkakibe' which is always held in the bachelors house or morung (hangseoki). The 'Kadeipeo' convenes the council (samakakibe) he and with the help of the village priest (Tingkupeu) he chooses elders to sit in the council. As a matter of fact all adult male persons above 30 years old are members of the 'Samakakibe'. Among the members of the council there is, besides, the headman, an assistant headman who performs the duties, of the headman in his absence. Then there is the 'tingkupeu' who is responsible for the public sacrifices and who conducts the religious life of the village. He is also empowered to fix the date of the gennas on which people abstain from work as well as the dates of festivals. Over and above there is a village crier (sabepen) whose duty is to proclaim to the villagers the decision of the village council on matters that accept the common weal as directed by the 'kadeipeo'. The council decides nearly all matters relating to the village and has jurisprudence over minor disputes, while complicated disputes normallv go to the District Council Court at Haflong. Disputes concerning land theft, inheritance of property, adultry, divorce etc., are disposed of by the 'Samkakibe' in accordance with their own tribal law and a dispute which can not be settled by the council is referred to the higher court of the district council.

Morung

The most notable feature of the social structure of the Zemis is the institution of the morung or the bachelor's houses. Their morungs have always become their pride and joy and the life-veins of their social and cultural activities. In even village there must invariably be a morung and if a big, two morungs for the comfort and convenience of village lands. In the Laisong villages there are two such morungs. The boys dormitory is known as 'hangseoki', while the one used by the girls is called 'leoseoki'. However, members of both the dormitories are collectively known as 'Kienga'. The girls have no such 'leoseoki' of their own but usually use the house of each members by turn.

Compulsory Membership

Every male member in the village should be a member of either of the two morungs, if their are two morungs in the village. The morung has members of all the clans and is not confined to one clan only. From the same house or family there can be members belonging to different morungs. It is not necessary to divide the number of houses for the purpose of membership but usually there is an approximate, if not equal balance in the strength of the membership in the two morungs.

Admission to morung

The method of admission to the Morung is a simple one. If a male child is born in a family, and member of either of the Morungs informs the father of the child that he should become a member of his (informer's) morung and that settles the question of the child's membership. As soon as a boy or a girl reaches the age of eight or nine he/she ceases to sleep in the respective dormitory. Girls work at home during the day time and use the dormitory only at night. In the dormitory they learn spinning, weaving, music and songs. No married man, not even the parents in whose the club is held far the night, ever enters it and only the village headman may drop in for a fatherly visit. If there is any other visit at all it is from a young man who comes stealthily at night to see his own sweet heart. Unlike the girls the boys spend the whole of their time in the hangseoki and go home only for meals or when they are ill. Sometimes, some of the boys exempt themselves from work in the fields and to nothing except to drink zau, gossip or do a little basketry work, play music, bathe and groom their youthful body for the favour of young girls. Indeed, it is a grand life, to which a married man looks back wishfully with regret, for the day a boy marries he ceases to be a member of the hangseoki and therefore he ceases to sleep in it. It should be noted that the kienga have their own leader known as 'kezeipeu' whom they themselves elect from amongst the village elders and who teaches the youths by precept and example. They are taught to make themselves perfect in hunting, fishing, fighting, and other namely arts. It is in the morung that the village young men are given training for their future. It is here that they learn to make baskets of different designs, learn musical instruments, rehearse folktales, learn the art of using spears, shields etc. The most important thing they learn here is the spirit of co-operation and unity and the realization that one must place the community's interests above one is self in order to succeed in life.

Resident Leader

Every morung has a resident leader or guide who lives in the morung itself, usually at the back side of the building especially allotted for him. He is appointed by the village elders. He should be an elderly person with specific views on matter common to the villagers and also be a man adopt in the art of compromise and reconciliation. He should be expert in basketry, cane works, music, folk tales etc. and lastly be very sociable for obvious reasons. He is appointed for indefinite periods. If he wants to quit the office he may inform the elders of the village who will in turn select some one of his type for the purpose. Lower in rank than the leader, there are two young men or youth leaders called harangmepeu selected from among the members of the morung by all the other members. Their function is to enforce the order or direction of the morung leaders. They are to see to the daily needs of the morung in matters like provision of firewood, water etc. and also to enforce discipline in the morung life. They may hold office indefinitely.

Hangseoki

The 'hangseoki' as a corporate body organizes dances repairs the village pipe line, make new water troughs, cleans the village paths, and constructs and repairs the existing paths. They may also be hired by a rich man to bring the harvest home or construct a new house and the payment either in cash or kind received, usually goes to the hangseoki's fund for feast during festivals. The payment depends on the volume of work which usually ranges between Rs. 20 to Rs. 30 in cash and ten to twenty baskets of paddy in kind. This corporate body also helps each member in turn to work in the fields which is ready for weeding or harvest.

No Class Distinction

Though there is no class distinction in the society yet women do not enjoy the same status as that of a man. Women have no part to play in public activities and it is only young girls who make only brief and formal appearance and that also with their club members (kienga). They never appear in a village durbar in person but are represented by a male relative. They cannot enter the meeting and it is immodest to see them in the boy's dormitory. Women have no legal rights at all and men are paramount in society. No man will eat a game killed by a woman for it is unclean and unnatural. Hunting is a man's job and no women participate in it. All works which require physical strength are men's responsibility while works like cooking, drawing water, cleaning the house etc. are always women's jobs.

Even at present in the non-Christian Zemi villages the hangseoki plays the same important part in it was in the ancient days particularly in those villages which are far away from the urban centres. Among the Christian Zemis, particularly those living in the Haflong area have clubs for the male and the female members, where boys and girls in their respective clubs learn songs, dances and games etc., and other activities from the elders. It is more in the nature of clubs in the urban area. In the interior Christian village, the morung system prevails particularly among the newly converts, who have recently accepted the new faith.

Ceremony and Beliefs

A married couple always looks to the day when they will have children. To them sons are most welcome but daughters too are equally treated.

Heteu

There is no professional midwife or dhai among the community. Child delivery is taken by some old woman in the family and, in the absence of each a woman, any other old women from the neighbourhood, is summoned to help in delivering the baby. The women are not paid for their work but she is only entertained with food by the members of the family. An expectant mother about to deliver a child usually breaks the necklaces of beads (heteu) that she is wearing on her neck and at the same time takes off all her clothes except the one which she wraps over the body like a shawl. She is kept separated from the rest of the household, her bed being separated and a separate hearth (hemibam) built for her though in the same room where the general hearth is situated. Zemis in the interior villages believe that if the father happens to be away from home the child waits for its father and will not be born till he arrives. Regarding birth much of the old customs have been disregarded by the Christian Zemis. Among the Christian Zemis the expectant mother about to deliver a child need not break the necklaces of seeds nor does she need to strip off her clothes. She is also not separated from the rest of the household as in the case of non-Christian Zemis. The old methods of delivery, are still followed by them.

Genna

Among the Christian and the non-Christian Zemis, immediately after delivery the women is given rice beer, rice and some chicken curry after the child and the mother are bathed and the naval cord is cut. The diet thus prepared is meant to compensate the stress and strain she bears during child birth. For five days or more the mother is fex exclusively on this diet and during this period, the husband as well as the members of the household observe genna among the non-Christian Zemis. That is they will not go to their work in other's fields. They must also live on the food available within the precinct of the house but not on the food which is brought from outside. If a male child is born then a cock is killed and if a female then a hen. There are some taboos connected with child birth in the family which are as follows :

Taboos connected with child birth

(*a*) The meat prepared for the mother should not be shared with the husband. Only the female members can share. Even small boys are not allowed as it is believed that when they grow up they will not succeed in sports like animal hunt, bird trapping etc.

(*b*) The husband should not go out to the jungles, jhums etc. before the elapse of 5 days.

(*c*) The baby cannot be taken outside through the front side of the house i.e. the side facing the village street before 5 days are elapsed.

(*d*) The water used for washing and bathing the baby should not be scattered here and there but be collected in a pit specially made for the purpose at the backside of the house and the mouth of the pit be kept closed to prevent to domestic animals like dogs, pigs, etc. from licking the water. This is done because of the belief that any one who does not carefully observe then rules of hygeine is more prone to bodily injuries like cuts etc., while in the field or during sports like hunting, animal chase etc.

(*e*) Formerly no outsider was allowed to enter the house before the elapse of 5 days after the child birth but now there is no such ban, this may be due to the urban influence, and is more found among the Christian Zemis.

(*f*) After 5 days the child is taken outside and its hair shaved by one of the elders of the village. A fowl is sacrificed during the operation. Formerly the sacrificial meat could not be taken by anyone except the mother of the child and a very old man or woman of the village. Now there is no such restriction. After the ceremony the husband can go out freely performing his normal duty.

At the end of the 5 days the mother is allowed to go out but only through the back door of the house since no one should see her going out. While going so she carries out all the cooking utensils, which have been used by her during the child birth, and when no one sees her, she throws them away behind the house, while performing this act, her husband keeps watch so that no body can look at his wife, even himself, while she does so. It is believed that by doing so the wife and her child will be free from the grasp of evil spirits, but if any one sees her doing so, misfortunes would befall on her, which may result in her death and of the child. After the performance of all these, the mother resumes her normal life and eats and drinks from the same hearth and the same utensils which the family use.

Twin Child

Twins which are of rare occurrence are well received by the members of the family. In case of the twins of the same sex the parents are congratulated and blessed. It is customary for the mother to clothe them in an identical manner, that is, the same variety and of the same pattern of design. But in cases where the twins are of opposite sexes wearing identical clothes are considered unlucky and it is believed that it may lead to the death of both the twins.

Tingwang

The birth of a child is dedicated to the Almighty God who is known Tingwang. When a male child is born, a cock is killed and offered to Tingwang whereas in the case of a female child a hen is offered. The offering is made by the eldest male member of the family. The naming of the child takes place usually after the ninth day of its birth.

Hezintak

After naming ceremony (hezintak) all relatives and friends are invited to a feast in which pork and zau are served. The name is given according to the wishes of the child's grandfather or relatives. Among the non-Christian Zemis the name given to a child is mostly considered from the point of view of the ancestral lines of the child's forefathers who were victorious in war or amassed wealth. The child is never given a name of a living relative as it is believed that the latter will die soon since a substitute bearing the same has been provided for this earth. So the names of dead ancestors are very popular in the community.

Baptise

Among the Christian Zemis the child is Baptised after one or two months or more and no sacrifice is observed in this respect. The Baptising ceremony which is done according to Christianity and consists of celebrating with rice beer and rice among the relatives and friends. Rice beer is not encouraged by the Christians but it cannot be given up by the converts who usually use it. The mother always carries her child on the back and continues to do so as she works.

Ear Boring

The ears of both boys and girls are pierced when they are about one year old. A sharp pointed iron is used for piercing the ear lobe. Ear-rings of metal are put on end some times when the parents have no means yet to procure ear-rings. Small prices of bamboo splits are inserted inside the lobe so that it may not disappear. No ear piercing ceremony is held by the community.

Pregnancy

Illicit pregnancy in the society is of rare occurrence but if there be a base, the elders of the village try to explore avenues to see if the boy, provided he is braced out and the girl can be united in matrimony according to custom. If they cannot be united then the decision of the elders of the village going against the boy will be final. Sometimes fines are imposed. The girl is not turned out of her house. Sometimes the family of the boy invites the girl to their house to come and give birth to the child in their house. This invitation from the end of the boy's family is considered to be a good social behaviour and it results in either compromise or marriage. But if the boy denies his association with the girl despite the fact that it is through him that conception taken place, then the girl after giving birth would go to the boy's family and hand over the child. The family of the boy will then take the whole responsibility of rearing the child at all costs. This practice is considered to be anything but honourable. Sometimes miscarriage or death of the girl takes place and this may amount to a very serious matter unless the elders of the village intervene. Sometimes the real culprit responsible for the pregnancy cannot be traced out by the girl because of her making associations with many youngmen. This is the case in which youngmen involve themselves with a girl of bad character, which is very rare.

The last of the persons making approach to her will then be responsible for the unwanted child. Possession of such a child usually tells upon the future career of that man. In the village no case of illicit pregnancy was found.

Marriage

In the past marriage relationships outside the members of the tribe was a taboo. But now this traditional ban has been relaxed perhaps owing to frequent contacts with the members of other tribes. Among the Zemis a man may also marry his father's sister's daughter though such kinds of marriages are regarded as unfertile. However, marriage with mother's brothers, or father's sister's son is preferable as such kinds of marriages are conducive to the strengthening of family ties between the two parties concerned. In the Zemi society one marries a girl whose clan is the same as that of one's mother or father. Again it is not considered to be socially expedient to marry a very close neighbour. The idea being that the family with whom they have had cordial relationships need not be explored for any help in times of danger or need he or they will come to help uncalled for. There seems to be another reason for this custom also. At the time of haggling over the bride's price the family of the bridegroom finds it hard to fix the price and to impose certain conditions and terms on the party. If the bride happens to be of different clan then the settlement of the price can be affected frankly and easily, it may be very high or very low. The higher the price, the dearer the value of their relationship and the lower the price will mean a psychological conquest of friendship for both parties.

To-day, the degree of marriage relationships, up to which marriage is prohibited among the zones is determined by the following social and other conditions.

No Sexual Intercourse in the same Clan

(a) Sexual intercourse between persons of the same clan is regarded as incest, whether the intercourse taken place before or after marriage. Such relations between persons of the same clan is against their social customs. One should not marry one's sister's daughter, aunt's daughter, uncle's daughter, and so on. It is also restricted to contract marriage with one's sister-in-law's sister. The two brothers of a clan can marry two sisters of the same family belonging to another clan, but is believed that their married life will be carried by the premature death of one of them husband or wife.

(b) At present there is no traditional clan enemy but in the past marriages were not contracted between two families if they were entertaining grudge, or having revengeful or enimical attitudes towards each other, left is legacy by the forefathers.

(c) It is prohibited to marry a member of a clan previously over taken by a unknown disease or who died by accident e.g. falling from a tree, or killed by a tiger, etc,

Consanguineous Marriage

The Zemis recognise the evils of consanguineous marriage which according to them may result in the child being born a mere or less physically deformed.

Marriage Age

The usual age of marriage is between twenty and twenty-five among the boys and fifteen to twenty among the girls. However, the boys are often found to marry at the age of twenty-five and above and the girls at the minimum age of marriage.

Marriage by Consent

Marriage by consent and at the same time love marriages are the usual practice. The boy himself choses the bride and after making his final decision he informs his parents.

Initiative from the Boy's Parents

The boy's parents send word to the girl's parents with a view to ascertain whether they will accept the proposal of marriage. After girl's parents agree to the proposal an answer to that effect is sent to the boy's parents. As a rule, both the parties concerned take ancestry as a guide in making the decision. Usually before giving their consent the boy's parents first try to ascertain whether the ancestor of the bride has been victims of unknown diseases, and whether they had met with accidents of a serious nature etc. Similarly the parents of the girl will also trace the family history of the boy in the like manner as is done by the boy's parents.

Gachipai

After everything has been decided, the girl's parents pronounce their acceptance of the boy's marriage proposal. The boy then set off for the house of the prospective bride on the fixed day, accompanied by his party which includes one old man (gachipai) who is also one of his relatives. The party takes with them a small quantity of rice and two or three gourd of zau. The food and the drink are shared by the members of the party together with the bride's parents at the latter's house. On this occasion the dowry is also fixed for the bride.

Question of Payment

After settling the question of payment, the bride's price which may be either in cash or in kind is brought over from the bridegroom's house. The bride's price in terms of money usually ranges from Rs. 200, to Rs. 400 and that in kind includes necklaces, cattle, mithuns etc. Sometimes even land is given as bride's price, but such practices are not found when a girl belongs to a different village. It sometimes happens that the bridegroom's party cannot pay the whole amount of the bride's price at a time. In such cases the party pays or hands over the bride's parents whatever amount it can afford and the balance may be paid or given after sometime, generally after the harvest. When both the parties are satisfied, then a pig is brought by the bridegroom's party and it is killed and its meat is taken by them. The bridegroom's party then fixes the date when the marriage is to be solemnised. The marriage is, however, performed on the day fixed irrespective of the bride's price has been fully paid or not.

Mpaumei

On the appointed day a feast is given in the house of the bride on which relatives and friends are invited. The bridegroom comes to the house of the bride with his relatives and they all partake of the food and drink provided by the bride's part. This feast is known as 'mpaumei'. A day or two after the feast the bridegroom and his party accompanied by the bride and her party leaves for the former's house. Before doing so, bride's father kills some fowl or pigs, the meat of which is to be taken to the house of the groom. An old woman (gechipai) acting as escort to the bridegroom accompanies the party to the house of the groom. On reaching his house and before the bride seats her foot in the house, the 'gechipai' makes the bride to step on a piece of iron placed just at the entrance of the house near the door. While doing so the 'gechipai' utters. "May the bond of your marriage be as strong as this piece of iron and may you both be happy and prosperous always." "On this day a feast known as 'Kahegiapeu' " is given in the house of the bridegroom.

Mpuimu

The bride usually makes a short stay at the house of her husband. During this period she is not allowed to use any of the articles she brought with her to her husband's house. Whatever she needs is provided from the husband's side. After some days the bride's father gives another feast known as 'mpuimu' in which the newly wedded couples are invited. On this occasion the wife receives the blessings of her parents, after which she and her husband go back to the latter's place and settle down. This completes the marriage rites and the wife can henceforth use any of her belongings which she has brought with her on the previous occasion.

Divorce

Though divorce is permissible it is rare to the community. When a man wants to divorce his wife within three years of their marriage all the property except the animals are divided equally between husband and wife. The wife must also return the bride's price to her divorced husband, childern born of their marriage invariably belong to the husband. If a wife leaves her husband only a short time after marriage, say about a year or so, all the property including the animals like mithun, cattle, fowl etc., together with the bride's price go to the husband or his parents. Where the wife seeks for divorce after two or three years of marriage the bride's price is not returned but only the personal belongings of the husband.

Adultery

If the divorce comes as a result of adultery committed by the wife, she or her parents must give one mithun if possible or else, at least a pig to the injured party, that is, the husband's relatives or part from the bride's price and either belongings of the husband. If a widow wishes to remarry after the death of her husband she is allowed to do so provided she receives permission from the late husband's relatives and provided also that she is still residing in her in-laws' house at the time of her second marriage contract. When she remarries all the usual ceremonies and practices are performed. A widow can marry her late husband's younger brother but not the husband's elder brother.

Death

The death of a person is announced by a village crier and friends and relatives flock to the house of the bereaved family. The body is washed in warm water with 'heneu', the bark of a certain tree which makes the water frothy when it is fixed thoroughly with water. The body is washed by warm water by members of the family of either sex depending on the sex of the dead person. It is then placed on a bed and covered from head to foot with the deceased's clothes. If the dead person is a male, the deceased's ceremonial garments are placed over the body. The family of the dead person kills fowl or pigs or both and prepares a feast. The feast is attended by the friends and relatives and those who engage themselves is making coffin and digging the grave. The dead is considered as one who goes on a long journey to the spiritual world. Hence provision of food is made for his use on the way. When preparation for the feast is ready, the watchman who is selected from those present, offers food and meat, especially the liver of animal killed on that occasion, to the dead. Rice and meat offered to the dead together with a gourd of zau is put in a basket and the watchman will bid the dead to take his spiritual land according to his wish. The relatives bring rice, meat and 'zau' and all their food and drink are presented to the deceased's family who on that day can eat and drink only that which is brought by the relatives. A portion of his food and drink is placed over the deceased's head as a share. The dead body is generally kept in the house for two days and sometimes even more depending on the liking of the deceased's family. All this time the deceased's family remain in mourning. Meanwhile, some members engage themselves (Kienga) in making coffin and dig the grave (hereu) either in the courtyard in front of the house are along the side of any one of the village paths. The coffin is made of wood and has no lid to cover it. When the dead person is a man his father-in-law or any of his elder male relatives stand on the left side of the body and spear is also placed on its left side. But if it is a woman a piece of black cloth is placed over the body. In both cases, however, a piece of hair is cut from the head of the deceased. When this preparation is complete the coffin is brought inside the house where the body covered with a piece cloth is placed. The dead body is duly wrapped with a piece of cloth and put inside the coffin and the household articles which has been used by the dead during his or her life time such as clothes, ornaments, spears, dao, hoe etc. are first placed near the coffin and are later carried to the grave. Articles including grains, seeds, meat, chillies and other things like boxes, clothes etc. used by the household are put on the graves but are not left there. They are taken back, after the burial, for use by the female relatives of the deceased. Besides these there are some other ceremonial articles though of no material value but are considered absolutely necessary to be put on the grave. These are the jaws of a pig which they believe would chase off the evil one who waits to devour the dead. Further they also place a little quantity of salt which they say the dead person will take to the new world, a piece of cloth which they think will deceive the evil one, some thorns to prick and kill the worms and a kind of umbrella made of leaves of plant to shelter him or her from the rain and sun. After the coffin is laid down in the grave, earth is heaped in and the grave is levelled. A memorial stone called 'herauchu' is raised over it and is also fenced with wooden poles. In respect of the burial of important persons like the head man, the priest a bamboo is constructed over the grave of the dead. One wooden post with some notches on it also raised. Each notch stands for some noble deed done by the dead person during his life time.

When every thing is complete, fowl, pigs and sometimes mithuns are killed by the deceased's family and a feast is given to friends and relatives. The blood of the animals killed is offered to 'Tingwang, the supreme being, that he may guide the departed soul safely to the unknown. The skulls of the slaughtered animals are hung on top of the fence or some kind of structure erected for this purpose. At right angle to this fence and on the opposite side of the grave a bamboo rail is constructed over which clothes, ornaments etc. of the deceased are placed and if it were a man, a spear is also struck into the ground. In the case of a woman, a little backete containing weaving implements, and also her ornaments like heads, ear-rings etc. are placed on the grave. A flat stone structure (herauchu) is also raised over her grave.

Death Ceremonies of Christian Zemis

Among the Christian Zemis although the death ceremonies are performed according to the Christian rites there are some of the old practice which are also followed. Thus when a person dies, the corpse is washed, clothed, digging of the grave and the preparation of the coffin is done in the same way as the non-Christians. A kind of feast is also offered to those present and those who helped in digging the grave and preparing the coffins. Before the burial would take a ceremony consisting of bible reading, songs and prayer is performed and the church elder or paster would conduct such ceremony. The coffin is taken to the grave for burial and before the coffin would be lowered down to the grave a simple ceremony of Bible reading and prayer is again performed. Over the grave a wooden cross bearing the name of the deceased and the date of death or sometimes a memorial stone (herauchu) is raised. After the burial is over, the church also organizes another ceremony in the death in which sermons, hymn songs and prayers are performed.

Spirit of the dead Man

The spirit of the dead is believed to be lingering in the dead man's house until it is forced to go away and leave the house. This is the reason why they offer food and drink to the ghost (herui) at every meal. The offering ceases only after ceremonial separation of the deceased's spirit from the rest of the family is complete, therefore, on feast times (hengimai) usually held to commemorate the dead, big bowls containing 'Heneu' are placed outside the house so that the ghosts may bathe themselves like the living and join in the celebrations. During such times all the things that the dead may require which have not been placed in the grave at the time of the burial, such as gourds, seed, clothes, various tools etc. are provided for the dead. When this is done the priest (tingkupeu) takes with him one fowl and proceeds to the top of the village where the fowl is sacrificed after that he comes down the main footpath and in a loud voice asks the ghosts to take their personal possessions and leave the place.

When the ghosts have done through the gateway to the land of the dead the 'tingkupeu' shuts the gate and returns to the village.

Un-Natural Death

Persons killed by wild animals and those who die during child birth as well as those who commit suicide (though suicide is very rare among the community), are not allowed to be buried within the precinct of the village. Instead, they are buried at some distance away from the village. However, the rites and ceremonies are nearly the same as those in the normal deaths. The difference lies in the fact that in accidental or suicidal deaths the flesh of the animals like fowl or pigs killed are offered to the evil spirits who are believed to be the cause of such misfortunes. The beads worn by the dead person can be taken off only by an old male relative of the deceased who at the same time buries the dead body. The flesh of animals killed in connection with such deaths is given to all youngmen and women. When a person dies from a fall, this cause is also taken as accidental and the rites and ceremonies are performed in the same manner as in the latter.

DRESS DWELLING AND FOOD

Dwellings

Villages are generally built on the slopes of hills and as such there cannot be much space to accommodate many houses. There is no clan wise clustering of houses. It should be noted that though the United Mikir and North Cachar Hills District Council passed a resolution regarding the regrouping of villages so that existing small villages may be replaced by bigger villages with a large number of people living side by side, the resolution is still not applicable to the Zemi villages where the average number of households are very small comprising only about 50 households in each village. All these villages look more of a hamlet and Laisong is the biggest village among the Zemi villages consisting of 124 households (according to 1961 census) and even in this village, houses are added together on the slope of the hill. From very early times Zemis adopted a system of cycle migration, when the villages were temporarily abandoned in the course of the cycle. Then at that time the boundaries or monuments were marked or memorized, and the jumping places where major sacrifices were performed and when heads taken in war here buried, was marked by an upright monolith. (Communication Man in India, 1948, Vol. 48. No. 102).

Bamboo Houses

The houses are single storeyed and stand on bare ground roughly levelled to form the floor after building. The roof is thatched, the sides almost touching the ground. This kind of roofing prevents the houses from being below off by strong winds. The houses are arranged in two rooms which lie on either side of the footpath facing each other. Each house has a small clearing in the front where their dead relatives are buried. Small uneven paths of sometimes steps connect the houses in the village. In most households where there is enough open spaces the little patches of maize or mustard are frequently found in the homestead ground. The house rests either on bambo or wooden supports. The walls of the buildings are of split, bamboo frames. Generally the house has only two rooms. One which forms the front room Kungduaki is meant for outsiders or strangers. This is also used as a storeroom where paddy, placed inside great baskets (Kelung) which are placed against the walls of the rooms. In this room pigs and fowl and the agricultural implements such as mortar (gepa), pestle (kemai), baskets (kelung), hoes (kepeu), daos (heka) etc. are kept. The second compartment is separated from the first by a plank wall on which there is an opening or door way. In this compartment there is the hearth (hemibam) which is made of three upright stones embedded in the earth forming a kind of a stand for the cooking pot. Generally by the side of the hearth there are some two or three bedsteads (zeira) made of split bamboo and raised about two feet from the ground. There are no windows and the doors are the only ventilation of the home. The home has usually three doors one at the front which serves as the main entrance, another at the back of the house and the third at either side of the walls. The doors usually measuring 5′ 6″ by 4′ are made of either wood or plank. Each house has the space in front of it surrounded with a low wall of slab of stones marking off its compounds. As there are no chimney so the smoke has to find its own way out of the house. The result is that the walls look black and dismal.

Kemarumbe

It is customary that a person who builds a new house receives every assistance he needs from his fellow villagers who are never paid for their labour but are entertained with rice beer and sometimes with food also. The owner of the house, on its completion, entertains those who helped to a feast known "Kemarumbe" literally meaning, 'trimming the front part of the roof'. This is so called because the grass on the front portion of the roof of the house is made to suspend or hang down low. The edge is then neatly cut or trimmed with sickles by young men of the village. With the assistance of neighbours, friends or relatives and the availability of the materials the construction of an average type of house does not require more than one or two days. On the day when work is completed the villagers are invited to a feast and the owner's friends and relatives join in the rivalry and partake of pork and rice beer (zou or zu) which are served together with the rice.

Utensils

The household utensils include among other indigenous ones such things as enamel mugs, bowls and plates, aluminium cooking post and occasionally brass dishes. These are the result of contact with the ur ban people. The principal indigenous household utensils are earthen pots for cooking (hegamli), wooden spoon (terui) wooden plates (ching kuak), cups or drinking vessels of bamboo (hepaipi ak) drinking vessels made of mithun's horn (buikepick), grounds for storing and carrying liquors (nrau), baskets, for storing and mixing liquor and vats, troughs and jars for fermenting liquor. Besides, there are inside the porch and the front rooms, the skulls of animals killed by the households in the chase or slaughtered by him on festive occasions. Brightly coloured insects and the plumage of birds are placed upon one of the cross beams to adorn the house. The houses are devoid of any piece of furniture or lavish decoration and thus are simple in both construction and design.

Modern Furniture

The Zemis living in Haflong town and working in the Government offices and who are better economically than the Zemi Nagas living in distant village from the town are found to be having furniture like tables, curtains etc. as found in the urban areas.

Hongseoke

The 'hongseoke' or the morung of the Zemi village consists of a big house as shown in the photographs. The methods of construction and materials are essentially the same as the other houses, the only difference being the largeness of the building. From the ceiling of the Hongseoke number of household materials like baskets, pots etc. suspended. In the centre of the morung is the hearth around which there are wooden planks on which the boys sit.

Dress and Ornaments

The Zemi Nagas show not much interest in the modern types of dress with the exception of those living in town and in plains who generally put on European dresses. They still love to wear their traditional dresses. Their clothes are richly coloured with beautiful and elaborate designs woven on them according to their fancy and skill.

Henipai

The male dress consists of a garment (henipai) which hangs down from the left shoulder, the front end reaching below the knee. Another piece of cloth known as 'peni' is fastened round the waist and the upper portion is secured to the body with a strip of a cloth called 'dindia'. Women's dress not so very different from that of man. A piece of cloth called 'aringmang' is worn round the upper portion of the body effectively covering the breasts. A kind of shawl called 'peingum' hangs down from the shoulders. It is to be noted that their traditional dress which they put on, especially the designs on their garments are not in any way related to status in the society at present. In earlier times the elaborate designs on the garments were related to the status in the society attained through participation in war, success in love-making etc. The Zemis who are living in the towns wear shoes and chappals, this is also observed among the Zemi's living, particularly the men folk, as compared to the females.

Male Ornaments

Among the men it is observed that a silver ring is worn on each ear and sometimes rings of metal specially made for the purpose are suspended from the earlobes. Sometimes a feather or a flower (mapa) is also worn along with the ear-rings. Necklaces of beads (heteuba) are also worn around the neck. The non-Christian Zemis who can afford to wear 'Teleiteu' (made out of conch shell) generally do so.

Female Ornaments

The women, are fond to wear ear-rings (kumchie) and necklace of beads (hetu), elephant task (teuba), piece of bone (telvil) or worn of mithan (buisangke) round the neck. They put on brass bracelets (heta) on their hands. The Zemis do not practice tatooing, the hair is nicely cut and in such a way that it covers both the ears while on the front side of the head, the hair is cut short. The hair styles of the Zemis differ from one individual to another depending on one's own choice. There are three types of styles observed among men.

Hair Style

1. Telap-pei : The hair is cropped very short only about half an inch in length so that it reveals the forehead as well as the ears and portion of the head at the back.

2. Pei-Suk : About half an inch above the ear the hair is cut at equal length all around the head so that it looks somewhat like a hat. The end of the hair is curled with the lips facing inward touching the exposed portion of the skin.

3. Negga peit : This type of hair style closely resembles the Angamis. It is like the 'pei-suk' style with the difference that the ends of the cropped hair are not coiled. In the centre of the head a small bunch of hair is grown long for the purpose of typing a white cotton ball (Kelang Kua).

Married Female

The unmarried females crop their hair short in the front just above the eye brows, then across the forehead more or less in a slightly semi-circular manner ending abruptly some distance behind the eye brows and thence trailing in thick, long strands round the head thereby concealing part of the face and the ear. This type of hair style is known as 'peibide'. Among the married women the hair at the back of the head is left as long as it would grow and it is plaited into two equal from the centre of the head. These braids are made into a knot at the back of the head. This type of the hair style is known as 'kakeibe'.

Common Hair Style

The primitive method of cutting the hair with a dao is still in vogue among the Zemis of the interior village and also the combs (timrau) of fine strips of bamboo are used by them.

The Zemis who are living in town or near the town are much influenced by the urban way of life and thus they use the scissors, combs, etc. for the hair do.

Food and Drink

Rice is their staple food and some vegetables either raw or cooked and meat are also taken along with rice. Vegetables includes leaves of certain plants and also tree roots and tubers. They eat the flesh of both wild and domesticated animals. Among them the most important are the cows, pigs, mithuns, goats, fowl and fish, especially dried fish and some species of wild animals as well as birds. Pork is their favourite delicacy. Mithun meat features well during festivals. The animal's fat is used as an eatable and also for preparing curry. Fats of animals (panan), after being boiled, is kept in a bamboo-pipe which is placed above the hearth for some days until the fat decomposes and gives off pungent smell, and later they are collected and stored. Dry fish (katiam) is also placed above the hearth as stored food. It has been stated that the intestines and blood of animals are boiled in water and eaten deliciously. This is in vogue only in interior villages, and not in town or in villages influenced by urban life. Just above the hearth a line is hung where large pieces of meat and fish are smoked and dried. They are usually preserved for a long time and when required, pieces are cut off and boiled or roasted on the fire for consumption.

Milk

Previously it was in vogue that, women especially young girls, should not take milk and mutton (J.H. Hutton, 1921,

p. 95) for it was believed that milk and mutton greatly increase sensuality and eroticism. Men should not take the head of a fowl for they fear that if they do so they would fall sown from the top of the trees. They also believed that eating the young shoots of the palm trees, which is sometimes used as vegetables, will make the eaters' hair curly. These believes are not prevalent among the Zemis of the present day.

Meal Time

Meals are generally taken three times a day, in the morning, at mid-day and in the evening. Morning meals are taken just before going to the field. When going to work the mid-day meal is taken along with, wrapped up in plaintain leaf and eaten in the fields. Evening meals are taken after returning home from the field. Tea is not much favoured in the villages instead rice beer is a favourite drink, it is almost the staple article of consumption. There are three varieties of rice beer or 'zau'. The mildest is 'dekrizau' which is prepared from millet, 'nduzan' is of medium strength and is prepared from rice fermented with yeast made of wild leaves or roots, the third variety is known as 'neñiakne' which is a kind of liquor prepared by distilling rice or millet and is the strongest one. The first variety is a common family drink while the second and third are used only in festivals and by men only. Each family brews its own rice-beer which is made almost daily to keep pace with an increasing consumption.

VILLAGE LIFE AND RECREATION

Fond of Dance

The Zemis of North Cachar Hills are very fond of dances. Dances have a place in their festivals and also on ordinary occasions forming a part of their recreation. There are a number of dances and each with a different name. They are named after the manner in which hands and feet are executed to resemble the movements of a bird or an insect or an animal. For example, nruirelians', known as 'cock dance', that is, the dance which resembles the trait of a cock ; 'gethinglim' or 'cricket' dance that is, a dance in which hands are moved to and fro. Somewhat resembling the movement of the insect, 'temangnetin' or the fly dance 'hetateulee or the Bare dance' which was usually done by men when defeating their enemies. All these dances are performed with the accompaniment of songs and music. Drums and cymbals are beaten at regular intervals while the singers array themselves on one side or form a circle so as to allow space for the dancers in the centre. As dancers have got different meanigs and functions so also their songs. Songs which are generally and commonly sung by both young and old alike may be classified as follows:

Songs

1. Heliamleu or dancing songs—They are composed and sung by young and old alike and are usually romantic.

2. Hereileu or war songs—Composed by old people about the pride of their life, their by gone days, usually sung in memory of the victory or defeat in war.

3. 'Neuleu' or legendry songs—Composed by old men to commemorate any significant event old days or that of a person who had done something notable during his life time.

4. 'Hekialeu' or songs about self—These songs are composed by old men of their eventful career while they were young and strong.

5. 'Hekialeu' or a duet—Composed by both young and old and is sung by young boys and girls together.

Games

Besides dances and songs, there are also various games played by both young and old for their recreation. Games are generally played during their festivals and sometimes also on ordinary occasions. Among the games usually played by the Zemis the most important are the following :

1. 'Hezua' or long jump : There is a mound of earth measuring about 4 feet in width and 30 feet in length usually in the centre of village. A slab of stone is laid at one end of the mound. The jumper runs toward it from some distance, pause for an instant on the stone for balancing the body and then jump. The distance is usually measured by the marks made by the feet where the jumpers land on the mound.

2. 'Teri' : It is a race run along the slope of a hill outside the villages, the destination being the centre of a village where a crowd awaits to receive the winner.
3. 'Hetung' : In this game a strong bamboo pole about 5 feet long is used and two or more combatants hold both ends of the pole and push the opponents backward until they fall down on the ground.
4. 'Hepua' : It is a wrestling competition between two persons, where one tries to lift the other by the waist and throw him to the ground.
5. 'Mapei' Kanbe : A big pole about 8 feet high well greased with fat is raised on the ground. On top of it is hung the head of a pig and the competitors try to climb up the pole and take away the pig's head.

Riddles also constitute some past times of both young boys and girls. Riddles are varied and are laden with meaning. As for example, to open the door of winds means to take fun ; to give water for curry ; to fish 'to hide hands' is to set traps for birds and animals or to hide some valuables 'to lose teeth' is to build one's own house ; to spread wings 'to build one's house with the help of friends and neighbours', 'to sit on the top of a tree but on the ground' is 'to pluck some branches of a tree for sitting on and rest on the ground,' but one's leg is to delay work ; 'to throw stone at the wood decker but miss it and hit the wood' 'to make an honest man scape goat. Sometime an enigmatic description of an object is given by a member of the party and the other member are asked to name that particular object.

The description given under leisure and recreation are based on field studies. Due to the impact of Christianity and urbanization, the modern games and sports like playing with balls, badminton etc. are finding way into the Zeme society particularly among the school going childern.

Sanitation Absent

Sanitation, in the real sense of the term, is totally absent in Zemi village. There is no drainage system in our around the houses and foul water finds its way on out tune village streets. In the interior villages there are no pit latrine or any lavatory and the nearby jungle is used for such purposes where pigs perform the task of sweepers. The Zemi villages which are nearby the urban centres are sometimes found to have the pit latrine system in some houses. As there is no dustbin all waste matters are scattered around the houses and rubbish is thrown carelessly along the village footpaths. Thus the village paths become filthy and stinky especially during the rains omitting foul smell.

As far as the persons are concerned they are clean and wash themselves frequently. Near every village washing places are always to be found where men and women stop tc wash their hands and feet on their way to and from the fields. The teeth are cleaned by brushing with a small stick ; usually the bark of a wild plant and rinsing with water. Soap is now in use in those villages which are nearer the town while in interior villages the bark of the tree which produces a foam like soap is used.

Before taking meals people usually rinse their hands with water. Wooden and earthen dishes are usually, though not thoroughly, washed after use. But earthen cooking pots and vessels do not receive such hygeinic treatment. These are generally rinsed with only a small quantity of water, since the villagers fear that too much washing of cooking pots and pans may cause the article to break too early.

SOCIAL WELFARE

No Urban Influence

The life of the Zemis remains much the same as to be expected of a community which has not been influenced by the urban ways of life, particularly those who are living near the urban centres, but even in such cases the rules of their traditional customs and manners still hunt them and are not therefore easily forgotten by them. Their tribal religion has undergone a slight change. This is due to the adverse economic conditions and other calamities which ruin their economy. Since their religion is mostly concerned with the performances of sacrifices of animals so it entails much expenditure. In the face of poverty and unavoidable hardships, it becomes easier if the restrictions and barriers imposed by their religion were removed as early as possible. So after such realization they are now gradually making some changes in their social customs and manners. They now believe that sacrifices to the gods should be limited to the bare minimum and that festivals which involve too much outlay of money be abandoned.

Outdated Agricultural Implements

With their outdated and worn out agricultural implements and tools they are forced to till the unfriendly and unyielding soil. Improvement in their method of cultivation is necessary and better seeds, better manures and improved implements are all the more necessary to better their economy. There is neither any co-operative society where the cultivator can offer his products for sale at a reasonable rate and avail the facilities of improving his lot, not does the community has any idea of it. Community development blocks which are meant to better the life of the rural people in every respect of their social and economic structure do not throw light on their community particularly in the interior villages. Education which is an important factor to raise the standard of the rural community seems to have little value to the community as is seen from the percentage of literacy. Hence one of primary needs of the community at present is a really efficient and cheap system of education that may give them a chance to get themselves acquainted with the world of knowledge and learning, particularly in the interior villages. There are some welfare agencies run by the Presbyterian Mission like free distribution of some medicines, and schools etc. at Haflong.

CHAPTER IX

TRIBAL RIGHTS AND CONFLICTS

SPEAKING broadly, it can be said that there are two polar orientations towards tribal development in India. The first can be called pragmatic and the second integral.

The first raises no ideological question and tries to tackle the tribal problem within the confines of a bureaucratic administrative framework. The second bases itself on ideological affirmation, presumes that the pragmatic approach is the end-result of a hidden power drive.

Looked at more closely however, the real situation present itself in a much more untidy guise than these two polar orientation would make us believe. This becomes manifest when one looks at the tribals in India and the manner in which they have been treated from a historical angle.

When the Aryans first entered India and found that the aboriginal populations were largely dark-skinned and more backward than themselves, they used the contemptuous term 'Dasyus' for them. But men like Risely, Grierson, Russell, Thurston, Enthoven and many others, despite their colonial interests, laid the foundations of tribal and linguistic studies in their vast compilations.

It is true that in the post-Independent phase India has become more conscious of her responsibilities. Towards the under-privileged segments of the country, that funds and personnel have been increasingly allotted to the task of tribal uplift, and that some measure of progress, social, economic and even political, has occurred among the tribal population of India.

On the other hand the London anthropologist and Indianist, Professor C. Fuerer-Heimendorf, has listed in a recent book a number of disadvantages from which the tribals have begun to suffer and to which, it seems, the authorities have been rather indifferent. Perhaps this is one reason why there is much talk these days of integrated tribal development projects.

More specifically, one notes that in Madhya Pradesh a special budget document on the tribal sub-plans was prepared to correspond with the needs of the tribal areas, that these areas were divided into three zones in accordance with the tribal concentration of population and that responsibility and accountability were located in each development department in order to prevent the diversion of funds from the tribal to the non-tribal areas.

Furthermore, agriculture development was given the highest priority and attention was directed to the restoration and preservation of the tribal rights in land, to make shifting cultivation more 'scientific', and to the improvement of other agricultural practices. So far as shifting cultivation was concerned, the Commissioner for Scheduled Castes and Tribes has suggested a multi-disciplinary approach to it ; but the State Government, it appears, dragged its feet in the implementation of this idea, and so lost the opportunity of bringing much land under permanent cultivation.

Apart from efforts at developing animal husbandry, at improving the co-operative movement, at expanding educational, medical and health facilities, at setting up cottage and village industries and the like in the plans, perhaps the most vital efforts were those aimed at improvements in the personnel and administrative set-up. Jawaharlal Nehru's directive, given long ago, that the tribals themselves should be trained to take up the work of tribal uplift still remains, by and large, to be fulfilled in all the tribal areas of the country.

Granting that funds will continue to be allocated for tribal development in India in a fairly generous measure, the tribal problem then becomes basically one of injecting in the non-tribal personnel, the Gandhian spirit of dedication and self-sacrifice in the first instance ; and in the second, of speeding up the implementation of Nehru's directive. Without these two desiderata, neither the pragmatic nor the integral approach will be of much avail.

The Tribal welfare committee recommended the following classification of the existing tribes of India :

(1) Tribal communities or those who are still confined to the original forest habitats and follow the old pattern of life.
(2) Semi-Tribal communities or those who have more or less settled down in rural areas and have taken to agriculture and allied occupations.
(3) Accultured Tribal communities or those who have migrated to urban or semi-urban areas and are engaged in modern industries and vacations and have adopted modern cultural traits.
(4) Totally Assimilated Tribals in the Indian population.

Distribution. The chief home of the tribes is in the barren and sparsely populated tracts of hills and jungles, corresponding in extent fairly closely to east Satapuras but encroaching eastwards and westwards along the Vindhyan range through the South of Madhya Pradesh Plateau on the eastern extremity of Gujarat. The only other tract where they are numerous are the outlying parts of Greater Assam range and the hilly country that divides Assam from Burma. The geographical distribution of aboriginals in India is reported as falling into three main regions in which they are concentrated :

Firstly, the tribal people are distributed all over the Sub-Himalayan region and the mountain valleys on the North-east India which merge imperceptibly with those of Burma in the south-east, i.e. Assam, Arunachal Pradesh, Meghalaya, Nagaland, Tripura, Manipur and Mizoram.

Secondly, the other major groups of the aboriginal tribes occupy the mountain belt between Narbada and the Godavari—the central barrier that divides the North from the Peninsular India has provided a shelter for these tribes from very ancient times. This region extends to the Santhal Pargana in the east, Hyderabad in the south and Rajasthan-Gujarat with a strong Bhil population in the west or north-west.

Thirdly, the third group is found chiefly concentrated in the southern most parts of the western Ghats stretching from

Wyndhas to Cape Comorin, i.e. south of the Krishna river below latitude 16° north. From the fact that they occupy the marginal areas and also from the records in the oldest Tamil literature of the Sangam period, they appear to be one of the most ancient and primitive inhabitants now living in India having been pushed by the intrusion of more advanced people into their present habitats, where safety and shelter were found against increasing pressure.

In addition to these three major zones, there are small groups in some parts of the country or within the Indian political boundaries. Of these the Andamanese and the Nicobarese who live in the Islands bearing their names, though separated from the mainland, are ethnically connected with them.

It has been observed that the aboriginal population has been decreasing rapidly. It may be pointed out in this connection that while the aboriginal population is under ordinary circumstances exceedingly prolific, the majority of them inhabit those parts of the country which are exposed chiefly to the ravages of malaria.

Secondly, there has been a real absorption of the tribes into Hinduism in the North-east plains and North-Cachar Hills.

Thirdly, the spread of Christianity among the tribes in Lushai, Khasi and Jaintia Hills as well as in the Madhya Pradesh and Travancore-Cochin has also helped in reducing their strength.

Fourthly, through acculturation—which is the process of change due to the contact with other people and it involves acceptance and adoption—when a tribe comes into close contact with civilization it may accept some of the traits of its neighbours so that their original traits gradually disappear and the tribal dialects are being replaced by Aryan languages and the tribal beliefs are giving way to the direct onslaught of the inhabitants of the plains.

It would not be inappropriate to deal here in brief with the factors which have made the contact of tribes with their neighbours easy. This contract may result from the following factors :

Existence of the mines and minerals in tribal areas in various parts of Bihar, Orissa, West Bengal and North-eastern India—coal bearing districts and iron ore mines encourage immigration of alien people, part of which must settle down and live in their new homes.

Emigration of tribal labour to mines and factories situated far away and to the distant plantations in Assam and West Bengal, which have attracted a considerable amount of contractual labour, the main cause of such immigration being land alienation or expropriation of the aboriginal peasant proprietorship.

The opening up of the tribal areas by a network of communications, railways and roadways has reduced the shyness of the tribal people with astonishing quickness and many landless families have settled down along the roads, while others make their living by catering to alien people domiciled in their midst.

The administrative officers, personnel of the Public Health Services, the forest officials and their agents, contractors, traders, merchants, touts, litigants, lawyers, the police and the Patwaris or revenue agents and others whose contact with the tribal people has been effective enough in producing discomforts and disintegration of the culture indigenous.

Amongst the new status symbols of the Gond adivasis are gods such as Krishna and Ganapati, which have replaced adivasi deities and animistic rituals. Country liquor such as *mosambi* and *narangi* has replaced the gentler, home brewed *mahua*. The traditional *langoti*, now looked upon as a dress of the country yokel, is being replaced by the more expensive pant and shirt.

The incidence of "dowry marriages" amongst the fast developing Gonds tribals, one of the three major tribal groups in the Chandrapur district of Maharashtra, is increasing. The custom was once alien to the Gonds but is now seen as a status symbol by educated adivasis who are trying to "keep up" with their non-tribal counterparts. The Gonds, like many other tribes of the central India adivasi belt, are torn by conflicting values. Mr. N.B. Naitam, Regional Manager, Tribal Development Corporation of Chandrapur district of Maharashtra, a Gond tribal himself, is aware of the identity crisis of his people, he makes it clear that for them, adopting a lifestyle is a part of the struggle for economic development and the struggle to compete with the rest of society.

The plus points in Naitam's life today are that he has a fridge, a television set and a radio at home and he is able to afford 'convent' education for his son. The minus points are that his son cannot speak the Gond dialect, and cannot live for even one day in their ancestral village, so used is he to urban comforts. Naitam himself cannot recall the traditional dress of his people, which he said is now only seen in pictures.

There is reason to believe that lopsided government policies are responsible for destroying the basis of adivasi culture. While on the one hand the government mouths slogans about preserving adivasi culture and encouraging development in tune with the adivasis' needs, in reality it is forcing them into the mainstream of Indian life at the cost of their distinct identity and culture.

In the Chandrapur area of Maharashtra, for example, there are three tribes—Bhil, Mahadev Kohli and Gond. Their problems according to Naitam, are largely economic, social and educational. Only 20 per cent own between one and a half to five acres to land and they cannot grow enough food to sustain themselves throughout the year. The only alternative occupation is building roads under the Employment Guarantee Scheme.

In the past Chandrapur area of Maharashtra was densely forested. Living of the products of the forests to which they had free access, the adivasis ate according to their needs, maintaining harmony with the environment and ensuring its replenishment with the enforcement of new forest laws and restriction on their entry into the forest, the basis of the adivasis survival has been shaken. This has encouraged the illicit felling of the trees through a major share of forest denudation is caused by timber merchants and the illegal activities of forest official. Some adivasis who still have agricultural land, have become increasingly indebted to money lenders, others have lost their land to money lenders. The few acres they owned could not sustain their increasing numbers. Although the Land Restoration Act recently enacted by the Maharashtra government has sought to restore the tenancy rights of the adivasis, they have not yet found freedom from bondage. The land is in the tribal's name, but money lenders continue to take a share of the harvest.

Despite the many provisions for scheduled tribes in government services, only a handful of adivasis are educated enough to take advantage of them. Only 11 per cent of Maharashtra's adivasis are literate. In Chandrapur, only two per cent are literate says, A.V. Bodhankar, retired joint director, Social Welfare, Maharashtra, who had worked as an administrator in adivasi areas. These are at least half a dozen graduates in most adivasi groups in Maharashtra, but they are now mostly clerks—their services are not being utilised for their community. Instead, uninterested officers have been sent to these tribal areas.

Recalling the proposal to write primary school textbooks in the adivasi dialects, Bodhankar says that this could have been used as a tool to strengthen adivasi culture. To this day, these textbooks are being mulled over by the scholars. Of the 200 primary schools for tribals in Maharashtra, 48 are run by the Tribal Development Corporation. Here an attempt has been made to employ trained local adivasi teachers who speak the dialects. In the other schools, non-adivasi teachers continue to teach in Marathi.

The corporation's only other major activity is providing interest-free loans for buying sewing machines or setting up cycle repair workshops. These activities do not strengthen traditional tribal occupations. Mr. Bodhankar reveals that 30 per cent of the funds allocated for adivasis are being used by fradulent groups claiming to be tribals. For example, a small community of Thakkars in Maharashtra have remained below the poverty line, while Thakkars from Rajasthan and UP have taken advantage of resources meant for them.

Similarly Lal Shan Shah, a Raja of the Gond tribe and former independent M.P., spoke of the threat posed by the gigantic Inchampalli and Bhopalapatnam dam projects in Madhya Pradesh, which will threaten the survival of thousands of adivasis. Not only are the projects going to benefit Andhra Pradesh more than Madhya Pradesh they are also going to displace thousands of adivasis and destroy the only surviving natural teak forest in the world.

The tribals are deeply disturbed by the governments continuing policy of destroying natural forests and replacing them with monoculture teak plantations of commercial value. This has destroyed the precious biosphere reserves of the country, not to mention the many rare jungle plants that hold medicinal value. "If forests are destroyed for the dams, we will die, our culture will die. Our gods are in these trees. The Mahua tree flowers not only provide our liquor but also our food. These forests are the breeding ground of wild bison. Where will they all go ? The Madiya and other tribes of Madhya Pradesh have not yet tasted the tea and sugar nor they have seen a train.

No doubt adivasi culture is intrinsically linked to the economic, social and environmental aspects of adivasi life. There is a clear evidence of changing trends in adivasi art forms. Some have retained the purity of the original, mainly because of their isolated existence, but the influence of urban culture was evident in the dress, dance and social comments of many others. The hill Madiyas for example, reacted with spontaneous pleasure when they come to the city stage, gasping at the sight of the vast audience and the bright lights. Their slow moving rhythmic dance and song, which conjured up images of the wind in the forest and the call of birds, would, however, can prove more enchanting in their village setting, rather than on a stage. The adivasi's performances can reveal their keen observation of nature. The creeping lizard, the lumbering walk of elephant, the loping stride of the deer and the bird pecking at grain can be marvellously mimicked by them.

As the adivasis move into the 21st century, their mute message, relayed through their art form, is clear. They do not want computers. They want the forest, the wild animals and birds that have inspired them and sustained them through centuries. Despite their surface urbanisation, every song, dance and other art form of the adivasis eloquently speaks of the circle of life and harmony therein.

Though the government makes statements about preserving adivasi culture, the very basis of the adivasis' existence is being shaken ; they are being torn by alien and conflicting values. But their songs and dances show that they don't want the harmonious circle of life disturbed.

It is not yet too late to save the tribes from the fate which an over-hasty and unregulated process of uplift and civilization has brought upon peoples in other parts of India. Most of the tribes still live as far as possible on forest produce and the spoils of the chase. But with ever-increasing restrictions on the use of the forest and the gradual deforestation of the country, these forest tribes are slowly but surely dying out, partly from famine and partly from loss of interest in life.

This decline is accelerated in another way by the opening up of communications. Many new diseases are imported against which no immunity has been evolved, since they did not form part of the environment to which the tribe is adopted, and the result is a staggering mortality from which there may be no recovery. The importation of veneral disease into the tribal districts of the country by outsiders has resulted in a disastrous infection of the Gond in that area.

In an admirable article, Mr. J. P. Mills discusses the evil effects of a narrow Christian Missionary policy. He points out how the American Baptist Mission in Assam has suppressed all the ceremonies of the Naga such as the great "feasts of merit" and all sacrificial feasts.

Unfortunately, the Indian aboriginal is all too ready to respond to the slightest hint that he should abandon his old culture and interests.

The undermining of old-established authority, of tribal morals and customs tends on the one hand, completely to demoralize the natives and to make them unamenable to any law or rule, while on the other hand, by destroying the whole fabric of tribal life, if deprives them of many of their most cherished diversions, ways of enjoying life, and social pleasures. The rapid dying out of native races is due more to wanton interference with their pleasures and normal occupations, to the marring of their joy of life as they conceive it, than to any other cause.

The life has gone from many villages. Due to the influence of Hindu reformers child-marriages have started, untouchables are despised, in some villages the women have lost much of their freedom. In the year 1939, J.H. Hutton suggested that to save the fascinating tribes in India, the first necessity is the establishment of a sort of National Park in each tribal district of India. These areas would enclose a wild and largely inaccessible part of the country that might have been created for the very purpose. This area should be under the direct control of a tribal commissioner. I see no reason why the tribal areas should be excluded or partially excluded as they are at present.

Inside the area, the administration should be so adjusted as to allow the tribesmen to live their lives with the utmost possible happiness and freedom. Courts and lawyers could be largely superseded and wide powers given to old tribal panchayats. The headmen should be leaders of the tribe, not agents of Government. Non-aboriginals should be required to have licences to visit them. No missionaries of any religion should be permitted to break up tribal life.

Many people in India suffer from the curious belief that the anthropologist wishes to keep primitive people "as they were" as materials for his research. But this is not true, the scientist is not interested in any particular grade of civilization. The anthropologist who has come to know and love the people he has studied well naturally desire the best for them.

What the tribe needs above all else is the restoration of the freedom of the forest. The Game Act has pressed heavily upon the tribe and has served still further to devitalize tribal life. It is a shame and a disgrace that a tribe that has lived for millennia by hunting should now have to witness the spectacle of any town people who can afford a licence coming into its country and slaughtering its animals for pleasure, while they who depend on their bows and arrows for food should have to hide them in their huts.

It would be a very good thing if the tribe were at least allowed an "annual hunt." It would have a revivifying effect on tribal life. The killing of hares should be permitted, and it should not be illegal to carry bows and arrows. Fishing should be freely permitted throughout the tribal areas. At present, subordinate officials get many a good meal by confiscating the tribe's catch. The dictatorship of these subordinate officials must come to an end.

This gloomy future could be averted by the creation of the National Park, or at least by handing over to the tribal part of the great tracts of forest that can never be exploited commercially. They should be allowed great freedom within their borders, provided that they observe the following conditions :—

1. Trees should only be cut in mixed forest or bamboo forest, more or less clear of sal.
2. It should be cut only on hill-tops and the middle and upper slopes of hills, and a protective belt should always be kept between the forest zone and shifting cultivation area line.
3. Each hill-slope should be laid out in small alternated strips, leaving untouched jungle in between.
4. Shifting cultivation should not be cut on ridges enclosing the head waters of important streams.
5. A rotation of ten years should be observed.
6. No jungle should be used either more or less than two years at a line.
7. The trees should be cut flush with the ground, and with a clean, not jagged, section.
8. The stools should be kept clear of combustible matter when the trees are fired.
9. A number of trees may be stripped of their branches, but a tuft of green should be left at the top of the tree.
10. At the end of third year, every tribe should undertake to plant a number of trees of special selected varieties in the jungle before he leaves it.

At least, these remarkable tribal people deserve more kindness and consideration than they have hitherto received. The grim example of the fate of the Australian aboriginal is before us. The findings of scientific anthropology should save India from repeating the mistakes of other nations.

BIBLIOGRAPHY

1. H. Risley, *The People of India (1904)*, p. 218 Census of India, 1931.
2. A.V. Thakar, *The Problems of Aborigines in India* 1941, p. 1.
3. Baines, *Ethnography*, pp. 112-113.
4. Shoobert, *Census of India*, 1931, p. 312.
5. Tallent, *Census of India*, 1921, p. 125.
6. Martin, *Census of India*, 1921, vol. I, pt. I, pp. 110-111.
7. Hutton, *Census of India*, 1931, vol. I, pt. I, p. 391.
8. V. Elwin, The Baigas, p. 519.
9. G.S. Ghurye, *The Aboriginals*, So called and Their Future, 1943, p. 21.
10. Dr. R.K. Das and S.R. Das, India's Submerged Humanity in Modern Review, 1955, p. 269.
11. Report of the Commissioner for Scheduled Castes and Scheduled Tribes, 1952.
12. I. Singh, *Development and Adivasis*, in Asian Labour, vol. I, No. 4, 1950. p. 52.
13. S. Chandrasckhar, *India's Population—Facts and Policy*, 1950, pp. 39-40.
14. K. Davis; *Population of India ond Pakistan*, 1951.
15. Hari, Mohan, *The Chero*, A study in acculturation, Bihar Tribal Welfare Research Institute, 1973.
16. Vol. I. Monograph Series Part V-B (iv) Buksa 1961.
17. Vol. XXII Manipur Part V—Ethnograhic notes on the Kabuis, 1961.
18. Vol. I, Monograph Series, Part V-B. The Dorla, 1961.
19. *Census of India*, 1971, A Pilot Study of Pasighat, Adis.
20. Vol. I, Monograph Series, Part V-B (iv) The Chenchus, 1961.
21. Vol. I, Monograph Series Part V-B (iv) The Lambadi, 1961,

22. *Census of India,* 1971, vol. I, Monograph Series. Parhaiya.
23. 1971, Series I, India, Monograph Part V, The Koraga.
24. 1971, *A Portrait of Population,* Assam.
25. 1971, *A Portrait of Population,* Nagaland.
26. 1971, *A Portrait of Population,* Manipur.
27. 1971, *A Portrait of Population,* Tripura.
28. *Census of India,* 1931, vol. III Part A and B : Ethnographic notes.
29. Indian Express, Jan. 25, 1986, *The Banjaras.*
30. Indian Express, Life Style, *The Bhuinyas* by Virendra Kumar.
31. Indian Express March 1986, *Tribal Rights* by Ajit Raizada.
32. Rupa Chinai, Express Magazine, March 1986, *Conflicts within the circle of life.*
33. Phunchok Stobdon, *Times of India,* Ladakhis.
34. Quarterly Journal, Manipur State Kala Akademi, 1981-85.
35. Pankaj Thakur, *India's north-east,* Prakash Publishing House, Assam, 1982.
36. Monoranjan Banerjee, *Primitive Men in India,* Indian Publication, Ambala, 1964.
37. Raghuvir Sinha, *The Akas,* Research Department, Adviser's Secretariate, Shillong, 1962.
38. Verrier Elwin, *The Kingdom of the Young,* Oxford University Press, 1968.
39. S.S. Shashi, *Himachal : Nature's Peaceful Paradise,* ISSD Publication, 1971.
40. S. Barkataki, *Tribes of Assam,* National Book Trust, India.
41. Narmadeshwar Prasad, *Land and People of Triba Bihar,* Bihar Tribal Research Institute, Ranchi, 1961.
42. Sir James Johnstone, *Manipur and the Naga Hills,* Gian Publishing House, Delhi, 1983.
43. Sarat Chandra Ray, Oraon Religion and Custom, Gian Publishing House, Delhi, 1982.
44. Verrier Elwin, *The Baiga,* Gian Publishing House, Delhi, 1986.
45. J.H. Hutton, *Diaries of Two Tours in Unadministered*

Areas East of the Naga Hills, Gian Publishing House, Delhi, 1986.

46. *Census of India,* 1931, vols. I and II.
47. S.T. Das, *The People of the Eastern Himalayas,* Sagar Publication, 1980.
48. S.T. Das, *The Indian Islands,* Cosmo Publications, 1982.
49. S.T. Das, *Tribal Life of North-Eastern India,* Gian Publishing House, Delhi, 1986.
50. S.T. Das, *Nomads of the Bay of Bengal,* National Publishing House, Delhi, 1986.
51. K.P. Bahadur, *Castes, Tribes and Culture of India-Assam,* Ess Ess Pub., Delhi, 1977.

ted commercially. They should be allowed great freedom within their borders, provided that they observe the following conditions :—

1. Trees should only be cut in mixed forest or bamboo forest, more or less clear of sal.
2. It should be cut only on hill-tops and the middle and upper slopes of hills, and a protective belt should always be kept between the forest zone and shifting cultivation area line.
3. Each hill-slope should be laid out in small alternated strips, leaving untouched jungle in between.
4. Shifting cultivation should not be cut on ridges enclosing the head waters of important streams.
5. A rotation of ten years should be observed.
6. No jungle should be used either more or less than two years at a line.
7. The trees should be cut flush with the ground, and with a clean, not jagged, section.
8. The stools should be kept clear of combustible matter when the trees are fired.
9. A number of trees may be stripped of their branches, but a tuft of green should be left at the top of the tree.
10. At the end of third year, every tribe should undertake to plant a number of trees of special selected varieties in the jungle before he leaves it.

At least, these remarkable tribal people deserve more kindness and consideration than they have hitherto received. The grim example of the fate of the Australian aboriginal is before us. The findings of scientific anthropology should save India from repeating the mistakes of other nations.

district of India. These areas would enclose a wild and largely inaccessible part of the country that might have been created for the very purpose. This area should be under the direct control of a tribal commissioner. I see no reason why the tribal areas should be excluded or partially excluded as they are at present.

Inside the area, the administration should be so adjusted as to allow the tribesmen to live their lives with the utmost possible happiness and freedom. Courts and lawyers could be largely superseded and wide powers given to old tribal panchayats. The headmen should be leaders of the tribe, not agents of Government. Non-aboriginals should be required to have licences to visit them. No missionaries of any religion should be permitted to break up tribal life.

Many people in India suffer from the curious belief that the anthropologist wishes to keep primitive people "as they were" as materials for his research. But this is not true, the scientist is not interested in any particular grade of civilization. The anthropologist who has come to know and love the people he has studied well naturally desire the best for them.

What the tribe needs above all else is the restoration of the freedom of the forest. The Game Act has pressed heavily upon the tribe and has served still further to devitalize tribal life. It is a shame and a disgrace that a tribe that has lived for millennia by hunting should now have to witness the spectacle of any town people who can afford a licence coming into its country and slaughtering its animals for pleasure, while they who depend on their bows and arrows for food should have to hide them in their huts.

It would be a very good thing if the tribe were at least allowed an "annual hunt." It would have a revivifying effect on tribal life. The killing of hares should be permitted, and it should not be illegal to carry bows and arrows. Fishing should be freely permitted throughout the tribal areas. At present, subordinate officials get many a good meal by confiscating the tribe's catch. The dictatorship of these subordinate officials must come to an end.

This gloomy future could be averted by the creation of the National Park, or at least by handing over to the tribal part of the great tracts of forest that can never be exploi-

ILLUSTRATIONS

1. Aka girls dancing.

2. An influential Aka youth with his Miji wife.

3. A mixed Aka dance.

4. Bringing firewood from forest.

5. The Aka Village Council.

6. Two little Aka friends.

7. The Aka Rani.

8. A group of boy dancers (Aka).

9. An Aka girl at the loom.

10. Aka girls husking and winnowing grain.

11. Apa Tani Women on balcony.

12. An Apatani.

13. Dafla Long House, Selsemchi.

14. Hari Village (Arunachal Pradesh).

15. Dimasa Kachari.

16. A Mikir woman.

17. A Kachari Man.

18. A Mikir peasant woman.

19. A Mikir man.

20. Mikir women.

21. Mikir peasant women.

22. Author with educated Kuki and Naga tribal girls.

23. Married Mikir girls.

24. The Bridal Pair (Mikir).

25. Mikir Maidens.

26. Kabui Martial dance.

27. A Khasi mother with her child.

28. Khasi women fetching water.

29. Garo Man ready for dance.

30. Garo mother from Meghalaya.

31. Garo-Chilok woman.

32. Mizo ladies with traditional dress.

33. Mizo dancer (Churachandpur).

34. Mizo woman fetching water.

35. A Mizo Belle.

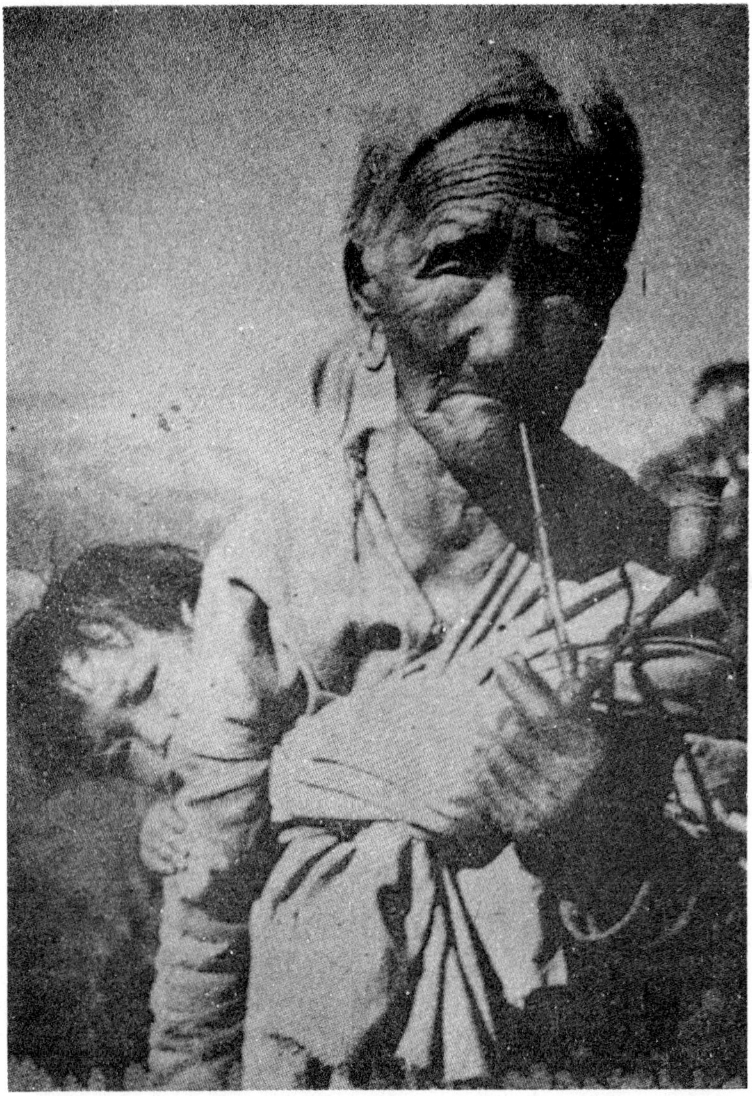

36. An old Mizo woman.

37. A Mizo.

38. Zemi Nagas.

39. Hero's House, Nagaland.

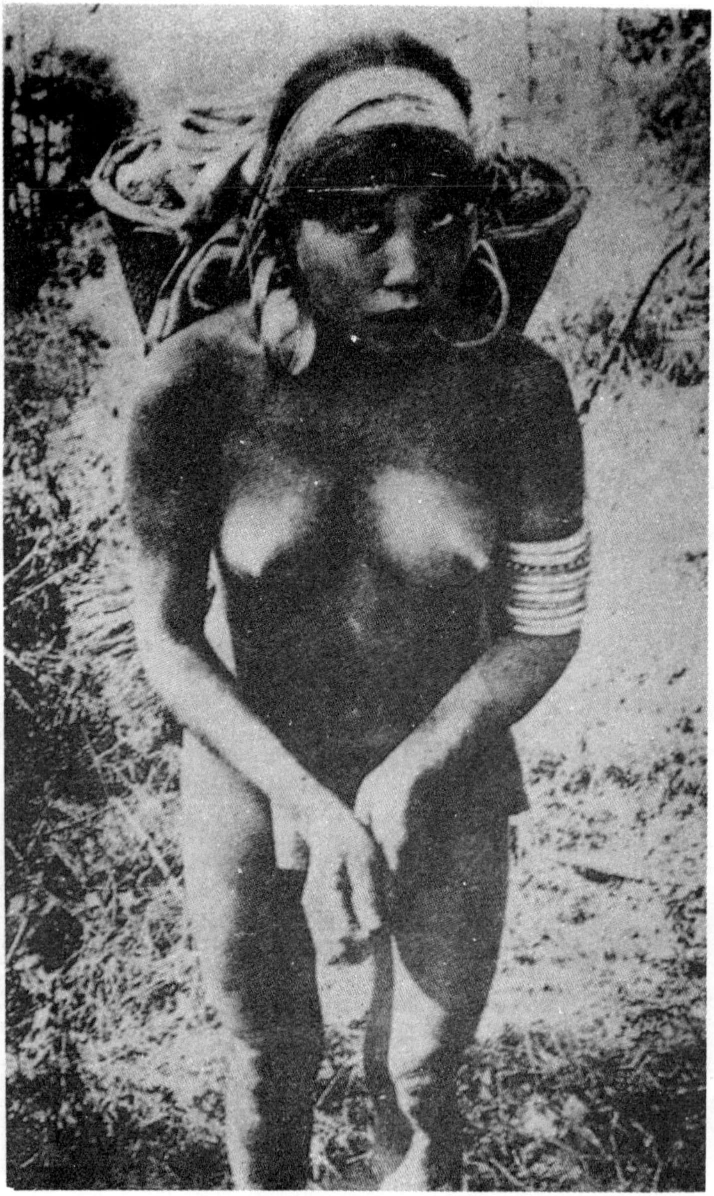

40. A Naga girl from Tuensang.

41. A Zemi Naga in a ceremonial dress.

42. A Portrait of Naga

43. An Angami village girl

44. A Konyak youth with the tattoo of a head-hunter.

45. Idu Mishmi chief in full dress.

48. Konyak Naga girl with blackened teeth.